Introduction

Over the 53 years since its publication in 1928, Walter Hough's "Collection of Heating and Lighting Utensils in the United States National Museum" has become a classic, an invaluable source of information for the collector and student of early lighting.

Bulletin 141, as it is more popularly known, was the result of many years of collecting, comparing and classifying the lighting and heating implements of many cultures, and tracing their histories. Hough was a pioneer in this field.

Walter Hough joined the staff of the Smithsonian Institution as a copyist in 1886, two years after he received his Ph. D. from West Virginia University. Eight years later he became assistant curator in the division of ethnology, department of anthropology, and later became head curator of anthropology, a position he held until his death in 1935.

The extensive collection of heating, lighting and firemaking devices in the Smithsonian Institution can be traced directly to Walter Hough's interest and collecting activities and to the interest he stimulated in others. One of the largest gifts made to the collection, the Virgil M. Hillyer collection of 1,250 Oriental, European and American lighting devices, was made three weeks after Mr. Hough's death. Shortly after receiving this impressive gift, the collection of heating and lighting implements was first placed on public view.

The examples were arranged primarily on the basis of Mr. Hough's system of classification, which in the lightinging exhibit began with the torch and continued through splint, rush and taper holders, utilarian candleholders, candelabra and lanterns. The section on lamps began with simple primitive lamps of shell and stone and extended through crusies and simple fat lamps, lamps with wick supports and spout lamps to American lamps of the 19th century for whale oil, lard, burning fluid and kerosene, to name the highlights. Most collectors follow this classification system in their own collections.

Walter Hough also wrote "The Lamp of the Eskimo" (from the Report of the United States National Museum), 1898; "Fire as an Agent in Human Culture" (Bulletin 139), 1926, and "Collection of Firemaking Apparatus in the United States National Museum" (from the Proceedings of the United States National Museum), 1928. All are out of print and difficult to obtain from antiquarian book dealers. Bulletin 141 stands as one of the outstanding contributions to the literature of lighting. It was the first such comprehensive book in the English language.

Bulletin 141 has long been out of print. For more than 30 years it has been all but unobtainable, and the price has steadily risen for the few copies that appear from time to time. Because of its value to collectors, the Rushlight Club has reprinted the book exactly as it first appeared. It has been reproduced by permission of the Smithsonian Institution Press from: United States National Bulletin 141, "Collection of Heating and Lighting Utensils in the United States National Museum," by Walter Hough, pp. i-vii, 1-113, Smithsonian Institution, Washington, D.C. 1928

Reprinting Bulletin 141 at this time is doubly significant in that it marks the beginning of the Rushlight Club's 50th anniversary year and coincides with the exhibit by the Smithsonian Institution of a major donation to its lighting collection by Preston Bassett, a long-time member of the Club.

About the Rushlight Club

The Rushlight Club was founded in November 1932 in Boston and is one of the oldest organizations dedicated to the study of one phase of antiquity. From its original handful of collectors and students of early lighting, the Club has grown into an international organization of more than 500 individual and museum members.

It was founded to "stimulate an interest in the study of early lighting including the use of early lighting devices and lighting fluids, and the origins and development of each, by means of written articles, lectures, conferences, exhibitions from private collections and if desired, through the medium of exchange, and its object shall be to collect, preserve, and disseminate these studies."

This latter objective is accomplished through the Club's quarterly bulletin, "The Rushlight," and through the publication of several books on the subject, including "Early Lighting - A Pictorial Guide," and the reprinting of a number of early catalogs on lighting.

The Club meets several times a year for lectures and discussions at appropriate sites where collections of lighting implements are maintained or where experts in the field are obtainable. Those interested in obtaining more information are invited to write: Corresponding Secretary, The Rushlight Club, P.O. Box 3053, Talcottville, Conn. 06066.

This reprint was made through the Publications Committee of the Rushlight Club, Harry W. Rapp Jr., Chairman. Other members of the committee are: Arlien and Charles Mc Gurk, Peg and Bill Dixon, Bette Rapp, Jane and Ray Schryver.

RUSH LIGHT
CLUB

November 1981

Library of Congress Catalog Number 81-84390
ISBN 0-917-422-04-x

SMITHSONIAN INSTITUTION

UNITED STATES NATIONAL MUSEUM

Bulletin 141

COLLECTION OF HEATING AND LIGHTING UTENSILS IN THE UNITED STATES NATIONAL MUSEUM

BY

WALTER HOUGH

Head Curator of Anthropology, United States National Museum

UNITED STATES

GOVERNMENT PRINTING OFFICE

WASHINGTON

1928

ADVERTISEMENT

The scientific publications of the National Museum include two series, known, respectively, as *Proceedings and Bulletin.*

The *Proceedings*, begun in 1878, is intended primarily as a medium for the publication of original papers, based on the collections of the National Museum, that set forth newly acquired facts in biology, anthropology, and geology, with descriptions of new forms and revisions of limited groups. Copies of each paper, in pamphlet form, are distributed as published to libraries and scientific organizations and to specialists and others interested in the different subjects. The dates at which these separate papers are published are recorded in the table of contents of each of the volumes.

The *Bulletins*, the first of which was issued in 1875, consist of a series of separate publications comprising monographs of large zoological groups and other general systematic treatises (occasionally in several volumes), faunal works, reports of expeditions, catalogues of type-specimens, special collections, and other material of similar nature. The majority of the volumes are octavo in size, but a quarto size has been adopted in a few instances in which large plates were regarded as indispensable. In the *Bulletin* series appear volumes under the heading *Contributions from the United States National Herbarium*, in octavo form, published by the National Museum since 1902, which contain papers relating to the botanical collections of the Museum.

The present work forms No. 141 of the *Bulletin* series.

ALEXANDER WETMORE,
Assistant Secretary, Smithsonian Institution.
WASHINGTON, D. C., *November 30, 1927.*

TABLE OF CONTENTS

LIST OF PLATES

28. Perforated lanterns, Europe; United States; small lanterns for special uses; arm lanterns, Moorish lantern, and ship's globular lantern.
29. Dark lanterns: 1, Philippines; 2, Korea; 3, entry lantern, United States. Japanese standing house and hand lanterns. New England lanterns connected with fisheries.
30. Rigging lantern, Gloucester, Mass. Pierced copper lantern, Germany.
31. Cinnabar lacquer table lantern, China. Carved wood Chinese lantern, and globular silk covered lantern, China.
32. Japanese bronze lantern; Japanese porcelain garden lantern.
33. Japanese, Egyptian, and Persian paper and cloth collapsing lanterns.
34. Collapsing lanterns with mica windows.
35. Church candlesticks, Europe and Near East.
36. Night light candles and holders.
37. Snuffer trays, snuffers, and extinguishers.
38. Spring candlesticks and other devices.

39. Firefly lighting devices: 1, 2, Firefly dark lantern and insect case, Java; 3, tree gourd perforated lantern, St. Vincent, West Indies.
40. Simple lamps and firefly lantern: 1, Shell lamp, Brittany; 2, shell lamp, Orkney Islands; 3, shell lamp, Ainos, Japan; 4, Chinese saucer lamp and stand; 5, Aleut beach stone lamp; 6, Eskimo pottery saucer lamp, Alaska; 7, firefly lantern, West Indies.
41. Simple and makeshift lamps from various localities; development of the Roman lamp from the saucer type, and a multiple wick terra cotta lamp.
42. Quasi-development of features of ancient classical lamp and the gutter lamp.
43. Ancient hanging lamps and stands.
44. Hanging float lamps and cup float lamp; 1, 2, Near East; 3, Philippines. Hanging float lamp and altar lamp; 1, Spain; 2, Damascus, Syria.
45. Moorish float lamps (7, 8) and wick channel lamps of other localities.
46. Turkish float installation, Persian float lamp, mica lantern.
47. Boxes of float wicks from Spain, France, and Germany.
48. Simple saucer lamps in various installations, Japan and China.
49. Tibetan butter lamp and Chinese pocket lamp candlestick; Tibetan temple lamps with simple saucer.
50. Hawaiian stone lamps.
51. Wick channel lamps: Near East, Europe, and North Africa.
52. Wick channel lamps: India and North Africa.
53. Wick channel lamps: India, Java, Europe, North Africa, and America.
54. Wick channel lamps, simple and two shell crusies.
55. Crusies of various types, Europe and United States.
56. Spout lamps: Italian lucerna. European and Philippine forms.
57. Spout lamps: Europe and Ceylon.
58. Wick tube lamps, European.
59. Single and double wick tube lamps, Europe and America.
60. Two wick tube installations, Europe and America.
61. Glass two tube lamps for burning whale oil; time indicating lamps, Europe and America.
62. Camphine-burning lamps.
63. Camphine-burning devices.
64. Inventive period lamps with flat wicks; candle lamps and American torch burner.

81. *a.* Stoves in combination with vessels: 1, hot-water biggin, United States; 2, coffee biggin, United States; 3, hot-water biggin, England.

    b. Various hot water devices: 1, shaving-water heater, United States; 2, wine heater by steam, China; 3, copper colonial teakettle; 4, hot-water vessel for warming food, Holland.

82. Preserving warmth and cooling devices: 1, 2, Calcutta water cooler, India; 3, Canton tea "cosey," China.

83. *a.* Fire fans: 1, Panama; 2, 4, Trinidad, West Indies; 3, Mexico; 5, 6, British Guiana; 12, Paraguay; 10, 11, Yucatan; 9, Morocco; 8, Spain; 7, Ecuador.

    b. Fire blowers and bellows: 1, 2, Japan and China; 3, India; 4, Spain; 5, England; 6, France; 7, United States.

84. Navaho double valve bellows, Arizona.

85. Primitive tongs: 1, California; 2, Apache, Arizona; 3, Havasupai, Arizona; 4, 5, Kiowa, Oklahoma; 6, Alaska.

86. Tongs of metal: 1, 2, Pivot tongs of iron, Spain; 3, antique fire-bearing tongs, Denmark; 4, 5, rod tongs, Japan; 6, spring tongs, United States; 7, hinged iron tongs, Pennsylvania.

87. Spits and grid, Virginia Indians (model).

88. Gridiron and adjustable trivet roaster: 1, tall roaster, Yorkshire, England; 2, wrought-iron gridiron, Virginia.

89. Gridirons, toasters, and roasters: 1, wrought gridiron, Belgium; 2, toaster, Virginia; 3, trivet roaster, England; 4, revolving gridiron, Belgium; 5, bent-rod gridiron, Virginia; 6, groove-bar gridiron, Virginia; 7, George Washington's field gridiron, Virginia.

90. Trivets: 1, perforated trivet, Pennsylvania; 2, trivet, Morocco; 3, trivet for heated iron, Flemish; 4, folding trivet, European.

91. Pothooks and hangers: 1, Adjustable pothook; 2, 5, suspending chains; 3, 4, 6, pothooks. All from Virginia. Ratchet pot hangers: 7, Finland; 8, Belgium.

92. Branding iron, iron rests, and curfew: 1, Branding iron, Virginia; 2–4, cast brass rests for iron, England and United States; 5, curfew, Holland. Waffle irons: 6, short iron, Charmian, Pa.; 7, long iron, Morgantown, W. Va.

93. Sadirons: 1, Pennsylvania; 2, Pennsylvania; 3, England.

94. Tripod paunch vessel for cooking, Teton Sioux, Dakota.

95. Cooking stones, griddles, and collapsible oven: 1, Baking stone, Hupa Indians, California; 2, ancient cooking slab, California; 3, cooking stones, Mexico; 4, pottery griddle, Mexico; 5, circular stone griddle, Morocco; 6, camp baker, United States; 9 camp oven, closed; 7, 8, iron tortilla griddles, Mexico.

96. Pueblo Indians cooking bread, Arizona.

97. Simple ovens: 1, Heap oven, Plains and other Indians; 2, slab cooking oven, Zuni Indians, New Mexico; 3, field oven, Hopi, Arizona; 4, mush-cooking oven, Hopi, Arizona; 5, dome-shaped mud oven, Mexicans and Pueblos; 6, earth stove of the Tibetans.

98. Spiders, Dutch oven, pottery oven, and steamers: 1, Spider of brass, England; 2, cast-iron spider, Alabama; 3, Dutch oven, Pennsylvania; 4, pottery griddle oven, Mexico; 5, rice steamer, Sumatra; 6, rice steamer, Simalur Island, East Indies.

99. Fuel: 1, Hay twists, South Dakota; 2, compressed peat; 3, 5, tubular compressed peat; 4, lightly pressed peat; 6, Buffalo chip, South Dakota; 7, prepared slab of Buffalo dung, South Dakota.

COLLECTION OF HEATING AND LIGHTING UTENSILS IN THE UNITED STATES NATIONAL MUSEUM

By WALTER HOUGH

Head Curator of Anthropology, United States National Museum

INTRODUCTION

The collection of heating and illuminating appliances in the United States National Museum was begun about 40 years ago by bringing together specimens from the ethnological series and from other material acquired by the Museum. The collection grew slowly, but about 1890 an effort was made to increase its scope. At present the collection numbers about 1,000 specimens. It is far from the required standard, yet it contains all the types needed to elucidate the history and ethnography of heating and illumination. Of the collection a series suggesting the development of lighting inventions was placed on permanent display in the museum. The specimens illustrating the earlier history of the development of these subjects were allocated to ethnology, while the series beginning with the age of progress were assigned to mechanical technology, which exhibits electric lamps and modern heating inventions. For illustration, however, some of the later forms are included. The collection is regarded as technological and no attempt was made to gather objects of art. The specimens are classified and described according to the way by which lighting and heating were effected.

As a logical starting point we may conceive that at some period of the past man took up the use of fire in response evidently to a human need. What need fire served in that early stage is surmise, but from observations of the use of fire among less advanced peoples it is deduced that what fire supplied was light, warmth, companionship, and perhaps protection from wild beasts. It will be seen that the quality of light giving is one of the most valuable adjuncts of fire. Doubtless in the earlier periods light was chiefly serviceable for the needs of what is conceived to have been quite a low state of culture. Adaptations of fire heat to the warming of the body or for cooking comes much later than light usages. For this reason the

1

subject of illumination and the development of light inventions beginning with the early camp fire is taken up first.

There is presented a synoptic series showing the steps in the development of illumination, which forms the basis of the classification so far as it concerns the evolution of lighting devices. The series mentioned is shown in plates 1 and 2 of this work:[1]

TORCH AND CANDLE

No. 1. Folded palm leaf used as a torch. East Indies.
No. 2. Stormy petrel, burned in the Orkney Islands for light_____ 178160
No. 3. Candle fish in a split stick, burned for light. Alaska_____ 178161
No. 4. Torch made of birch bark. Iroquois Indians_____ 178162
No. 5. Torch made of split fat-pine knots. Virginia_____ 129997
No. 6. Torch made of a bundle of slivers of fat pine. Southern Indians_ 178163
No. 7. Torch made of dammar gum wrapped in palm leaves. Malays___ 76727
No. 8. Torch or "link" made by soaking rope in resin. Europe in the
        Middle Ages_____ 178164
No. 9. Torch composed of cords soaked in fat or wax. Europe, six-
        teenth century_____ 178165
Nos. 10 and 11. Cord soaked in fat or wax, coiled, for lighting. England_ 178166
No. 12. Rush soaked in grease, forming a primitive candle. England__ 178167
No. 13. Stick smeared with grease for lighting. Mongolia_____ 178168
No. 14. Mass of fat formed upon a stick, around which is wound a wick
        of fiber. Kashmir, India_____ 175141
No. 15. Tallow dip with rush wick, later cotton. Northern Europe.
No. 16. Candles formed of wax; wick of fiber. Japan and North
        Africa_____ 128246, 178169
No. 17. Molded candles. Patent candles of stearine, paraffine, and wax,
        and decorated candles. Nineteenth century_____ 178171

LAMP

No. 1. Firefly lamp. Perforated tree gourd in which fireflies are con-
        fined for light. West Indies.
No. 2. Lamp made from the skull of a sheep_____ 178186
No. 3. Lamp. Pecten shell with oil and wick of rush pith mounted on
        a forked branch. Ainos, Japan_____ 178187
No. 4. Lamp. Unworked beach stone, with concavity, supplied with fiber
        wick and oil. Aleuts, Alaska_____ 13017
No. 5. Lamp. Hollowed beach stone with moss wick arranged along
        one edge. Eskimos, Alaska_____ 16900
No. 6. Lamp. Fusus shell suspended. Orkney Islands_____ 178188
No. 7. Saucer lamp with shallow grooves for wick. India.
No. 8. Lamp. Terra cotta saucer. India_____ 164920
No. 9. Saucer lamp with pinched-up spout for wick. India.
No. 10. Stone lamp with pointed spout. Kashmir, India.
No. 11. Lamp of terra cotta. Reservoir almost closed over; spout for
        wick. Roman_____ 74561
No. 12. Lamp of terra cotta. Reservoir closed over; spout for wick.
        Roman _____ 175583
No. 13 (1). Lamp. Designed to furnish oil to the wick under pressure.
        Cape Cod, Mass. Colonial period_____ 151483

---

[1] Extracted from Synoptic Series of Objects in the United States National Museum Illustrating the History of Inventions, by Walter Hough. Proc. U. S. Nat. Mus., vol. 60, No. 2404, 1922, pp. 5, 6.

No. 14 (2). Lamp of brass. Reservoir mounted on rod and stand; several spouts. Italian_____ 129400
No. 15 (3). Lamp of glass having two tubes, for burning lard or whale oil. United States. Eighteenth and early nineteenth centuries_____ 130610
No. 16 (4). Lamp, with chimney, draft around the wick, and oil under pressure. Argand's invention. United States_____ 130667
No. 17 (5). Lamp. "Fluid" or camphene, burned by means of wick and tubes and without chimney. United States_____ 178189
No. 18 (6). Lamp, with chimney and Argand burner, oil under forced pressure of a spring. France_____ 130669
No. 19 (7). Lamp, with chimney; burner ventilated; tubular wick, raising refined petroleum by capillarity. United States, 1876_ 73829
No. 20 (8). Gas burner. United States_____ 178190
No. 21. Electric arc lamp. (No cut.) The familiar arc lamp would appear here.
No. 22 (9). Incandescent hood for gas burner. Welsbach's invention__ 178192
No. 23 (10). Incandescent electric lamp_____ 178191

TORCH AND CANDLE

This series epitomizes the development of the candle, beginning with the use of fireflies and the burning of the fat bodies of fishes or birds, and of faggots of resinous wood. Continuing, the series shows torches, consisting of rudely aggregated slivers of wood or sheets of bark, torches of more careful manufacture, torches made of wax or resin inclosed in palm leaf forming an exterior wick, torches of rope or cords soaked in wax or resin, the crude beginning of the candle, and follows through formed candles, dipped candles, and molded candles, terminating with the elegant art candles of the present day.

While the line of development has proceeded from the rude torch to the candle, the steps marked by the specimens in the series are suggestive, embracing devices employed by many different peoples and at divers times. Following the torch in the line of development comes the lamp, which separates from the stem of the torch at a period when oils and fats came to be used. This may have occurred after the domestication of animals whose fat was available; at the time of the discovery of mineral oils, or of the utilization of vegetable oils, such as that of the olive and coconut.

TORCH

The torches in the Museum collection come from peoples who have made little progress in the arts of civilization or have survived in use among civilized peoples not in contact with progress. Naturally the smoky torch was suitable only for out-of-door illumination, but smaller splints of resinous wood could be used without discomfort indoors.

The torch may be considered as the most primitive device for artificial illumination. It can be as simple as a brand taken from the camp fire or as elaborate as those prepared for a Roman funeral or the artistic flambeaux of the Middle Ages. For a long period the torch was the only form of illuminant known to humanity. It is also the most ancient beginning in illumination.

It will be seen that the series has at the beginning several usages of materials for light, which are included as steps in development. These are the use of fireflies, and the burning of the fat bodies of fish and birds or of fat faggots of wood or bunched palm leaf. Strictly speaking, these may stand at the beginning of either the torch or lamp. Before the making of torches for a definite use for light there is little to more than suggest the earliest stages.

It is necessary to exercise caution in explaining the devices which might be classed on account of their simplicity as belonging to the stage when the first steps were made in the use of artificial light. A device may be a temporary expedient assuming a primitive character though not representing a period or tribal usage; it may represent a beginning acculturation, or a decayed survival. In the earlier stages habitual use is not likely to be well established and we have uses as events and not in a regular sequence.

As the development of the arts of life gradually went on at different rates in especially favored and unfavored regions the torch took part in this growth or remained simple, according to circumstances. As the demand increased for lighting within the house other devices were necessary, and these led toward the candle. In civilized countries torch makers found that rope imbued with wax, resin, or tar formed a rigid though crude torch, which the English called link. These links entered into the picturesque night life of European cities, and with the links came " link boys," extinguishers, and link rests, the two latter perhaps remaining on the walls near the entrances of great old buildings. As an example of a somewhat remarkable survival, one of these links was found in use on a railroad in Spain in 1892. It is a section of coarse fiber rope dipped in resin. (Plate 3, fig. 10, Cat. No. 178164; Walter Hough. 27.6 inches (70 cm.) long.)

Torches made by the aggregation of rodlike materials, as cane, seem to have preceded the flambeaux formed of a bundle of cords dipped in inflammable materials. It appears that such cords preceded the candle and it is probable that their use dates rather far back into classical times. Individual cords of greater or lesser length became the taper. The taper was coiled in plain or fanciful ways, or laid in vessels, some of them resembling the reservoir of a lamp on a stand. The taper required constant attention in drawing up sections for free burning. In Virginia the taper light was called " pull up," an apt descriptive term. An excellent specimen is shown in plate 3, figure 9 (Cat. No. 204264), Fauquier County, Va.; Dr. Thomas L. Settle; 15 inches (38 cm.) high. While the use of the taper was general in Europe, the only introduction to America was in the English colonies and particularly in Virginia.

In plate 3 are grouped specimens showing some of the important steps in the development from the torch to the candle which may be described in detail. At the lower right (fig. 14) is a piece of bark of the Mexican candle tree, *Jacquinia pungens*, which is naturally so waxy that a small piece will give a good temporary light. This torch material has been much prized in Mexico, probably from ancient times. The most valued torchwood in the earlier stages of culture and persisting to modern times is derived from coniferous trees. There are many references to pine torches in classical literature and these often ascribe a sacred character to the wood and mention its use in rites. A similar observation is true for Mexico. In general the nations within the distribution of the pine knew the value of its fat wood for light. The specimen pictured (fig. 13) was collected near Richmond, Va., about 1890. Known in Virginia as "lightwood," fat or heart pine was formerly burned in a pan stuck into the side of the fireplace in the kitchen of the better class of families and is even now used for light in the cabins of the poor white people and negroes. (Cat. No. 129907; gift of Rev. R. Ryland.) In olden times in Louisiana a familiar sight was negroes carrying on the head bundles of lightwood for sale in New Orleans. Plate 3 also contains in figure 11 a mass of resin attached to a rod used by the natives of Africa (Cat. No. 169176); J. H. Camp; 16 inches (40.5 cm.) long. In comparison note the candle, Figure 12, the Chinese form of which is called lobstock. This candle is made by winding a cord wick around the end of a piece of the stalk of some plant and forming over it a mass of tallow. It was collected in Kashmir by Dr. W. L. Abbott. (Cat. No. 175141; 10 inches (25 cm.) long.)

The practice of using natural sources, either animal or vegetal, as light producers has doubtless many examples which have escaped observation. Fortunately, a few of these have come within the horizon of modern scientific observers. Especially interesting is the use within the memory of man of the fat body of the stormy petrel as a complete torch or lamp by the Shetland and Blanket Islanders. This bird is small but excessively fat. It is recorded that when caught the petrel ejects oil from its digestive tract. The custom in the Shetlands was to thrust a wick down the dead bird's throat, apply a light, and thus produce a feeble illumination in the somewhat cheerless huts of the islanders. (Pl. 4a, fig. 1, Cat. No. 153887, Shetland Island; Edward Lovett.) The bodies of the great auk, *Pinguinis impennis*, an extinct bird of the North Atlantic, were sometimes used for fuel and incidentally for light. So far as may be ascertained the petrel and auk are the only birds which were employed within recent times for illumination. Joly in his work, Man before Metals, states that the Danes of the Mitchen-middens employed a wick of moss, one end of which was buried in the stomach of a great penguin (*Pinguinis impennis*) which is laden with fat (p. 197). Fish have been so used, the most striking instance being the candle fish, *Thaleicthys pacificus*, called eulachon, a salmonoid surf fish of the northwest coast of America. Quite generally the Indians along this coast used the candle fish for light. The candle fish is excessively fat. The custom was to place a dried eulachon in the cleft of a split stick and apply a light. It is doubtful whether a wick was necessary. One observer mentions the use of a bark wick, thus bringing the device nearer to a primitive candle. (Pl. 4*a*, fig. 2; Cat. No. 178161; Walter Hough.) Dr. C. A. Q. Norton informed the writer that the Penobscot Indians of Maine pursued the same method with suckers taken from the river. The use of fish as fuel is more common and was no doubt a customary source of light. The tail of the dogfish was cut into strips and burned for light off the banks of Newfoundland by fishermen. The mutton fish, which was captured off the coast of New Zealand, was used as a torch. The informant, I. B. Millner, has observed this use. Dr. Franz Boas informs me that the Kwakiutl Indians of Fort Rupert, British Columbia, threw fish oil from a kelp-weed bag onto the fire to produce a temporary bright light. One of these bags of the tubular sea weed, in flattened condition, from the Makah Indians, Neah Bay, Wash., is in the museum. (Cat. No. 73753; James G. Swan.)

The torch proper is taken up at the stage when materials were aggregated into a definite form for the particular use—in other words, a manufactured product. This may result quite simply as a palm leaf crushed into a bundle and dried. (Pl. 1, fig. 1, Cat. No. 209351, Philippines; Gen. J. M. Bell.) This device has, however, a suggested primitive phase of industrial beginnings. In the area of distribution of the large grasses it is quite natural that bundles of canes should be tied together and used as a torch in many places. The Peabody Museum, at Cambridge, Mass., has such a contrivance from a prehistoric cave deposit in Kentucky. (Cat. No. 150845.) In the Truk Group, Caroline Islands, a bundle of natural canes tied with strips of vegetal material served as a torch. (Pl. 4*b*, fig. 1, Cat. No. 206274; F. H. Moore; 24.8 inches (63 cm.) long.) In the East Indies split bamboo torches were used by fishermen and others. One of these, from Mindanao, southern Philippines, is shown in

Plate 4b, Figure 1. (Cat. No. 325617, Philippine Commission, 39.4 inches (1 m.) long.) In this class is a torch of strips of apparently palm spathe tied in a cylindrical bundle used by the Javanese and called *abor mantjoung* in native dialect. (Cat. No. 128017, Java; Bureau of Arts, Paris, 29 inches (73.6 cm.) long.) Another specimen is made of long splints of fat pine bundled together to form an especially effective torch for outdoor use in the wind. This torch was collected from the Choctaw Indians of Louisiana. (Cat. No. 178163; Walter Hough.)

In the birch tree area bundles of dry bark are rolled up to form a torch for the woods or for fishing. (Cat. No. 178162, Iroquois Indians; Walter Hough.) On the information of W. W. Rockhill, the Chinese make torches by crushing bamboo and twisting it into a rope, the crushing of the fiber rendering it more inflammable. No resin or other aids to combustion are added as in the European link.

Another class of torches has a wide distribution in southeastern Asia and in western and central Africa. They consist of cylindrical masses of resin bound up usually in palm leaf, pandanus leaf, and palm spathe. Apparently the first notice of them was given by Sir Alfred Russell Wallace, who records seeing them for sale at Ternate. This torch is common in Malaysia. It would appear that this type is coincident with the distribution of the dammar tree, which produces the resin used in the torch. Specimens were received from Singapore about 50 years ago by the United States National Museum. They are encased in pandanus leaves and tied with rattan. The handle is a continuation of the leaf below the resin bound into small compass. (Pl. 4b, fig. 2, Cat. No. 76727, Singapore; U. S. Department of State, 16.5 inches (24 cm.) long.) Plate 3 depicts a group of resin torches, except Figure 1, described later. Figure 2 is a simple packet of dammar wrapped in palm leaf, from the Karens of Burma. (Cat. No. 175194; Mrs. U. B. White; 18.9 inches (48 cm.) long.) (See pl. 7 for Siamese form.) The third specimen is spindle-form, wrapped in palm leaf and tightly bound with many turns of split rattan. It is evidently the work of a professional Siamese torch maker and reflects the meticulousness of Siamese art. (Cat. No. 175979, Trong, Lower Siam; Dr. W. L. Abbott; 34.5 inches (84.5 cm.) long.) Figure 4 is a large resin torch from the Philippines. It is encased in palm leaf and spirally wound with rattan. It is lighted at the lower end shown in the plate, the twisted loops at the upper end being for temporary suspension. (Cat. No. 232826, Moros of Saranaya, Rio Grande, Mindanao; Maj. E. A. Mearns, U. S. Army; 40 inches (102 cm.) long.)

In one locality in the New World the resin torch is found. The type was collected at Arima, Porto Rico. It consists of a roll of resin about the size of a candle and is incased in palm spathe. It appears to be the successor of torches made by the Caribs from the "gum of a sandal," described by De Rochfort before 1665. (Fig. 5, Cat. No. 219403; Dr. J. Walter Fewkes; 11.8 inches (30 cm.) long). Figure 6 is a resin torch from the Gaboon River, Africa. It is wrapped in palm leaf and tied with a pliable strip of some plant. (Cat. No. 164872; A. C. Good; 37 inches (94 cm.) long). For a large resin torch from the Congo see Plate 4c. Figure 7 is a resin torch of palm spathe inclosing a mass of fiber saturated with resin. The spathe casing is fastened at intervals with wooden pins. In several parts of Siam resin-soaked fiber is used as torch filling. In Burma rattan wood soaked in rock oil was used as a filler. (Cat. No. 175977, Trong, Lower Siam; Dr. W. L. Abbott; 22.4 inches (57 cm.) long). Figure 8 is a dammar torch wrapped in pandanus leaf. (See pl. 4b.) (Cat. No. 76727, Singapore; 16.5 inches (42 cm.) long.) The largest resin torch which has come to notice is from Loango, French Congo. It is a cylinder of compact resin wrapped first in palm leaf and incased in basketry consisting of strips of cane interwoven with a continuous spiral of rattan. This torch was used in fishing, traveling, and in fetish rites. (Pl. 4c, fig. 1, Cat. No. 152631; Carl Steckelmann; 52 inches (132 cm.) long.) A cylindrical mass of resin folded in pandanus leaf and resembling the Burmese specimen, shown on Plate 3, Figure 2, is from Siam. The resin is of reddish color, not homogeneous, and burns with a bright yellow light quite smoky and with a pleasant odor. (Pl. 4c, fig. 5, Cat. No. 178243, Siam, C. E. Eckels; 13¾ inches (35 cm.) long). Another Siamese torch, short and thick, is shown in Figure 4. It is covered with thick rugose leaf and filled with resin-coated fiber. It is held in shape by loops of rattan. (Cat. No. 235901, Siam; Government of Siam, 1907; 16⅛ inches (41 cm.) long.) Figure 2 is a smaller resin torch from the Philippines. It is filled with granules of resin. The wrapping is pandanus leaf in several thicknesses to facilitate combustion. The binding is a spiral of rattan simply fastened off at the ends. (Cat. No. 232826, Moros of Mindanao, P. I.; Maj. E. A. Mearns, U. S. Army; 28 inches (71 cm.) long.) Plate 4c, Figure 3, is a resin fetish torch from the Gaboon River, Africa, collected also by A. C. Good.

A widespread form of illumination which is classed as a torch is the candlenut device. Meats of the candlenut are strung on a strip of bamboo and the top meat being lighted burns down to the next below, and so on. On account of its universality among the Polynesians the torch has been assigned as a characteristic culture appanage of this race. It has, however, a wider distribution than the *Aleurites triloba*, the tree furnishing the nut. This is seen in a similar use of palm nuts among the Tule Indians of San Blas, Panama.[2] The presence of this device in the New World seems anomalous and could be explained by acculturation, the oriental contact with Panama having been long continued. So far as known no other torch of this type has been observed in America. (Pl. 4b, fig. 3, Cat. No. 327508; Richard O. Marsh; 18.9 inches (48 cm.) long.)

TORCH HOLDERS

Torch-holding devices have an interesting history, not so familiar as the multitudinous candleholders, nevertheless covering a period about which much is yet to be learned. A torch is usually conceived of as an object to be held in the hand and requiring the attention of one man. Traveling or hunting parties must delegate some member or servant as bearer and caretaker of the torch. About the camp or living place the temporary torch offers no difficulty when ingenuity was sufficient to provide for it. Where torches are used to supply light in ceremonies held on moonless nights and without the great fire which illuminated primitive rites, some need would be apparent to make the torch stationary. This would imply a marked advance over early culture. Such devices are observed among uncivilized peoples and as survivals. These devices are crude and appear as extemporaneous as the various makeshifts to mount the candle, mentioned later. The problem of setting up the torch is in line with the problem of installing the candle in a later stage of progress. It is noteworthy that the installation of the resin torch in the Simalur Islands, East Indies, shows a considerable advance, paralleling that of the candle and simple lamp in an advanced social stage. The first form consists of a rattan bent into a bow, the ends fastened to parallel strips of wood. The strips are sprung out and a resin torch inserted. The frame resembles a bamboo lamp of Chinese derivation seen in the Philippines. The other specimen is carved from light wood. It consists of an upright set up at one end of a flat long-oval base. The upright has a mortise cut through it about the middle, and through the hole are slipped two thin strips of wood, acting as a clamp for the resin torch. It will be seen that the principle of the clamp is applied in both specimens. A more primitive clamp is found in the split stick for the insertion of a torch used in the Philippines. (Pl. 5a, fig. 1, Cat. No. 216338, Sigoeli, Simalur Island; Dr. W. L. Abbott; 22 inches wide, 23 inches high (56 cm., 58.5 cm.). Pl. 5a, fig. 2, Cat. No. 216339, Sibabo Bay, Simalur Island; Dr. W. L. Abbott; 28½ inches high, 10 inches by 18 inches base (72.5 cm., 25.5 cm. by 45.75 cm.).)

---

[2] H. W. Krieger. Material Culture of the Tribes of Southeastern Panama. Bull. 134, U. S. Nat. Mus., Washington, 1926.

There is now encountered a great and unnoticed change in the materials used in lighting. Splints of resinous wood supplement torches and the holders of these splints form a subject of particular interest. Splint torches or candles, as they have been indiscriminately termed, indicate that social progress demanded the proliferation of lights for special places and uses, and that the camp fire, house fire, and torch had grown inadequate for social needs. In effect, special lighting is being taken into the house. The date when this gradual development became noticeable is not certain. Traces of the usage are found in the later bronze age, and bronze torch holders with two clasping arms were found in the tomb of Tut-Ankh-Amen. In the collection of the late Henry J. Heinz, of Pittsburgh, is a trifid bronze stand allocated to Egypt, which appears to be a torch or splint holder. (Pl. 5b, fig. 1, No. 992, Heinz collection.) The Museum possesses a specimen of Etruscan origin found in Italy and dating from the middle of the first millennium B. C. It consists of a tripod and shaft, on the apex of which is a four branch portion, each arm terminating a cleft leaf in which splints were put for burning. It has been suggested that the central spine held the shallow dish used in the wine throwing game of Cottobus, but there is no trace of a junction. (Pl. 6a, fig. 1, Cat. No. 147695, Italy; Dr. Thomas Wilson; 28 inches (71 cm.) high.)

It is surmised that the large series of splint holders about to be described represent survivals from the iron age. As would be anticipated from the metallurgy of northern Europe, most of the specimens are from that region. They are in the simplest form, strips of iron bent into flat loops and provided with spike ends for attaching to the wall or other support. In the clefts were placed splints of pine. (Pl. 5a, figs. 6, 7, Cat. No. 167866–867, Finland; Hon J. M. Crawford; 8.3 inches (21 cm.) wide.) These simple forms of iron bent into clefts have their prototypes in the iron age. There has been found in a site of the Hallstadt period, early iron age, in Court St. Etienne, Belgium,[3] a much bent bar of strap iron which is identified by its discoverer as a sort of grate. This specimen may be related to the splint holders described. With this in mind, the status of the family of rude iron splint holders appears clear, and their variety to be the result of simple folk invention. A rod of iron with a double cleft at one end and a spike at the other shows a device for fixing to an overhead beam, forming a primitive splint chandelier. (Pl. 5a, fig. 3, Cat. No. 167865, Finland; Hon. John M. Crawford; 15 inches (38 cm.) long.) Another is for socketing on the end of a staff. It has two divergent horizontal clefts and a basket made by four upright spikes, probably to hold a billet of split wood or

---

[3] Records of the Past, vol. 11, 1912, p. 123.

possibly a candle, as seen in later forms. (Pl. 5a, fig. 4, Cat. No. 237687, Salaberg, Lower Austria; P. J. Schock; 6.3 inches (16 cm.) high.) A wooden stand splint holder gives a suggestion of devices which may be effected in the absence of iron. It consists of two strips of wood mortised together at the top of a cylindrical staff with square cross shape joined base. The clefts are charred from ignition of the burned down splints, showing that the wooden holder required frequent attention. (Pl. 5a, fig. 5, Finland; Hon. John M. Crawford; 15.8 inches (36 cm.) high.) An iron splint holder set in the top of a cylindrical wood upright arising from a square, heavy wooden base provides a light to be set on a table or other raised flat place. (Pl. 5b, fig. 2, Cat. No. 167861, Raisala, Finland; Hon. John M. Crawford; 12.2 inches (31 cm.) high.) Another form for standing on the floor is ingenious and shows a considerable advance in wood working. It consists of a block base with two uprights having grooves cut on the opposing faces. The tops of the uprights are held by a mortised piece through which slides the upright bearing the iron holder. The upright is notched and the lower end is mortised in a crutch which slides in the grooves. A latch fastened to one of the bars forming the frame engages the notches on the sliding upright and thus the light may be raised or lowered. (Pl. 6a, fig. 2, Cat. No. 167859, Finland; Hon. John M. Crawford; 39.4 inches (1 m.) high.) The entry of the candle is shown by an iron having a splint cleft in combination with a candle socket. This is an interesting example of history written in things. The candle, made of valuable food fat, is subsidiary at first to the cheap splint, and was probably burnt on special occasions. (Pl. 6b, fig. 5, Cat. No. 167865, Finland; Hon. John M. Crawford; 4.6 inches (12 cm.) wide.) There appears to have been in Finland a fortunately undisturbed conservatism which preserved precious relics and customs of past times. Much of the folk material in the Crawford collection might serve as illustrations of early Aryan arts and industries.

Splint holders of pincer form with one arm weighted to produce pressure on the splint constitute another type. This type shows an advance on the simple bent iron cleft which gives uncertain adjustment of the splint. The pincer type gives a grip on the splint similar to the grasp of the fingers. So far as may be ascertained, the joining of two pieces of metal in apposition on the pivot hinge principle was not practiced in the Bronze Age or in the prehistoric Iron Age. The hinged splint holder must then be assigned to the historic period. This device is seen in a floor splint light which has a cross-shape base and an upright of wood perforated at intervals for the reception of an iron spike, part of the iron splint pincers, by means of which the light could be raised or lowered.   (Pl. 6b, fig. 1, Cat. No. 150884, Surrey, England; Edward Lovett; 35 in. (89 cm.) high.) Another specimen dating in the seventeenth century consists of an oak pole rising from a block of the same material.   The splint holder has a rather large ball counterpoise at the end of one arm. (Pl. 6b, fig. 3, Cat. No. 150410, Surrey, England; Edward Lovett; 33.7 inches (86 cm.) high.)   An example from Scotland, where it is called "Peer man," is of cast iron.   It has a heavy counterpoise. The specimen, being of cast iron, is not as old as the other examples. (Pl. 6b, fig. 6. Edward Lovett.)   As candles in the British Isles were preceded by fir splints and fatted rushes, some of the lighter holders were used with the latter illuminant.   When tallow candles with rush wicks came into use the " clip," as the holder is called, was fitted with a candle socket at the end of the counterpoise. History here repeats itself as in the Finnish splint holders described, but at a later period apparently.   Specimens are shown on Plate 6b, Figure 4 (Cat. No. 150382, from Surrey, England, collected by Edward Lovett, and Figure 8 (Cat. No. 178799 from Antrim, Ireland), by the same collector (8 inches (20.3 cm.) high and 9.7 inches (24.5 cm.) high).   An excellent specimen of splint and candle clip with adjustable rack comes from North Germany.   It is of wrought iron.   The lower end of the notched iron bears the socket and clip.   The support is a rod of iron with a loop at the upper end and a stirrup for engaging the ratchet at the lower end.   (Pl. 6b, fig. 2, Cat. No. 289195, Germany; Mrs. Rose Gouvernor Hoes; 24.2 inches (61.5 cm.) long.)

A specimen which might be regarded as a curiosity of the Patent Office was a pine knot burner, devised and patented by J. Price, December 18, 1839.   The time honored candle dish is seen as a basis of this invention, the columnar burner represents the candle and the slide was a device of long ago.   The holder for pine knot wood is perforated with heart design.   The specimen is of normal size and made of brass and tin.   (Pl. 64, fig. 1, Cat. No. 251738, United States; U. S. Patent Office; 12.2 inches (31 cm.) high.)

Loosely called torch, a number of open-air lighting devices are in the Museum collection.   Among these are basket torches which have ancient use and which survived in the whaling industry as late as 1880.   These baskets were of strap iron strongly riveted.   One old specimen is square and shows signs of much use.   It was probably suspended overboard by a bail from the rigging and fed with the cracklings left after rendering the whale oil.   It thus gave light to the Homeric slaughterings of the mighty whales.   (Pl. 7a, fig. 1, Cat. No. 75358.)   Other basket torches had long handles and could be placed to advantage for illuminating the work on an old-time whaler. In the fisheries collection is an iron basket at the end of a long iron rod socketed in the extremity of a wooden pole. This appliance was called "Torch Dragon" and was used in mackerel fishing to attract the fish to the seine. (Pl. 7a., fig. 3, Cat. No. 57,829, Gloucester, Mass.; U. S. Fish Commission.) Fishing torches for placing in the bow of a canoe are of various materials and variously installed. Broadly, they are torches used by peoples unacquainted with metals and those having metals. In the first case the torches are bundles of bark, canes, or slivered wood. In the second case a basket of iron, or lantern, or a so-called torch with wick may be used. In the first class the birch bark torch of the northern Indians may be cited as an example (pl. 7b). The model canoe was made by northern Algonquians and the group composed in the Museum laboratory. The other, almost as primitive, but made of iron, is a fishing torch holder from Finland. This apparatus consists of a block of wood fitting in a thole in the bow of the boat and bearing a bent piece of iron having three U-shaped loops riveted to it. In these loops was laid the torch or lightwood. (Pl. 7a, fig. 2, Cat. No. 167864, Antrea, Finland; Hon. John M. Crawford; 23.2 inches long, 6 inches wide (59 cm., 15 cm.) A torch displaying considerable ingenuity was used on the whalers about half a century ago. It consists of a can with handle and match case combined, the lid of the can having a long handle, a shield, and an iron rod with a burner of perforated and plain iron plates attached to the end. In use, the can was charged with the illuminant, apparently rape-seed oil, the burner always bathed in the oil, withdrawn, lighted with a match, and replaced in the can, and smothered out when the exigency was over. To obviate any gas pressure, an air vent was led in a tube from the bottom of the can. The specimen was presented in 1882 by C. A. Williams and Co. (Pl. 8a, fig. 4, Cat. No. 75370, New London, Conn., collected by J. Templeton Brown; 14.2 inches (36 cm.) high.)

On account of a survival of usage in the open air the name torch is applied to vessels having a large wick burning oil. In reality these belong in the single-wick type of lamps and mostly are modern. Of these, torches carried in political processions are familiar examples. One of these, rudely made of tin and fitted with a gas-pipe wick tube, is said to have been carried in a torchlight procession during the Lincoln campaign. (Pl. 8a, fig. 5, Cat. No. 289457; Anton Heitmuller; 4.6 inches (12 cm.) dia., 7.8 inches (20 cm.) high.) Another, more elaborate, is a flare torch of tin painted red with long tubular handle. Air is blown through the flame by means of a tube, the mouth of which projects from the handle. (Pl. 8a, fig. 2, Cat. No. 251476; U. S. Patent Office; 24.4 inches (62 cm.) long. Patented August 1, 1876, by I. W. Shaler.) A hand torch of sheet iron with brazed joints and cast handle riveted on is from British Columbia, where it is said to have been used by miners and other frontiersmen and sold by the Hudson Bay Company. (Pl. 8a, fig. 3, Cat. No. 326755, British Columbia; Walter Hough; 9.8 inches (25 cm.) high.) An interesting torch of tin with brass wick tube was used on mackerel fishing boats at Gloucester, Mass., in 1882. It has a tube below for fitting on a staff. (Pl. 8a, fig. 1, Cat. No. 54384; U. S. Fish Commission; 6.3 inches (16 cm.) diameter, 8.6 inches (22 cm.) high.) A heavy cast-iron torch used formerly by engineers and others on railroads was recently received. It has cast on one side " P. R. R. Bayton Malleable Iron Co. X1028." (Cat. No. 325618; Walter Hough; 9.3 inches (23.5 cm.) high.)

CANDLE

The crude torch and the flambeau passed out among civilized peoples in the course of progress, but one of the elements of the flambeau survived as the taper. This waxed or fatted cord was burned in vessels like lamps or wound in a coil or on a support presenting many forms due to expediency or taste. The taper was very useful, and indeed still may be found on sale where fashion and conservatism demand the use of sealing wax. In European countries the taper still has a cult use.

The rôle of the taper in the development of the candle may have been important. There is probability that the southern European candle had the taper as ancestor. The conditions were complete for such a development. In northern Europe, however, the candle is clearly a development from the fatted rush. The far eastern Asiatic candle has still another origin, also using pith of the rush as a wick. There are thus seen three avenues of approach to the invention of the candle traceable at the present. It is not to be concluded that these are all. The candle is a device which depends on conditions, principally on the stage of human advance in culture, and, therefore, given flocks and herds for the production of abundant suitable fats, the candle may have arisen, but it must arise out of earlier uses of substances for light. This combination of circumstances could have assembled in the early Bronze Age among peoples favorably situated. Some of the commercial tapers purchased about 35 years ago are shown in Plate 8b. Figure 8 is a slender white taper wound in an ingenious way to uncoil through an aperture in the holder. (Cat. No. 167065, Seville, Spain; Walter Hough; 2.4 inches (6 cm.) diameter.) Figure 7 is a bundle of thicker taper of unbleached beeswax from north Spain, purchased at an almacen, or store, selling ecclesiastical objects. (Cat. No. 167062, Burgos, Spain; Walter Hough; 1.6 inches (4 cm.) diameter, 3.1 inches (8 cm.) high.) Figure 5 is a bleached wax taper coiled on a wooden support sold by stationers and known as " Pomeroy's coiled taper." (Cat. No. 150431, Washington, D. C.; Walter Hough; 2.7 inches (7 cm.) high.) Figure 6 is a wax taper coiled to fit a holder, through the opening of which it can be easily drawn up as needed. (Cat. No. 167062, Burgos, Spain; Walter Hough; 1.5 inches (4 cm.) diameter.) The taper is found still in use in the float lights or night lights, in wax matches, and in the long cords used in the almost obsolete gas lighter. Small candles called tapers will be discussed under candles.

TAPER HOLDERS

Such appliances as have survived depend on the use of the taper for special purposes such as sealing letters or for a temporary small light. In one specimen the familiar clip with spring is seen. (Pl. 8b, fig. 2, Cat. No. 289449; France; Anton Heitmuller; 5.1 inches (13 cm.) high.) In this specimen to install the taper coil the screw top and clip were taken off, the taper slid over the upright, and the clip replaced. The extinguisher attached to the clip by a chain is missing. A very old Italian taper holder of fine ironwork has a clip with spring. The clip is mounted on an upright rod arising from a square table with ornately cut edge and four curved legs with ball feet. Around the rod the taper is wound and brought up to the clip. This taper holder appears to date late seventeenth century. (Pl. 8b, fig. 1, Cat. No. 168311, Italy; G. Brown Goode; 5.5 inches (14 cm.) high.) Another form has a receptacle for the taper, which is drawn up through a bell-shaped orifice. The extinguisher has an arm fitting into a small tube somewhat as the candle extinguisher to be described. (Pl. 8b, fig. 3, Cat. No. 324719, Washington, D. C.; E. D. Tabler; 3.1 inches (8 cm.) diameter, 2.7 inches (7 cm.) high.) Another is of openwork brass of elaborate decoration. It has an extinguisher on a chain. (Pl. 8b, fig. 4, Cat. No. 167662, Italy; G. Brown Goode; 2.3 inches (6 cm.) diameter, 3.5 inches (9 cm.) high.)

CANDLE MAKING

In the remarks on the development of illumination the growth of the candle was considered from the standpoint of invention. There follow notes on the materials and processes of the industry.

The materials for candles are not many. In nature vegetal substances preponderate over those available from animal sources, yet only in a few places have vegetal fats and waxes been used for candles, and most of these sporadic attempts belong to the modern period. In China and Japan, however, is seen a replica of the western candle industry based mainly on valuable illuminating substances derived from the tallow tree, *Stillingia sebifera*, of eastern China, and the *Rhus succedanea*, of Japan. In both cases the wax or "tallow" occurs on the seeds as in the *Myrica cerifera*, from which myrtle wax candles are made occasionally in eastern North America. The process of extraction is similar, freeing the wax from the seeds by means of heat and pressure. The Chinese tree tallow has a rather low melting point, below summer temperature, and it is found necessary to put on such candles a substantial coating of beeswax or insect wax. In southern China candles of animal fats are so covered.

The *Cocus pela*, or Chinese wax insect is found on the *Ligustrum japonicum*, *L. obtusifolium*, *L. tibola*, and *Rhus succedaneum*. The eggs are gathered from nests on the above trees in the fall and kept wrapped in reed leaves. At the beginning of May the eggs are placed upon the proper trees, usually *Fraxinus chinensis*, where they hatch about the 1st of June and begin wax making. In September the wax is scraped from the twigs where it has been deposited, melted with boiling water, and cast into cakes. It is a white crystalline substance resembling the best spermaceti. It melts at 152° F. and is thus suitable for summer candles. The *Cocus pela* is a relative of the lac insect, which produces a valuable product known as shellac.

This is an interesting example of man's skill in adapting the habits of insects to his needs. So far as the candle is concerned, the industry is aided by the products from two insects, the Cocus and the bee.

It appears that the beeswax candle has a fairly ancient history in the West among the historic nations. While there is evidence that the ancient Aryans practiced apiculture, using dome-shape hives of coiled straw, there is no basis for the belief that candles were used. Candle making in China applies notable skill in the industry. The first requirement are slender rods finished from bamboo and tapered from base to point. (Pl. 9a, fig. 1, Cat. No. 325619; Chinese Centennial Commission, Philadelphia, 1876.) The next in order is a spill or tube of paper wound spirally, with rush pith forming the wick (fig. 5). This is slipped on the bamboo rod. The Chinese thus solved the problem of the high-capillarity wick. (Pl. 9a, fig. 2, Cat. No. 325619; Chinese Centennial Commission, Philadelphia, 1876.) The combination is then dipped in the melted wax or fat and cooled alternately until a candle of the caliber required is secured, forming the finished candle shown in Plate 9a, Figure 3 (15.7 inches (40 cm.) long). The pink candles of graded size (figs. 6–10) are made by the same method as are the large candles. In the latter a vegetable stem is used instead of a bamboo rod upon which the rush pith wick is wound. (Pl. 9a, fig. 4, Cat. No. 93478, Ningpo, China; Royal Gardens, Kew, England; 8 inches (20.5 cm.) long.) This specimen is wax incased, green, and ornamented with characters, as is the other specimen. (Pl. 9a, fig. 11,

Cat. No. 93479, Tung Cheng, China; same donor; 11 inches (28 cm.) long.) The latter is softer and apparently is of tree tallow.

Japanese candles follow generally the methods of Chinese manufacture. It is more than probable that the art of making candles was introduced from the older country. The candles made by the Japanese are more accurately and neatly finished than the Chinese. They are frequently beautifully decorated. The industry also was most carefully organized in every detail. An ingenious method of molding candles in paper tubes was worked out by the Japanese.

In the Western Hemisphere a number of local or domestic industries connected with wax yielding trees and plants may be noted. The bayberry, *Myrica cerifera*, of the eastern coast of the United States produces a waxy substance which in the earlier days of the country was made into candles by economical housewives of New England. It is said to have been discovered by a New England surgeon who made it into candles and introduced it into medicine. The Indians made no use of the wax, as stated by Pere Lafiteau in his work of 1724. In Middlesex, west side of the Connecticut River, near Haddam, is Candleberry Hill. There is tradition of the use of the wax from berries here to make candles during the Revolution. The method of extracting the wax was to fill a kettle half full of water, put in bayberries and boil them. The heated mass was then put in a bag over a kettle of water and strained. As the water cooled a film of wax consolidated on the surface. This was the desired wax. The wax was not only used in making candles but wax mixed with tallow to harden the candles made for summer use. The wax was also sold in drug stores. The cylinders employed in the early graphophones were made of this wax.

Candles were made in Brazil from wax from the Ceroxylon, or wax palm. In northern Brazil the *Klopstockia cerifera* (*cornauba*), produced a useful wax, as does a Myrica in Peru. The *Virola sebifera* (*dari*), a large tree growing in Demarara, bears seeds from which candles equal to wax was made. Specimens of bayberry candles from New England are Cat. No. 229926; Alice Morse Earle. Rude candles of myrtle wax, made by natives of Puerto Plata, Santo Domingo, are Cat. No. 29923. (Charles A. Frazer; 12.2–15 inches (31–38 cm.) long.) An account of bayberry wax is found in Scientific American Supplement.[4]

Rush candles in the British Isles preceded the candle with textile fiber wick, and followed the fatted rush which was used in the clips described. Rushes were gathered, the cortex peeled off, exposing the pith except a small strip of the outer covering which was allowed to remain to sustain the fragile pith. These were dipped in hot fat

---

[4] Sept. 1, 1883, p. 6385.

and put away to season. (Cat. No. 150410, Surrey, England; Edward Lovett; 14 inches (35.5 cm.) long.) They were later " dipped " by the usual domestic process for tallow candles. Rush wicks, even with part of the cortex left on, were not strong enough to pull in molds, hence such candles were dipped, a method preceding the use of molds.

Tinned iron candle molds are comparatively common, and many are seen in collections where they point out that formerly candle making was an important domestic industry. In reality the molds represent a method of economy among our ancestors in that small amounts of fat could be worked up into candles with the molds when required. Generally on the plantations, where a great many candles were necessary, sufficient were made for the whole year by dipping, which was far more expeditious than by molds. Candle dipping was usually coincident with the butchering of the winter stores of meat, at which time much fat was accumulated.

The molds shown range from 3 tubes to 24 tubes. The 3-tube specimen has lost the stand. (Pl. 10, fig. 1, Cat. No. 127281, Lynchburg, Va.; Mrs. Ed. Hunter; 9.7 inches (24.5 cm.) high. Fig. 2 has 6 tubes. Cat. No. 298359, Virginia, Dr. P. B. Johnson; 10.8 inches (27.5 cm.) high.) The 8-tube specimen retains the stand. The tubes are less tapered than in the examples described. (Fig. 3, Cat. No. 126825, Virginia; Mrs. G. Brown Goode; 11 inches (28 cm.) high.) The 24-tube mold has handles on two sides and the tubes are only slightly tapered. (Fig. 4, Cat. No. 175464; Morgantown, W. Va.; Walter Hough; 11 inches (28 cm.) high.)

Slender candles called tapers have still a general currency for religious use. As suggested, these are survivals of the flambeaux tapers cut into lengths for a definite use. They are intended to be carried in the hand and rarely or never are sticks designed for them. Plate 9b figures a number of these tapers. Figure 1 is a bundle of mocoluteori used in the Roman carnival. They are very slender and of white wax. (Cat. No. 154308, Italy; G. Brown Goode; 9 inches (23 cm.) long.) Figures 2, 3, and 4 are bundles of tapers sold in the churches and used by the devout in processions and other ceremonials. The tapers in Figure 2 are rather large and of natural yellow wax. Those of Figure 3 are long and slender natural wax. Figure 4 are red tapers. (Cat. No. 238067, 238070, 238068, Manila, P. I.; Philippine Commission; 12.6 inches (32 cm.) long, 13.4 inches (34 cm.) long, 10.2 inches (26 cm.) long.) Figure 5 is of a bundle of white, red, orange, yellow, pink, and green tapers bought at Madrid, Spain, and used in Christmas festivities in 1892. (Cat. No. 166996; Walter Hough; 7.5 inches (19 cm.) long.) Figure 6 are small candles of red, white, and green wax and called tapers. They were " bought (and freely burned) in the Great Golden Pagoda at Rangoon, Burma, December 30, 1885," writes the donor. (Cat. No. 129532, Rangoon, Burma; Rev. C. H. A. Dall; 3.8 inches (9.5 cm.) long.)

There are a number of candleholders connected with special occupations and of much human interest. These show invention off the beaten track and are examples of the adaptiveness of the plain people. About the domestic textile industry there are needs for special lighting and a number have been used. The weaver, for instance, plying her loom in the twilight hours or on dark days had a thin S-shape iron candlestick with a hook to hang it conveniently before the work. (Pl. 6b, fig. 7, Cat. No. 178798, Antrim, Ireland; Edward Lovett; 18 inches (46 cm.) long.) The brewer had a candleholder cut from a block of wood with hand grasp, socket in the middle and an awl point at the other end for thrusting into casks. (Pl. 11a, fig. 4, Cat. No. 178361, Washington, D. C.; George Woltz; 7.9 inches (20 cm.) long.) Another form of iron with a vertical and horizontal spike leg was useful in many places from the holds of New England ships to the barns of New Jersey. (Pl. 11a, fig. 3, Cat. No. 25937, Gloucester, Mass.; A. McCurdy Crittenden; 4.5 inches (11.5 cm.) long.) Western hard rock miners used a candlestick having a spring socket, a hook, a loop handle, and a long spike which on emergency could be or was reported to be useful as a dagger. (Pl. 11a, fig. 2, Cat. No. 129836, Colorado; Edward Wyman; 9.8 inches (25 cm.) long.) The miner's candlestick seems to have attracted American inventive spirit, for several improvements on the older form are in the collection. One specimen of excellently finished ironwork has a hinged spike with pivoted stop, which when folded down allows the candle to be hung to the hat by means of the hooks. The patent was granted September 4, 1877. (Pl. 11a, fig. 5, Cat. No. 251460; U. S. Patent Office; 7.7 inches (18.5 cm.) long.) Another is a miner's folding candlestick with a knife blade incorporated. (Pl. 11a, fig. 1, Cat. No. 251466; U. S. Patent Office; dated April 3, 1883. 8.2 inches (21 cm.) long.) During the Civil War in the United States the bayonet sometimes had a more peaceful employment than its designed purpose as a candlestick. Fortunately, the caliber of the bayonet and that of the candles used at the period agreed, but any adjustment necessary could be made with a bit of paper. (Pl. 11b, fig. 2, Cat. No. 325620; Walter Hough; 20.5 inches (52 cm.) long.) The Northern lumberjacks had a device suggesting the bayonet candlestick. The candle was held in the cleft of a sharpened stick by a strip of birch bark. Model from a drawing by David I. Bushnell, jr. (Pl. 11b, fig. 1, Cat. No. 325621, 23.4 inches (59.5 cm.) long.) The famed Gloucester fisherman in the eighties used a tin candle dish furnished with a long, sharp iron spike for sticking in a convenient wooden wall. A pair of these is in the fisheries collection of the National Museum. (Pl. 11a, fig. 6, 7, Cat. No. 54416, Gloucester, Mass.; J. W. Collins; 10.2 inches (26 cm.) long.) They were used in the hold in storing fish.

It has seemed necessary to use the name pricket candlestick for the candlestick having a spine on which the candle is stuck and socket candlestick for the common type used to-day. In practice it suffices to understand that candlestick means the socket type. The pricket type is found in eastern Asia and Europe. The surviving European examples are almost entirely ecclesiastical and large, for placing on altars. The pricket would suffice for holding the candle on stationary candlesticks, but for ambulant candlesticks the socket would seem better. The Museum has an excellent specimen in the form of a seven-branch wrought-iron processional candelabrum with prickets. The stem is expanded into a disk, and below is a socket for a staff by which the lights were carried. The specimen is of the fourteenth century. (Pl. 12, fig. 3, Cat. No. 176329, France; S. B. Dean; 32.5 inches (57 cm.) high, 13.3 inches (34 cm.) wide.) Two pricket church candlesticks of European provenance are figured in Plate 12. Figure 1 is of heavy bronze with large base and a drip catcher above, in the center of which is the spike. (Cat. No. 289421, Hildesheim, Germany; Anton Heitmuller; 20 inches (51 cm.) high.) This specimen may be taken as type of the massive roundel church candlesticks of the north. Figure 2 is a Spanish example of carved wood skillfully plated over with sheet iron, painted and gilt. Altar candlesticks of this sort are sometimes very large and are frequently observed in Spain. (Cat. No. 289421, Spain; Anton Heitmuller; 19.3 inches (49 cm.) high.) A spike stick two-arm iron wall light of the fourteenth or fifteenth century is represented as driven between the stones of a wall. This rare specimen is of handwork in soft iron, is very strong, and of graceful outline. (Pl. 13, fig. 3, Cat. No. 169094, England; S. B. Dean; 11 inches (28 cm.) wide.)

Asiatic pricket candlesticks are practically confined to China and Japan, and are usually representations of mythological beings. The candlesticks accompanying the ceremonial set used in ancestor worship at present may be excepted. The bronze figure holding a vase with flower candlestick appears to be one of a pair employed a long time ago in such worship. It is from the Henry J. Heinz collection, Pittsburgh, Pa. (Pl. 12, fig. 4, Cat. No. (1748 Heinz), China.) The pricket is observed on a finely made folding candlestick from Japan and a stork standing on the back of a turtle and bearing a branch in its bill. (Pl. 13, fig. 1, Cat. No. 248625, Japan; Eleanor Wallace; 15.3 inches (39 cm.) high, and fig. 2, Cat. No. 315086, Japan; Mrs. John Van Rensselaer Hoff; 11.5 inches (29 cm.) high.)

WOODEN CANDLESTICKS

Specimens of wood are not common, perhaps on account of the thought of risk of burning. Most of those in the Museum collection are from parts of Finland, secured at a time when a most interesting primitiveness was observed in the life of the folk. Plate 14, figure 7, is a joined candlestick of wood with an iron socket. This candlestick was whittled from wood in a way to suggest turning. (Cat. No. 167862; Hon. John M. Crawford; 10.1 inches (26 cm.) high.) Figure 9 is made from a multiforked branch, with the socket cut out of the stem. (Cat. No. 167863, Finland; Hon. John M. Crawford; 5.8 inches (15 cm.) high.) Figure 10 appears to be a very old specimen cut from wood. (Cat. No. 167941, Finland; Hon. John M. Crawford; 5.8 inches (15 cm.) high.) Figure 8 is a candlestick turned from walnut and used in the church of the Seventh Day Adventists at Ephrata, Lancaster County, Pa., many years ago. (Cat. No. 4,812; Miss Concordia W. Myers; 7.8 inches (20 cm.) high.)

CANDLESTICKS OF EARTHENWARE AND STONE

Ruder forms of unglazed pottery and examples cut from soft stone are presented here. They are folk craft not depending in most cases on a customary form such as appear at the time of the trades. An interesting specimen is a cylindrical block of chalk with central candle socket. This was used by the Brandon, England, gun-flint makers for measuring time while at work. Chips of flint were stuck in the candle at one-hour spaces previously determined. (Pl. 14, fig. 1, Cat. No. 211911, Brandon, England; Edward Lovett; 2.7 inches (7 cm.) diameter.) Figure 3 is cut from sandstone and rudely ornamented with parallel scores representing rain. Rude stone candlesticks have been collected from several of the eastern Pueblos. They are of course post-Conquest and appear to have been used in the Mission churches. (Pl. 14, fig. 3, Cat. No. 234749, Jemez, Pueblo, New Mexico; Mrs. Matilda C. Stevenson; 5 inches (12.7 cm.) diameter.) Figure 2 is an earthenware candlestick slightly glazed, with drip catcher and hole for ejecting the stub end. (Cat. No. 115797, Indian potters of San Pedro, Mexico; Edward Palmer; 3.2 inches (8 cm.) diameter.) Figure 5 is an earthenware dish candlestick which is quite effective for its lowly use. (Cat. No. 73893, Merida, Yucatan, Mexico; Louis H. Aymé; 4.4 inches (11 cm.) diameter.) Figure 6 is a candlestick pinched out of clay and baked. It was used by the Indians of Santa Cruz, Mexico. (Cat. No. 175565; Edward Palmer; 3.3 inches (8.5 cm.) diameter.)

Figure 4 is an earthenware figure of a reclining Bacchus supporting a floriated candle socket. This is a modern conception. (Cat. No. 129408, Italy; Mrs. E. S. Brinton, 4.1 inches (10.5 cm.) long.)

GLAZED POTTERY AND GLASS CANDLESTICKS

The candlestick on its material side reflects to some extent periods of culture and phases of art. A North African candlestick of earthenware glazed and decorated with ornamentation in deep blue is a worthy exhibit of native handiwork and art. (Pl. 15, fig. 1, collected at Tetuan, Morocco, by Dr. and Mrs. Talcott Williams; 16.3 inches (41 cm.) high.) As a rule, earthenware candlesticks offer great difficulties in manufacture and are, therefore, not so common as those made of finer materials by modern processes of manufacture. Among the almost infinite kinds and conditions of modern candlesticks it is possible to touch but few and those of the average within the means of the average people. One example of a highly glazed stoneware is shown in Plate 14, Figure 14. It dates about 1870 and was made in Hungary. (Cat. No. 325622, Centennial Exposition, Philadelphia, 6.7 inches (17 cm.) high.) Porcelain was a favorite medium for candlesticks. The pair shown in Plate 14, Figures 11 and 12, are of Liverpool china and date about 1820. (Cat. No. 317638, England; Mrs. N. L. White; 8.3 inches (21 cm.) high.) The pair marked Figure 15 on the plate are German, probably (Royal Saxon) Meissen, and date near 1800. (Cat. No. 289428, Germany, Anton Heitmuller; 8.3 inches (21 cm.) high.) Figure 13 is of dark green cut glass of Bohemian manufacture, about 1840. (Cat. No. 300321, Czechoslovakia; Mrs. C. E. Danforth; 10.6 inches (27 cm.) high.)

SILVER AND PLATE CANDLESTICKS

The technic of the brass worker is radically different from that of the silversmith. The brass worker descends in the line of the bronze and cast-iron workers of antiquity, while the silver worker emerges with the pattern maker (perhaps of lamps) of old Rome. The difference is between casting and beating or pressure. It is understood, of course, that brass was often beaten in the method of silver and copper, but neither of the latter was cast as a practical method of working. The candlestick figured on Plate 16, Figure 3, is a case in point. It is an old Sheffield Baroque candlestick made of sheet copper silvered by rolling that metal with copper by the well-known Sheffield process. The socket roundels, swell of the stem, are formed by spinning, beating, or other processes and joined to form the candlestick. (Cat. No. 311537, England, Elizabeth S. Stevens; 11.7 inches (30 cm.) high.) The base of this candlestick is loaded and covered with coarse green baize. Two pairs of desk candlesticks of silver are good examples of the silversmith's art and skill in design. The pair to the left had the Victorian hallmark of 1886 and the initials of the maker, J. K. B. These are no doubt a copy of earlier Georgian silversmith's work. The base is loaded with cutler's cement of resin covered with an iron plate. (Pl. 17, fig. 2, Cat. No. 311534, England; Elizabeth S. Stevens; 5.2 inches (13 cm.) high.) The second pair are the antithesis in design of the first pair, showing a circular base and a stem of soft curves. The base is loaded with a cast-iron plate. (Pl. 17, fig. 2, Cat. No. 311535, (no mark); 5.5 inches (14 cm.) high.) More ornate candlesticks are Sheffield with mark, probably 1800, and appear to follow the French style of Louis the Fourteenth. (Pl. 17, fig. 4, Cat. No. 311531, England; Elizabeth S. Stevens; 10.2 inches (26 cm.) high.) The middle pair are plate, Rococo in style, and follow the art of Louis Sixteenth, the stem showing the return to classical art. (Pl. 17, fig. 5, Cat. No. 311532, England; Elizabeth S. Stevens; 12.6 inches (32 cm.) high.) The third pair of Sheffield plate are called Chippendale; that is, following the conception of that master designer. The sockets are oblong rectangular. The bases are weighted and the bottoms covered with green baize. The date of these candlesticks is believed to be near 1770. (Pl. 17, fig. 6, Cat. No. 311530, England; Elizabeth S. Stevens; 10.4 inches (27 cm.) high.) At one period many candlesticks were made in France from designs furnished by sculptors, sometimes by eminent artists who may have been in need. The period perhaps coincided with that of pottery figures and groups, which must always be regarded as an unwarranted departure from the true field of ceramics. To some extent the same may be said of the candlestick miniature groups in silver and brass which served mainly to increase the supply of scarcely useful bric-a-brac. A pair of these is shown in Plate 17, Figure 1, representing a camel bearing a fanciful candle socket. This pair is marked Reed and Barton and simulates silver. (Cat. No. 311651, United States; Elizabeth S. Stevens; 4 inches (10 cm.) high.)

CANDLESTICKS OF PEWTER

Not so many pewter candlesticks have come down from the period of their use. Pewter, on account of its liability to distortion and the care required to keep it presentable, and also the economic demand for old pewter for other uses, had a tendency to become scarce. One of the best specimens of pewter candlestick is that which belonged to Col. Joseph Warner, of the Massachusetts Colony, exhibited in the collection of the Society of Colonial Dames in the historical collection of the U. S. National Museum. (Cat. No. 486, Massachusetts; Mrs. Marcus Benjamin; 8.5 inches (21 cm.) high. Pl. 16, fig. 1). Two old German pewter candlesticks from Hildesheim are in the collection. They are enameled, except on the rings in red and yellow, respectively. No marks are observed on these specimens. (Pl. 19, fig. 19, Cat. No. 289427; Anton Heitmuller; 7.7 inches (19.5 cm.) high.) The Chinese used pewter candlesticks on the altar of ancestor worship, some elaborate and some plain. These are pricket candlesticks. (See p. 20.) (Pl. 18, fig. 1, Cat. No. 75344; Chinese Centennial Commission, Philadelphia, 1876; 13.3 inches (33.5 cm.) high.) A pair of handsome candlesticks in metal resembling pewter, shown on Plate 18, Figure 2, are of English manufacture and appear to be Georgian, or after a Georgian model which was probably in silver. (Cat. No. 311678, Elizabeth S. Stevens; 7.8 inches (22.5 cm.) high.)

CANDLESTICKS OF BRASS

It is really a short time comparatively since the socket candlestick took its place as an important feature of house furnishings. The Romans left candlesticks in the débris of the ancient Roman station of Saalberg, Germany, but it was many centuries before they became usual in Europe. Brass, the useful alloy which was known in India in the third century B. C., became widely disseminated. More lamps, candlesticks, and religious objects were made of brass than of any other metal. It would seem not beside the mark to term the period following the Bronze Age and before the wide distribution of iron the Age of Brass. There is no doubt that brass candlesticks are the oldest form of this lighting device in metal. It is difficult, however, to date the common brass candlestick except special patterns which have arisen generally at a late period in various cultured countries. The roundel sticks seem to go back very far and are molded from wood turned patterns, which accounts for their resemblance to products of the lathe worker's art. Candlesticks of the roundel type, which may be assigned to the American colonial period and subsequently, have an oblong rectangular or square base with truncated or rounded corners, cut separately and joined to the stem. Plate 19, Figure 16, is a colonial mantel or table candlestick of brass. (Cat. No. 216269, Pennsylvania; Anton Heitmuller; 8 inches (20.5 cm.) high.) There appears to be no data as to when the manufacture of candlesticks of this type was discontinued. It may be hazarded that it was about 1860, near the period when coal oil struck a disastrous blow to the candlestick industry. Replicas, however, have been occasionally made to supply a certain demand. The specimen (pl. 16, fig. 2) appears to be in this class. (Cat. No. 311538, United States; Elizabeth S. Stevens; 11.8 inches (30 cm.) high.) Figure 4 is a solid brass cast of the turned wood model more slender and graceful than those described and tastefully ornamented. (Cat. No. 311,-539, England; Elizabeth S. Stevens; 10.7 inches (27 cm.) high.)

This specimen is not old, but is probably a replica of an older candle-stick. Another ornate pair shows how far variation may be carried on the old turned wood model. (Pl. 19, fig. 17, Cat. No. 325911, England; M. L. Turner; 10.8 inches (27.5 cm.) high.) There are many solid cast brass candlesticks with slender roundel stem and oblong rectangular base with claw or ball feet, of which the date is not ascertained. Some of the specimens in the collection are much worn and damaged, more so than the English baluster type, and appear old. (Pl. 19, fig. 18, Cat. No. 290442, France; Mrs. C. E. Bates; 10 inches (25.5 cm.) high.) Brass candlesticks in general are provided with a simple device for pushing up the candle ends in the socket for economical burning. This is a rod passing upward through the stem and terminating in the socket with a disk. When this device began to be utilized is not ascertained; also there is no information as to whether it was patented. If not, it was applied to candlesticks before the establishment of patent offices.

CANDLESTICKS OF HAMMERED IRON

A familiar iron candlestick of early times in America was a widely accepted type because it was indestructible and serviceable to the limit of early ideas of economy. It had a cupped base, a straight tube with a slide, and a rim around the top provided with a hook for hanging up or for carrying. On occasion this candle-stick in virtue of the cupped base was used to scrape hogs at the butchering and also could be used to cut out cookies. (Pl. 19, fig. 15, Cat. No. 75359, Bainbridge, Pa.; George Bean; 6.1 inches (15.5 cm.) high.) A candlestick prized by collectors is variously assigned to Switzerland, Germany, and the Tyrol. It is really a remarkable piece of seventeenth century ironwork, showing the art of the painstaking craftsman unmindful of time. The specimen is dated 1709. It shows ancient survivals from the splint clip in its spring arm and the hook for hanging. (Pl. 20, fig. 2, Cat. No. 130655, Switzer-land; Goldsborough and Co.; 11.4 inches (29 cm.) high.) Another type familiar in collections and frequently copied is of hammered iron. It consists of a lobed base, a short column from which rises a spiral surmounted by a ring with a hook. In the spiral works a candle socket with a guiding hook allowing the candle to be moved up and down, a feature in advance of candle slides and not bettered before the advent of the spring candlestick. (Pl. 20, fig. 1, Cat. No. 168313, Germany; S. B. Dean; 10.2 inches (26 cm.) high.) The specimen dates about 1700 and shows some relationship to Figure 2. This type of candlestick was called "Martin Luther." Rude wrought-iron candlesticks are somewhat common. These, like the betty lamps, were exhibits of the skill of the local smith, who not infrequently wished to show what he could do. One of these has a ring base to which three prongs at the lower end of the stem are welded. The drip catcher is large and has a hook extending down from one side, answering as a handle and hanger. (Pl. 20, fig. 3, Cat. No. 289432, United States; Anton Heitmuller; 5.6 inches (14.5 cm.) diameter, 9.1 inches (23 cm.) high.)

CANDLESTICKS OF CAST IRON

About 1870 cast iron was the medium for many art works. It had, however, only a temporary vogue, although the material, especially in the hands of the Russian artist-artizans, was capable of producing fine results. Among the works in cast iron were candlesticks generally showing the worst phases of Rococo art. These are regarded with disfavor by collectors and not many find a way into their hands. The specimens shown are German and consist of two candlesticks and two candle dishes, one of cast iron and another of cast brass showing the same class of work and of the same period. (Pl. 19, fig. 13, is a candlestick, Cat. No. 300383, Germany; Mrs. C. E. Danforth; 7.1 inches (18 cm.) high.) Figure 12 is a similar specimen without dripcatcher. (Cat. No. 300384, same locality and donor; 6.4 inches (16 cm.) high.) Candle dish (fig. 14), also from the same donor, is a good example of the art overloading of the period. (Cat. No. 300385, 8.1 inches (20.5 cm.) long.) Figure 11 is of heavy cast brass, trefoil design. (Cat. No 301540, Germany; Library of Congress; 6.8 inches (17.5 cm.) long.)

CANDLE DISHES OF METAL

The candle dish expresses the need of a less formal furnishing than the candlestick. It not only insures the means of carrying the candle about but provides a catch-all for drip as a concession to cleanliness. Candle dishes were made of sheet iron tinned or otherwise, copper, brass, and silver, or silver plate. Plate 19, Figure 4 is a specimen boldly hammered from copper. The handle is pierced for hanging the dish as a sconce. (Cat. No. 317216, Mexico; Harry S. Bryan; 4.6 inches (11.5 cm.) diameter.) In contrast is a dainty French candle dish of repoussee silver. (Pl. 19, fig. 5, Cat. No. 317637; Mrs. N. L. White; 4.3 inches (11 cm.) diameter.) Figure 6 is of hammered and chiseled brass with saucepan handle riveted on. It is dated 1785. (Pl. 19, fig. 6, Cat. No. 168318, England; S. B. Dean; 5.5 inches (14 cm.) diameter.) A neatly made specimen of sheet iron crimped on the border is from Nantucket, Mass. It has a ring for the finger. (Pl. 19, fig. 7, Cat. No. 129904; F. B. Smith; 6.5 inches (16.5 cm.) diameter.) The next figure is an ornate dish of Sheffield plate with an aperture in the stem for snuffers (Pl. 37) and a socket in the ring for the extinguisher. (Pl. 19, fig. 8, Cat. No. 130666, Baltimore; J. S. Russell; 6.3 inches (16 cm.) diameter.) Figure 9 is a sheet-iron candle dish tinned, from Hanover, York Co., Pa. (Pl. 19, Cat. No. 151462; T. W. Sweeney; 6.9 inches (17.5 cm.) diameter.) The last figure is a typical brass candle dish widely familiar to the older generation of Americans. (Pl. 19, fig. 10, Cat. No. 289447.) United States; Anton Heitmuller; 6.1 inches (15.5 cm.) diameter.) An unusual candle dish is boat shape of sheet brass, the handle having been applied at one side. (Pl. 19, fig. 1, Cat. No. 311867, Holland; Elizabeth S. Stevens; 8.8 inches by 5.5 inches diameter (22.5 cm. by 14 cm.).) Another excellent specimen is of sheet brass, oval, and well ornamented with punched work. The handle terminates in a hook. (Pl. 19, fig. 2, Cat. No. 311866, England; Elizabeth S. Stevens; 7.8 inches by 5.4 inches diameter (19.7 cm. by 13.5 cm.) Figure 3 (pl. 19) is a candleholder which slides into a slot in the candle dish.

CANDLESTICKS WITH WIND GLASSES

Glass protectors for candlesticks were in use for a long period in America. They resemble in shape the lamp chimney formerly used, but much larger. They were, it is presumed, the largest piece made by the glass blower. Well-to-do families in the States which were the Colonies would possess and carefully treasure these "hurricane glasses," as they were called. These glasses were imported from England, where they were made, and decorated in floral designs with the wheel. It was customary to set these hurricane globes in a drafty hall or on the portico to protect the candle from the breeze. (Pl. 21, fig. 5, Cat. No. 315102 (candlestick, No. 251722); Mrs. John Van Rensselaer Hoff; 9.8 inches (25 cm.) diameter, 22 inches (57 cm.) high.)

Candlesticks were often fitted with graceful flaring glass protectors, the bases of which had a brass collar fitting around the candle socket. (Pl. 21, fig. 6, Cat. No. 309022, United States; Mrs. Abby Knight McLane; 18.8 inches (48 cm.) high.) Such candlesticks are again coming into use for decorative effects. Another obsolete form, but of the modern period, is seen in a candle stand with glass globes. It consists of a pair of spring candleholders of Palmer's invention about 1845 running on an upright support and adjusted with a screw. It is of white brass. (Pl. 21, fig. 4, Cat. No. 315103, England; Mrs. John Van Rensselaer Hoff; 22 inches (56 cm.) high.)

CANDLE ARMS

Candle arms are in the form of rigid brackets or brackets hinged on pins or extensible. The form of candle installation reaches back to an uncertain date, certainly before the fifteenth century. Its use

has survived for special purposes to this day. An interesting specimen of Spanish iron candle arm of the fifteenth or sixteenth century
was collected in Seville, Spain, in 1893. It is said to have hung
over the entrance to the convent of the Santa Trinidad at Seville,
the square cross painted partly red and blue being, it is alleged, the
sign of that convent. The monogram is also worked in the scroll.
The arm shows traces of paint and gilding. (Pl. 20, fig. 4, Cat. No.
325623; Walter Hough; 13.8 inches by 13 inches (35 cm. by 33 cm.).)
An extension arm of wrought iron of Belgian manufacture is shown
in Plate 20, Figure 5. The specimen has five pivoted sections. The
candle socket with drip catcher is set at the end of the arm. (Cat.
No. 168320, Belgium; S. B. Dean; 18.5 inches (47 cm.) long.) A
more elaborate specimen of old ironwork consisting of five pivoted
sections is from Nuremburg, Germany, and is probably early eighteenth century. (Pl. 20, fig. 6, Cat. No. 168321; S. B. Dean; 18.5
inches (47 cm.) long.) The third specimen is an extensible brass
candle arm cut out and joined by modern methods. Such arms were
used on desks and pianos. (Pl. 20, fig. 7, United States; Charles
D. Walcott; 18.9 inches (48 cm.) long.)

CANDELABRA

Ascending in the scale from the stemmed utilitarian candlestick
is the candelabrum or arm candlestick, connoting luxury and taste
with the basal idea of more light. An interesting brass two-arm
candelabrum in the collection dates from the early eighteenth century. It is Dutch, has an openwork stem of conventional vine and
leaves, and has a punched tracing on the base. (Pl. 22, fig. 1, Cat.
No. 311528, Holland; Elizabeth S. Stevens; 10.6 inches (27 cm.)
high.) A specimen in brass of unusual design has three candle
sockets on floriated brackets moving on a rod stem arising from a
basin. This fine specimen is evidently a floor candelabrum. (Pl.
22, fig. 3, Cat. No. 289420, English; Anton Heitmuller; 26.3 inches
(67 cm.) high.) One of a pair of French Empire candelabra regarded
as rare is shown in Plate 22. The base is square, the column
of ormolu brass topped with a half globe on which stands an exqui-
sitely modeled bronze Cupid holding up a combination of bow,
quiver, arrows, and two candle sockets. The work is executed
with the greatest regard for detail. (Pl. 22, fig. 2, Cat. No. 311533,
France; Elizabeth S. Stevens; 14.6 inches (37 cm.) high.) Another
interesting example of candelabrum of Rococo style is in the collection. It is of ormolu brass, with four arms set in the sides of
a mirror erected on a marble base. Arising from the apex of the
mirror is an openwork cup holding a flower receiver of fine blue
glass delicately shaped. (Pl. 22, fig. 4, Cat. No. 311541, France;
Elizabeth S. Stevens; 24 inches (61 cm.) high.)

SCONCES

These candleholders have never reached any considerable importance in the field of illuminating devices, but as aids in decoration have played a great part. They are the origin of the side lights used for the double purpose of lighting and beautifying dining rooms of modern houses. One of the early and simple forms of the sconce is shown in Plate 21, Figure 2. It is of sheet iron and has the dignified aspect of good work and design. (Cat. No. 129905, Nantucket, Mass.; F. B. Smith; 9.5 inches (24 cm.) high.) A good example of folk art is shown in the Dutch brass sconce with three candle sockets. The decoration is in repoussé. (Pl. 21, fig. 3, Cat. No. 233136, Holland; Walter Hough; 8.5 inches (21.5 cm.) wide, 10.2 inches (26 cm.) high.) A Rococo sconce in silvered copper with mirror has a detachable candle socket on a curved arm. The pair is of German workmanship. (Pl. 21, fig. 1, Cat. No. 311543, Germany; Elizabeth S. Stevens; 17.9 inches (45.5 cm.) high, 14 inches (35.5 cm.) wide.)

CHANDELIERS

Chandeliers have followed the development of illumination and therefore represent every type from the rush light to the electric light. They are described together here for convenience of treatment. The earliest chandelier in the collection is a noteworthy example of high-class English ironwork. It is described as a rush chandelier of the thirteenth-fourteenth century. Although this date may not be insisted upon, the specimen is apparently very old and a remarkably pure and consistent design. It is conjectured that bundles of fatted rushes were set in the perforated drip catchers at the end of the arms. (Pl. 23, fig. 1, Cat. No. 169098, England; S. B. Dean; 31 inches (79 cm.) diameter.) The chandelier with lusters shown in Plate 24a is English, early nineteenth century. It is of bronze gilt and consists of a stem with four crowns graded in size, the great crown with arms being supported by ornamental brackets. Three chain festoons with unusual links hang from the head into which the stem is screwed. The chandelier had eight candle arms fitted with cut-glass drip catchers. (Cat. No. 328624, Morgantown, W. Va. (Va.); Walter Hough; 45 inches (114 cm.) long.) A small chandelier of brass, Rococo in art, comes from Germany and dates about the middle of the eighteenth century. (Pl. 25, fig. 1, Cat. No. 289430; Anton Heitmuller; 18.1 inches (46 cm.) long.) Several Turkish chandeliers were secured at the Chicago World's Fair in 1893, and hung in the Arts and Industries Building of the National Museum. They are interesting specimens of ironwork, but especially so in the character of the lighting apparatus. This consists of glass cups with knob base set in arms riveted to the crowns, as the circular elements are termed. A tripod of wire bearing the wick is placed in the cup and water poured in to the required depth and on the water oil sufficient to allow the wick to emerge. This describes the customary Mohammedan oil-water lamp. (Pl. 26, Cat. No. 325625; Turkish Commission, World Columbian Exposition, Chicago, 1893; about 4 feet in diameter, 8 feet high.) From the Centennial Exhibition at Philadelphia in 1876 there was received through the courtesy of the Chinese Imperial Commission a magnificent chandelier in general effect blue owing to the mosaic of kingfisher feathers with which it is incrusted. The chandelier has arms and large and small rings for installing the lights. These were porcelain simple saucer lamps with rush wicks. (Pl. 24b Cat. No. 169334, 72 inches (183 cm.) long.) About 1830 camphine or "burning fluid" was introduced. This predecessor of gasoline was prepared by distilling turpentine over lime (see p. 68). The camphine chandelier shown on Plate 25, Figure 2, is of gilt brass and has a reservoir from which the fluid was delivered to the burners by gravity. (Cat. No. 127167, Lynchburg, Va.; William F. Page; 36 inches (92 cm.).) What may be called a sconce-candelabra is shown in Plate 23, Figure 2. It is of heavy cast brass and of German manufacture, about the seventeenth century. Gift of Mrs. E. S. Brinton, 12.8 inches (32.5 cm.) long and wide.

LANTERNS

Under this head will be classed lanterns as devices for protecting and transporting light, and exhibiting types of illumination inventions grading from the candle to advanced oil-burning lamps. It is apparent that those who newly possessed the candle must meet the problem of protecting this clear but fragile light from boisterous airs when carrying it about in the open. This was met by inclosing the candle in an apparatus capable of diffusing the light yet affording the flame sufficient protection. When these prime conditions were met yet other conditions, demanded by the uses to which the lantern was to be put, the place it was to be used or installed, as well as the requirements of taste, arose and were fulfilled. As to the origin or origins of the lantern nothing is known. The zone in which paper and sometimes textiles are used to cover the lantern may be centered in China; the zone of this cloth rendered transparent and employed usually on collapsing lanterns is Persia; horn, glass, and punched metal lanterns may be assigned to Europe. This may mean three origins of the lantern. Plates of horn as lantern windows were practically more serviceable than glass and transmitted sufficient light for ordinary needs. An English horn "lanthorn," a name which shows the connection of horn with this lighting apparatus, is figured on Plate 27a, Figure 1. In common parlance

such a lantern is called " Guy Fawkes," from some legendary asso-
ciation with that detested character. It is well and strongly made
from sheet iron, has a ring for carrying, three dormer ventilators,
and a door with catch. A rush candle is shown in the socket. This
quaint specimen is about 150 years old. (Cat. No. 130435, Wiltshire,
England; Edward Lovett; 17.3 inches (44 cm.) high.) An old horn
candle lantern which had belonged to United States Government
ship stores was found at Alexandria, Va. This specimen is somewhat vaguely given the date of 1812, but may well be older. It is
ventilated through the apex of the conical top and the carrying ring
band has a shield against the heat. (Pl. 27a, fig. 2, Cat. No. 325626;
Walter Hough; 18.9 inches (48 cm.) high.) At a later date sheets
of mica came into use and had advantages over horn. The specimen
is a two-wick tube lamp lantern of sheet iron, square in form with
pyramidal top perforated for ventilation. It has a large band handle which distinguishes the arm lantern. Date about 1830. (Pl. 46,
fig. 3, Cat. No. 178444, Alexandria, Va.; Walter Hough; 17 inches
(43 cm.) high.) A folding lantern used in the World War has
mica plates (Pl. 34, fig. 1). Concerning ventilation of lanterns it may
be stated that there are draft orifices below and above the light of
all except perforated lanterns. Perforated lanterns have been used
in America since colonial times and in Europe date much earlier.
A typical example of sheet-iron hand-punched in patterns is shown
in Plate 28a, Figure 3. The top is conical, like an extinguisher, and
has a circular handle and shield. The lantern has an ordinary candle
socket and also a "burn-all" consisting of five pieces of wire set in
a circle in a little pan for catching the drip and beneath a wooden
plug for fitting in the candle socket. This ingenious device was a contrivance of the original owner of the lantern, Dr. Charles McLane.
The lantern dates somewhat before 1795. (Cat. No. 175597, Morgantown, W. Va. (Va.); Fred C. Hough; 15 inches (38 cm.) high.) A
very old punched copper hand lantern comes from central Italy.
The top is conical, the handle missing. The decoration is in
perforated designs and repoussée. Around the base of the candle
socket were eight small holes for ventilation. The handle is of
wrought iron riveted to the side of the lantern. The specimen is
probably sixteenth century. (Pl. 28a, fig. 4, Cat. No. 324438, Italy;
John W. Butler; 12.4 inches (34 cm.) high, 7.6 inches (19 cm.)
diameter.) A rush light shade protector with perforations was
used in England about the beginning of the nineteenth century.
This protector had a door but no top. A cup containing the tube
socket was set in a receptacle on the bottom. (Pl. 28a, fig. 1, Cat.
No. 150412, Croydon, England; Edward Lovett; 13 inches (33 cm.)
high, 8.6 inches (22 cm.) diameter.) A Moorish candle lantern

with glass panes shows artistic perforations in the top and base. The top is bell-shape and has a circular band handle. The material of this artistic lantern is tinned iron. (Pl. 28c, fig. 3, Cat. No. (149), Tetuan, Morocco; Talcott Williams; 17.3 inches (44 cm.) high.) Lanterns with glass globes came into use about 1820, so far as known. They were installed with either candle sockets or wick tube lamps for burning fish oil. The circular handle was for slipping over the arm or for the hand. Most of the specimens are japanned. Some of this type are protected with a wire frame or the globe is held between the top and bottom by a locking device or sometimes cemented at the top. Of these (pl. 28c, fig. 5) is a small globe lantern with wire handle and a hook for hanging on the dashboard of a vehicle. The globe is blown glass. The lamp is two-tube, with screw cap, and is removed by pressing two springs. The specimen was placed about 1812 by the donor. (Cat. No. 175581, Poland, Me.; W. P. Damon; 10.3 inches (26 cm.) high.) An arm lantern in the collection has an octagonal cast glass globe and is protected with wires. The bottom with candle socket is slid on over two pegs and slightly rotated to catch the pegs in a horizontal slot. The date is about 1820. (Pl. 28c, fig. 1, Cat. No. 130322, Morgantown, W. Va.; Ashbel Fairchild; 15.3 inches (39 cm.) high.) Another of about the same period has the octagonal glass globe cemented to the top and bottom. The glass two-tube lamp is removed by rotating it until two spurs coincide with two slots in the circular frame. (Pl. 28c, fig. 4, Cat. No. 175582, Poland, Me.; W. P. Damon; 12.6 inches (32 cm.) high.) A more ornamental form has four beveled plate-glass sides, a square base and top, and an arm ring. It is fitted with a flat wick kerosene lamp with a spur wheel wick ratchet. The bottom is hinged and may be turned down for attending to the lamp. The older lanterns were without this device. (Pl. 28c, fig. 2, Cat. No. 292696, United States; Isobel Rives; 12.5 inches (32 cm.) high.)

The transition from lanterns described to what became of the accepted form of lantern for many years is evident in different types. The old types persisted until the use of kerosene, when all lighting devices were profoundly modified. Invention perfected the tubular lantern in the eighties and it was the current form for many years and still has an immense sale. It is light, strong, reasonably wind proof, and is the last word in effectiveness. A predecessor of the tubular lantern was used by the United States Fish Commission in 1870. The lantern was patented December 1, 1868, has a glass tube held in a bow frame, suggesting the modern tubular **farm** lantern, and a two-wick tube burner set in a lamp which is **inserted** in the base of the lantern and held with spring clamps. The use of the wick tube at this late date is unusual. Another, about the same date, has a two-tube wick burner and the globe is protected by a sturdy wire frame to withstand the strong buffets of sea work. The lamp is removed by slightly turning the base, disengaging a spur pin from a slide. The lantern was patented March 15, 1890, by Howard and Morse, New York. Another lantern in the collection, not figured, has a glass globe protected in a wire frame. Within the glass globe is another of green glass. A flat-wick kerosene lamp supplied the light. Patented May, 1877, by Cash and Baron. Cat. No. 325629, East Coast; U. S. Fish Commission; 17.2 inches (44 cm.) high.) There is some question whether this is the first signal lantern with colored glass. Small lanterns for various employments are in number and many kinds, no doubt, have disappeared. An attractive little lantern secured in Spain in 1892 is said to have been used as a light in hunting for snails. It is an oil-burning lantern with single tube, the top and sides glazed, the top resembling the *louvre*, or chimney opening turret of old Spanish architecture. (Pl. 28*b*, fig. 1, Cat. No. 166990, Madrid, Spain; Walter Hough; 8.2 inches (19 cm.) high. A tumbler converted into a small candle lantern was made and sold in New England many years ago. These oddities are seen in most illumination collections. (Pl. 28*b*, fig. 3, Cat. No. 75384, New Bedford, Mass.; J. F. Brown; 8.2 inches (21 cm.) high.) Lamps for vehicles are and were in endless variety. As a subject for study lights connected with transportation offer a wide field. The specimen shown is a japanned carriage lantern of 1850. The lamp has one tube for heavy oil. There is a quadrille reflector at the back and an anular reflector around the light. (Pl. 28*b*, fig. 4, Cat. No. 325630, United States; Walter Hough; 8.2 inches (21 cm.) high.) The small lantern, Figure 2, is of the punched variety of sheet iron and is for a single-tube lamp. It appears to be quite old. (Pl. 28*a*, Cat. No. 167069, Madrid, Spain; Walter Hough; 7.5 inches (19 cm.) high.) So-called "Dark Jacks" or detectives' lanterns may be introduced with a Korean dark lantern which consists of a globular shell of basketry covered with paper decorated with circular characters and with a circular opening. The handle is of wood, turning on a wire leading to the interior, and from the end of the wire hangs a candleholder mounted in a gimbel frame by which the candle is erect, no matter in what position the lantern is held. This is regarded as the height of ingenuity and is alleged to have been invented long ago in Korea. (Pl. 29*a*, fig. 2, Cat. No. 273018, Seoul, Korea; H. C. Whiting; 14 inches (35.5 cm.) diameter, 16.9 inches (43 cm.) high.) Filipino fishermen use a somewhat similar lantern of calabash with a curved wood handle and rim sewed on at the mouth, but merely a suspended pottery lamp of antique shape is suspended within. (Pl. 29a, fig. 1, Cat. No. 283062, Tarlac, Luzon; Philippine Commission; 9.5 inches (24 cm.) diameter, 15.8 inches (40 cm.) high.) The dark lantern which antedates the electric flash light by perhaps several centuries was a device affected by guardians of the peace and it is said also by robbers. The specimen shown on Plate 27b, Figure 6, the oldest in the collection, is of French make, early eighteenth century. It is of good craftsmanship, the fluted turret being a difficult piece of work. The glass is bowed and is probably a later substitute for the horn pane. A candle was the means of illumination. In these lanterns of the earliest type the glass is mounted in a cylinder turning within the outer case and moved into position for light by rotating the turret. In this case the handle is rigid; in modern forms the handles fold back. (Cat. No. 311656, France; Elizabeth S. Stevens; 10 inches (25 cm.) high.) In point of age Figure 3, Plate 48, is next. The mechanism is as in the French specimen and it is also for candle. The handle is in two parts ingeniously fitted to slide together into flat position. The lantern is made of brass. (Cat. No. 168125, Italy; G. Brown Goode; 6.7 inches (17 cm.) high.) Another of modern type with bull's-eye of glass has also a collapsing handle and a two-wick tube lamp. The slide moved by the turret shuts off or admits the light through the lens. The back of the interior is tinned as a reflector. This feature is found in most of the dark lanterns. This specimen was used in the Armory Square Hospital during the Civil War. (Pl. 27b, fig. 4, Cat. No. 247659, Washington, D. C.; A. Haas; 6.3 inches (16 cm.) high.) Figure 2, Plate 27b, has a double turret with flutes, two wire handles, and a strip on the back for hanging the lantern inside the coat. This device brings the lantern nearer to comparatively modern police methods. This lantern dates 1845–1858. The slide is moved by a peg and slat and not by the turret. (Cat. No. 204894, Boston, Mass.; C. A. Q. Norton; 7 inches (18 cm.) high.) A two-tube wick lamp was used. Another similar specimen with candle socket is of black japanned tin. It was made by J. G. and W. Lord, Birmingham. (Pl. 27b, fig. 5, Cat. No. 316255, England; Walter Hough; 6. 9 inches (17.5 cm.) high.) A fine lantern of thick copper and embodying the principle of the dark lantern is in the collection. The light aperture is furnished with two plates of horn. The slide is moved as usual by turning the top and held by a button which slides in a slot when the lantern is open and shut. The lantern has a candle socket and two short tubular ventilators on either side of it. (Pl. 27b, fig. 1, Cat. No. 290447, probably English; Mrs. C. E. Bates; 14.4 inches (30.5 cm.) high, 6 inches (15 cm.) diameter.)

Ships' lanterns in the collection are a small part of the number which have been used in sail-bound commerce and other occupations on the sea. They serve, however, to convey an idea of the character of such lanterns employed on ships before the age of invention. Especially prized is a large rigging lantern whose lines of strength and dignity are due to the skill of a master designer of many years ago. Some ship in the New Bedford whaling fleet possessed this lantern. The body is hexagonal and the panes of glass protected by a grid of iron bars. The turret is in two parts, covered with a hood, above which is the suspending ring secured around the end of an iron rod passing down through the lantern and secured in the bottom. There are three candle sockets on the floor. The gracefully curved handles on either side of the turret were not only useful but add greatly to the completeness of the design of the lantern. (Pl. 30, fig. 1, Cat. No. 75376, New Bedford, Mass., J. T. Brown; 21.3 inches (54 cm.) high.) A small and comparatively new rigging lantern with glass panes, handle of wire, and one candle socket, comes from New Bedford, Mass. It is built of sheet iron and painted green. This square lantern was used on fishing schooners in 1882 and before. (Pl. 28b, fig. 2, Cat. No. 75375; J. T. Brown; 13.4 inches (34 cm.) high.) A Danish ship lantern with octagonal base glazed, a circular superstructure with ventilators, and a hood of fluted metal is shown in Plate 27a, Figure 3. The lamp burns heavy oil and has a circular wick installed around a tube as in the Argand and raised by a rod lift having a spur. The lamp is inserted in the base of the lantern by the pin and slot method. Within the lantern, resting on pegs, is a chimney with wide flange and polished to serve as an aid to ventilation and as a reflector. The lantern is excellently constructed of tinned sheet iron. The lantern was made by Lehmann, Kjobenhavn; no date. (Pl. 27a, fig. 3, Cat. No. 178199; L. M. Turner; 19.3 inches (49 cm.) high.) A ship's lantern of exceptional quality is shown as Figure 6, Plate 28c. The lantern lamp has a flat wick, but heavy oil was the fuel used. The globe is large and held between the top and base by the wire frame. The lamp is removed from below by the peg and slot method. The material from which the lantern is made is brass. The hood and base perforations are high-class work. The date is about 1840. (Cat. No. 325631, Alexandria, Va.; Walter Hough; 14.6 inches (37 cm.) high.) A curious lantern for hanging in an entry was collected in New Bedford, Mass., in 1882. The two-tube burner places this specimen earlier and in the heavy-oil period. The door is at one end. There are two reservoirs with two burners on each. The lantern is glazed and strongly protected by wire guards. The lantern is made of tin and painted green. The ventilating chamber has a trough-like shield open at the ends. (Pl. 29a, fig.

3, Cat. No. 75371, made by J. A. Tripp, collected for the U. S. Fish Commission by J. T. Brown; 16.5 inches (42 cm.) wide, 15 inches (38 cm.) high.) A lantern used in catching eels and employed by the fishermen of Noank, Conn., in 1876, is triangular in shape and has a triangular lamp of copper fitted with brass, ventilated kerosene burners. The lantern is made of wood and tin and has an inverted pannikin over the ventilator. (Pl. 29b, fig. 4, Cat. No. 29365; James H. Latham; 21.6 inches (52.5 cm.) wide, 23.2 inches (59 cm.) high.) A lantern for placing on a shelf for illumination of halls, stores, etc., has two reflectors, two tin lamps fitted with brass ventilated burners of the 1865 patent, and flask chimneys of lead glass. It is made of tin painted red and is glazed on three sides. Four ball feet, a wooden handle, and a wire slide to fasten the door are fitted to the specimen. (Pl. 29b, fig. 5, Cat. No. 325632, New England; U. S. Fish Commission; 17.3 inches (44 cm.) wide, 21.6 inches (55 cm.) high.) A fine specimen of European artistic lantern of the seventeenth century is in the Andrews collections. The lantern was a studio property of the late Eliphalet F. Andrews, the artist, who lived in Washington many years and who studied in Germany. The lantern is of pierced brass with copper facings to hold the glazing of horn or glass. It has three ball feet, a dome turret terminating in a ball, and a circular band handle. The bottom is chased with double eagle design. There is a single candle socket set in the middle of a pan, which is set on a dowell in the middle of the bottom. (Pl. 30, fig. 2, Germany; E. F. Andrews Collection, National Gallery of Art; 21 inches (53 cm.) high, 8.3 inches (24 cm.) diameter.) Lanterns of the Chinese and Japanese enter intimately into the life of the people and reflect the art and taste inherent in their culture. More forms of the lantern are found in these countries than in any other. A lantern of carved teak shown on Plate 31, Figure 2, was received from the Chinese Commission at the Centennial Exhibition at Philadelphia in 1876. The carving is painstakingly done and the joining is excellent. The design is evidently from a metal vase. A valence of brocade with heavy fringe hangs from a cornice-like projection. Other tassels, embroidered ornaments, and fringes of silk and beads decorate the lantern. The glasses are decorated with characters and color. The lamp is missing, but evidently was placed in the bottom by the peg and slot method. (Cat. No. 325633, China; Chinese Centennial Commission; 43.8 inches (111 cm.) long.) A more familiar Chinese hanging lantern has a hexagonal carved wood frame set with various size panes of painted frosted glass. From the six carved arms projecting from the upper part of the lantern hang streamers of silk with enamel placques bearing silk fringes. The lamp is European. The ratchet head is marked " P " above " Harvard " and below "A." It is of brass and has a ventilated burner which takes a flat wick of proper width and pulls it into a circular wick. Apparently the lamp dates 1876, but no patent stamp is visible. The lamp is raised and lowered by counterpoise chains. (Cat. No. 127832, China; T. B. Ferguson, 1887; 19.7 inches (50 cm.) diameter, 21.7 inches (55 cm.) high.) A table lantern in cinnabar lacquer, finely finished, and a noteworthy specimen of this characteristic work, is in the collection. The light chamber of the lantern is hexagonal and surmounted by an openwork section, and is supported on an elaborately worked stand. (Pl. 31, fig. 1, Cat. No. 309062, China; E. W. Keyser; 19.8 inches (50.5 cm.) high, 7.5 inches (19 cm.) diameter.) Japanese monumental lanterns of stone and bronze are widely known and form a pleasing note in garden and parks in many places far from their point of origin. In them is installed a tiny light which is more a guide than illumination.

A Japanese bronze lantern in the Museum, perhaps not an important specimen, illustrates this feature of art in Japan. The specimen is a Japanese toro, made in Tokio, 1850–1875, and is a copy of a larger lamp made since or about 1600. The base is circular, decorated with four panels bearing the seven gods of good fortune, in bas-relief. The shaft is of hourglass shape, decorated at top and bottom with bands of fretwork, about its middle is a collar bearing a bas-relief of the Japanese water dragon, above and below this are lotus leaves in low relief. The capital is circular, its lower part decorated with lotus leaves, its center with a band bearing bas-reliefs of the ape, cock, rabbit, and dragon (four of the twelve zodiacal signs). The lantern is ribbed or melon-shaped with five reticulated panels bearing the Shogun's crest (three mallow leaves) and bas-reliefs of four sages. One of these panels is hinged to open as a door, and is fastened with a latch in the form of the mythical bird, the hoho. The Shogun's crest is repeated in gilt on the bands at top and bottom of the lantern. The top is hexagonal, pagoda-shaped; the terminals of the ribs are projecting, up-curving dragon heads, with double tongues; beneath each is hung a wind bell similar to those hung at the eaves of the Buddhist temples. Between the ribs are bas-reliefs of sages. The underside of the top is ornamented with incised lines in their conventional forms of clouds. The apex is a representation of the jewel or sacred pearl enveloped in flames (the conventional form of representing it). The form of the toro is an evolution of their ancient symbols of nature. "*Cha*," or earth, is represented by the sacred pearl; "*Ka*," *or wind*, by the cloud-decorated top with its wind-clappered bells; "*Ka*," *or fire*, by the lantern; "*Wa*," or water, by the shaft decorated with the water dragon and lotus leaves; "*A*," *or earth*, by the base, with its bas-reliefs of earthly gods. (Pl. 32a, Cat. No. 94556; Edward Greey;

46 inches (117 cm.) high, 18.5 inches (47 cm.) diameter.) Another is a garden lantern of pottery with a light green glaze. This specimen is in four sections, and, like all lanterns of this type, is not provided with glass, but when necessary translucent paper is used to cover the open spaces. (Pl. 32b, Cat. No. 94312, Japan; Japanese Department of Education.) The *andon* or night light used in Japanese houses is an attractive piece of furniture. It consists in some instances of a circular light wooden base with four uprights bearing a paper-covered frame in two parts, which can be rotated one upon the other to open or close the lantern. The saucer lamp of brass with rush pith wick is set on a crossbar within the lantern. In a drawer in the base are kept the rush wicks. (Pl. 29b, fig. 1, Cat. No. 325635, Japan; Romyn Hitchcock; 12.6 inches (32 cm.) diameter, 32 inches (81 cm.) high.) Another specimen is square, and a sliding sash admits of opening the lantern. (Pl. 29b, fig. 2, Cat. No. 128236, Tokio, Japan; Japanese Department of Education; 10.3 inches (26 cm.) square, 31 inches (76 cm.) high.) A similarly constructed lantern is called *bonbori*. It has a handle projecting from the base. (Pl. 29b, fig. 3, Cat. No. 128245, Japan; Japanese Department of Education; 6 inches (14.5 cm.) diameter, 9.8 inches (24.5 cm.) high.) Among the lanterns for special uses in Japan are the *bajo* with extension of whalebone in the handle carried on horseback; the *gifu*, a most attractive lantern, from which is swung a wind bell; and the *umihari*, held when opened out in a curious extension frame and carried when walking at night. (Pl. 33, figs. 1, 2, 3, Cat. Nos. 128241, 128242, 128239; Japanese Department of Education; 20 inches (51 cm.) high—central figure.) The Chinese lanterns having a bamboo frame covered with silk is very attractive. The strips are pivoted at the ends in wooden rings and the cage so made is slipped over two iron rods arising from the turned wood base. By pressure on the top ring, somewhat as in an umbrella, the cage, which has been covered with filmy painted silk, is bowed out to the extent desired. (Pl. 31, fig. 3, Cat. No. 262641, China; Dr. Hugh M. Smith; 38 inches (96.5 cm.) high.) Collapsible lanterns have been widely used in the East and are apparently originally Persian. A fine specimen is of oiled linen, the folds held by wire secured by stitching. The top and bottom sections which hold the lantern when collapsed are of brass. The top is beaten up into 12 large and 14 small bosses and the surface is chased in fine dotted lines. The bottom is also elaborately covered with a chased design and small perforations. The handle and hook are ornamented. The candle socket is in the middle of a small cup riveted to the bottom. The specimen was received in 1869. (Pl. 33, fig. 5, Cat. No. 7552, Shuster, Persia; donor unknown; 15 inches (38 cm.) diameter, 30.5 inches (77 cm.) long.) A Japanese collapsible lantern, the

folds held by slender bamboo rings, is shown in Figure 6. The covering is tough oiled paper. The pricket candleholder has a drip catcher. The case is *percé à jour* chased. The top aperture is covered with a lid having a trifid floral crest as a central design. The bottom is chased with cloud designs. (Cat. No. 317682, Japan; Mrs. N. L. White; 4.7 inches (12 cm.) diameter.) Figure 4 is a Turkish collapsible lantern of folded white linen with no crease support. The case is of tinned sheet iron punched in linear pattern, the work being crude. (Cat. No. 74597, Egypt; Dr. George W. Sampson; 5.5 inches (14 cm.) diameter.) A collapsible pocket lantern almost of vest-pocket size was patented by Mr. Minor January 24, 1865. This lantern is most ingeniously hinged and the parts stowed in small compass so that it is a puzzle to open it up. The windows, which are only two on account of the exigencies of folding, are glazed with mica sheets. The lantern includes a small pocket for reserve candles and a sanded surface for scratching matches. (Pl. 34, fig. 2, Cat. No. 325636, United States; gift of the Misses Long; 2.9 inches by 3.1 inches, 5.1 inches high (7.5 cm. by 8 cm., 13 cm.) During the World War a folding lantern was issued to the United States forces. This was the Stoneridge lantern patented in 1908, folding into a compact bundle, and easily set up. The windows are glazed with sheets of mica. The candleholder is a wire-rack device which is the last word in burning candle ends. (Pl. 34, fig. 1, Cat. No. 325637, Washington, D. C.; Walter Hough; 14.2 inches (36 cm.) high.)

CHURCH CANDLESTICKS

In this great field the collection has only a few scattering examples. Some of these are shown under other headings (pl. 12). Of hand specimens there is a bishop's candle dish held for him by a deacon for the service after mass in the Roman Catholic Church. (Pl. 35, fig. 3, Cat. No. 325638; donor unknown; 10.6 inches (27 cm.) long.) A five-branch terra-cotta candlestick is included in the History of Religions collection. It is yellow brown in color and is excellent work. The candle cups screw into the arms. (Pl. 35, fig. 4, Cat. No. 152245, Italy; G. Brown Goode; 7.5 inches (19 cm.) diameter, 9 inches (23 cm.) high.) Like the baluster brass candlesticks described are those shown in Plate 35. This pair was used in a Jewish synagogue in Palestine. (Pl. 35, figs. 1, 1a, Cat. No. 315251; E. Deinard; 8.7 inches (22 cm.) diameter at base, 24.8 inches (63 cm.) high.) An excellent specimen of metal art affected by Persian influence is shown in a mosque candlestick of Moorish origin. (Pl. 35, fig. 2.) The material is brass treated to produce the shade of bronze, except the collar on the stem and margin of the socket. The surface is beautifully ornamented with chisel work in various patterns incorporating Arabic characters. While unique in design, the candlestick may be classed with the turned or baluster type. (Cat. No. 154459, North Africa; F. Keller; 13.4 inches (34 cm.) diameter at base, 23.6 inches (60 cm.) high.) Church candles which depart from the baluster type are most common in German art. This remark excludes candlesticks as individual expressions of artists and refers to candlesticks of usual pattern. An exceptionally fine specimen of German art is shown in Plate 35, Figure 6, from an old church at Hildesheim. The metal is bronze, the stem voluted, the base decorated with a pleasing design in relief produced by repoussee and outlined by graving. (Cat. No. 289422; Anton Heitmuller; 7.9 inches (20 cm.) diameter, 10.2 inches (26 cm.) high.) Another, probably older, is of worked brass, the voluted stem resting on an octagonal drip catcher, and the base formed into lobes. (Pl. 35, fig. 5, Cat. No. 311525, Germany; Elizabeth S. Stevens; 6.3 inches (16 cm.) diameter, 7.5 inches (19 cm.) high.) Figure 7 is of sheet brass with no drip catcher, a flat similar base, and an octagonal foot. The specimen is ornamented with repoussee work. (Pl. 35, fig. 7, Cat. No. 311524, Germany; Elizabeth S. Stevens; 6.3 inches (16 cm.) diameter, 7.5 inches (19 cm.) high.) Figures 5 and 7 appear to be complete and Figure 6 seems to lack the ornamental ledge at the top of the stem, unless this candlestick dates before it was customary.

NIGHT LIGHT CANDLES AND HOLDERS

For a considerable number of years squat candles of greater diameter than ordinary were made by candle manufacturers for use as a night light. In these the wick was held in a clip at the base of the candle to prevent it falling over when the candle burned low. Receptacles for burning these candles varied from a simple glass cup to elaborate night lights. Plate 36, Figure 2, is a candle as described. (Cat. No. 178181, Syracuse, N. Y.; Walter Hough; 1.9 inches (4.7 cm.) diameter.) Figure 1 is a brass holder like a dish candlestick. (Cat. No. 289425, England; Anton Heitmuller; 5.2 inches (13 cm.) diameter.) Figure 4 is a wine glass adapted as a holder and pierced for ventilation on one side (Cat. No. 315498, England; Mrs. Julian James; 9 inches (23 cm.) high), and Figure 3 shows a high-class installation for the night light in art glass brought from England but probably Venetian (Cat. No. 326725; the Misses Long; 7.2 inches (18 cm.) diameter, 10.2 inches (26 cm.) high). The ordinary night light used floating oil on water, as a lamp is described under its class, page 51.

TIME CANDLES

Time candles, called "King Alfreds," have been made in England as a reminder of the legend that the "Good King" first made these recorders of the fleeting hours. It is told that Alfred, feeling the great need for a more accurate division of the day into the three periods which he had allotted for his regimen, namely, eight hours for prayer, eight hours for sleep, and eight hours for work, devised a time candle. It is necessary to read into the legend at this point that Alfred by experiment found the amount of wax or tallow which, when made into a candle, would burn a certain time. It is told also that in order to preserve his candles from draft Alfred surrounded them with transparent horn, and it is gathered from this that he was the inventor of the lantern. The time candle figured in Plate 15, Figure 2, was made in London about 1890. They were sold as curiosities. (Cat. No. 152594, England; Edward Lovett; 11.4 inches (29 cm.) long.) The custom of auction by candle is recorded in numerous instances in England. In deference to the language of ancient conveyances some tracts of land are periodically sold in this manner to this day.

SNUFFERS, SNUFFER TRAYS, AND EXTINGUISHERS

It may well be surmised that the first snuffer was the index finger and thumb dextrously manipulated. It also seems true that snuffers were, for the above reason, not in considerable demand during the early periods of the candle. Old English snuffers were crude, consisting of two short rods of hand-forged iron expanded a bit at one end to form opposing faces, coming to a sharp point at the distal end, and pivoted like the rush clip. The elaborate and artistic specimens coming at the height of the candle as an illuminant form a vivid contrast to these. At this period luxury required a separate tray for the snuffers, or a candlestick with tray and a divided stem through which the snuffers could be thrust. The candlestick might also have a hole in the handle in which the arm of the extinguisher was to be stuck. Separate trays varied from inexpensive to costly. A familiar variety to former generations was of sheet iron lacquered and painted with floral designs. (Pl. 37, figs, 1, 3, Cat. No. 311870, Pennsylvania and the Colonies; Elizabeth S. Stevens; 10.3 inches (26 cm.) long.) Toward the other extreme is a Sheffield plate tray with ornamental border of silver. (Pl. 37, fig. 7, Cat. No. 303804, England; Isobel Lenman; 9.4 inches (24 cm.) by 4.3 inches (11 cm.).) A spoon-shape cast-brass tray with three ball feet and handle with a ring expresses the ideas of a Dutch artist designer. (Pl. 37, fig. 8, Cat. No. 168319; S. B. Dean; 10 inches (25.5 cm.) long.) Another, of cast brass, is bilobed and has four ball feet and a handle loop like that of the candle dish. (Pl. 37, fig. 12, Cat. No. 311504, England; Elizabeth S. Stevens; 7.7 inches (19.5 cm.) long.) An attractive brass candlestick with divided stem and tray for the snuffers is shown on Plate 37, figure 9. (Cat. No. 311540, European; Elizabeth S. Stevens; 3.3 inches (8.8 cm.) by 6.1 inches (15.5 cm.); 6.3 inches (16 cm.) high.) Another of Sheffield plate shows the divided stem and the placing of the extinguisher. Rarely have the candlestick, snuffers, and extinguisher been kept together. (Pl. 37, fig. 11, Cat. No. 311536, England; Elizabeth S. Stevens; 6.5 inches (16.5 cm.) by 4.9 inches (12.5 cm.), 3.9 inches (10 cm.) high.) Generally the snuffers which have survived are too large for the receptacle in the candlestick, which points to their use on trays and perhaps the later date of trays. Snuffers are with or without legs, and all have a sharp point for regulating the wick except Flemish specimens. The earlier forms simply pressed the fungus or charred portion of the wick between the two flat faces. Later forms pressed the fungus into a box inclosure, obviating the disagreeable odor. Still later, near the decline of the candle, a spring at the pivot was introduced and the final effort produced a spring partition which closed off the fungus into a separate chamber. Plate 37, figure 4, is a springless snuffer of brass. (Cat. No. 311869, England; Elizabeth S. Stevens; 6.3 inches (16 cm.) long.) Figure 5 is an artistic pair of brass with spring. (Cat. No. 311868, England; same donor; 7.3 inches (18.5 cm.) long.) Figure 2 is an artistic pair in silver and steel with spring partition as described. (Cat. No. 300846, England; Groce's Hardware Store, Washington, D. C.; 7.3 inches (19 cm.) long.) Figure 6 is a quaint, highly artistic Flemish snuffers of cast brass which appear clumsy in comparison with the English specimens. (Cat. No. 326314, Belgium; Kendrick Scofield; 7.7 inches (19.5 cm.) long.) Extinguishers also exhibit divergent grades of art, and, like snuffers, might be considered a refinement when a puff would extinguish a candle as effectively. The collection is without a pole extinguisher such as were used for candles placed in high situations, as in chandeliers. The specimen (pl. 37, fig. 10) is an elaborately ornamented example in brass. (Cat. No. 311874, France; Elizabeth S. Stevens; 2.4 inches (6 cm.) high.) The specimen attached to candlestick Figure 11 is of Sheffield plate and has an ornamented tip.

MODERN IMPROVEMENTS ON THE CANDLESTICK

About 1845 an Englishman named Palmer made improvements on candles and candlesticks. Palmer's device on the candlestick consisted of a spring placed in the tubular stem. The candle was thrust down, the tube compressing the spring, and was held by a locking cap which held the upper end of the candle. The cup, corresponding to the old candle socket, was choked. The candle was forced up by the spring as it burned, so that there was no excess to form a drip. A good example of excellent English brass work is shown in Plate 38, Figure 5, embodying Palmer's patent. (Cat. No. 168322; S. B. Dean; 13.3 inches (34 cm.) high.) A candlestick to which this device has been applied is Figure 6. It is of fine yellow brass and of superior design. The ring indicates that a glass bell formerly belonged with this specimen. The lower end of the tube has been closed with a threaded cap, as in Palmer's candlestick. (Cat. No. 168314, Scotland; S. B. Dean; 8.7 inches (22 cm.) high.) Figure 7 is of Sheffield plate. In this example a tube bearing the socket slips into the stem and can be raised to candle height. This is evidently a gravity device which acts like Palmer's spring pressure. It is not known whether this antedates Palmer's patent. The fittings show that a bell of glass was installed on this candlestick. (Cat. No. 325639, England; Walter Hough; 8.7 inches (22 cm.) high.) "Green's Arctic lamp patent," so called, used Palmer's device and had attached to the shade holder a cap on an arm which could be tripped, falling down and extinguishing the light. (Pl. 38, fig. 1, Cat. No. 178371, England; Paul Brockett; 10 inches (25.5 cm.) long.) As a side light on the small economies of the candle period are shown various simple devices for saving candle ends. Plate 38, Figure 2, shows a nickeled-iron extra socket for holding a candle end in the candle socket. (Cat. No. 325641, Paris, France, 1892; Walter Hough; 1.7 inches (4 cm.) long.) Another, Figure 3, clutches the candle with numerous arms adjusted by an encircling ring with scalloped edge. (Cat. No. 292508, Austria; 1.2 inches (3 cm.) long.) A handmade brass candle-end burner is from Scotland. (Pl. 38, fig. 4, Cat. No. 169096; S. B. Dean; 3.6 inches (9 cm.) long.) In 1892 there could be bought in Paris several forms of these *brulé tout*. One of these, of turned alabaster, has a slender spike upon which the candle end could be impaled for burning.

PRIMITIVE LAMPS

There has been shown in a previous section (pl. 2) the suggested line of development of the lamp. The line begins at a period when it is conceived that light apart from the camp fire and set up in a vessel of its own had not come to be a human need. For a long time the human societies which had fire were satisfied with the torch, and as they advanced, almost imperceptibly on the whole, the torch gradually became improved and put to new uses.

No art of man is ever in the same state of advancement throughout the world at any one time; thus an areal survey of the culture of the tribes in the torch period would reveal in use every grade of torch, depending on many things which may be brought together under the term " environment." For instance, a tribe may live in an isolated environment and another on a natural migration line of culture. It will be seen that progress in the arts will differ in the respective tribes.

The lamp, on account of the fuel, the wick, the need, and the knowledge used in its invention, is extremely complex. Although the rude lamp may seem simple, all these requisites are present in its make-up. It follows that the lamp is a newcomer compared with the torch. It also appears that the lamp, on account of its deceptive simplicity, and in reality its complexity of invention, as mentioned, would arise only when advance had been made to a certain grade of culture. This would imply that the lamp originated in a few favored places, while the torch might originate at any camp fire in the world. As to the antiquity of the lamp, the evidence so far furnished points to the Mediterranean culture area, the eastern portion, where the oldest examples have been found. The lamps discovered by Howard Carter and his efficient coworkers in the tomb of Tut-Ankh-Amen are float lamps and sometimes are combined with a torch stand. As told by Doctor Breasted, the find dates 3,250 years ago. In the Assyro-Babylonian region a lamp shaped like a boot, having a channel cut from the instep to the toe, can be traced 3,400 years. These are the oldest lamps which can be dated. The actual origin of each of these lamps is much farther in the past.

As to the inventions, or rather light usages, standing about the origin of the lamp, there are the making of a quasi lamp of the fat body of the petrel and of the candlefish, and, nearer to nature, the firefly lamps. The bird and fish have been placed at the beginning of the torch, not as a scientific contribution to origin but as suggestions (p. 2). The firefly lighting may be placed nearer in suggestiveness to the lamp because something must be devised to contain the insects, but the container is rather a lantern. This interesting episode in illumination having no bearing on the development of illumination is the only example of the use of a natural light by man. In the tropical parts of the new world a large beetle, *Pyrophorus noctilucus*, 1 to 1¾ inches long, furnishes a remarkably brilliant light. A constant light is emitted by two circular areas on the thorax and a powerful intermittent flash from the abdomen. In the range of this insect the inhabitants make many recorded uses of the light of the pyrophore, "light bearer." One of the oldest specimens in the Museum collection is a firefly lantern from the West Indies. It is in three circular diminishing stories made by setting small rods in square pieces of wood with truncated corners and leaving a door in each story. The lantern is suspended by a hook. (Cat. No. 5631, West Indies; John Varden; 15.1 inches (38.5 cm.) high; pl. 40, fig. 7.) Another specimen is a jicara or tree gourd perforated and furnished with a cord for suspension and a rude door. This is such a specimen mentioned by Humboldt, who saw it in use on a ship sailing from Cumana on the north coast of Venezuela. (Pl. 39, fig. 3, Cat. No. 153182, St. Vincent, West Indies; F. A. Ober; 7 inches (17.7 cm.) high.) From Java comes a curious firefly lamp said to have been used by a burglar. It consists of a small shallow wooden dish having wax on the bottom, to which fireflies taken from a cane tube were stuck. A lid pivoted at one end closes over the dark lantern. (Pl. 39, figs. 1 and 2, Cat. No. 175615, Djok-ja Karta, Java; Miss Eliza Ruhamah Scidmore; 2 inches (5 cm.) long.

It has been suggested somewhat fancifully that the skull of an animal may have been used as a vessel for the lamp in the early stages of the invention. A skull would furnish a suitable reservoir, but there is no evidence of the use of entire skulls for lamps even as a makeshift. There is, however, abundant data on the use of shells for the purpose. It would be safer to originate the lamp from shells of suitable form than from any other natural products. Shells which have been converted into lamps would have suggested to the early inventors the spout lamp, the smooth-lipped clam, the simple dish lamp, and the scallop the grooves in which the wick might be rested. In the Orkney and Shetland Islands a *fusus* shell was hung horizontally with cords and the wick drawn along the natural channel. This primitive lamp was in common use by the islanders. (Pl. 40, fig. 2, Cat. No. 151147; Henry Balfour; 6.5 inches (16.5 cm.) long.) Another method of hanging the shell lamp is by a single cord. A saucer lamp formed of one valve of a pecten shell is in common use by the Aino of Yezo, Japan. It is an inseparable companion of the box fireplace of that people set up in spread prongs of a split stick stuck in the earth or in a forked branch. In it was burnt fish oil by means of a fiber wick, as in the equally simple Japanese saucer lamps. (Pl. 40, fig. 3, Cat. No. (4838), collected by Romyn Hitchcock; 5.7 inches (14.5 cm.) diameter.) There is a great transition of culture between the Aino shell lamp and the artistic lamp of decorated porcelain from China, but no improvement. (Pl. 40, fig. 4, Cat. No. 175863, China; W. W. Rockhill; 6.9 inches (17.5 cm.) high.) A shell lamp from the south coast of Brittany is probably a reminiscence of the early use of shells as light vessels. It has, however, been assembled with iron wire and follows the idea of the familiar crusie with drip catcher. (Pl. 40, fig. 1, Cat. No. 151646; collected by Henry Balfour; 4 inches (10 cm.) diameter.) Some examples of simple lamps of pottery show the probable migration of Chinese forms and are figured on Plate 41a. Figure 9 is a pottery lamp of glazed ware from the Shan States, Burma. (Cat. No. 164922; collected by Henry Balfour; 2.3 inches (6 cm.) diameter.) Figure 11 is a pottery dish from Singapore. (Cat. No. 167556; A. H. Webb; 4.1 inches (10.5

cm.) diameter.)   Figure 15 is a pottery saucer lamp with stem and dish foot. (Cat. No. 167556; Singapore; A. H. Webb; 3.1 inches (8 cm.) high, 4.7 inches (12 cm.) diameter.)

Eskimo lamps furnish examples of great simplicity and of extreme interest as they are the only aboriginal lamps in the Western Hemisphere. They have been monographed by the writer.[5] It is seen that there are two distinct types of lamps in the Eskimo area: The simple saucer lamp of Asiatic origin, and the wick lip or ridge lamp, apparently indigenous to America. Plate 40, Figure 6, is a pottery lamp with ridges around the interior, from the Yukon delta, Alaska. (E. W. Nelson, 5.1 inches (13 cm.) diameter.) Plate 41a, Figure 4, is a small example of the long wick edge lamp of soapstone. The wick is powdered moss laid along the edge and in contact with the oil. (Cat. No. 64223, Hotham Inlet, Alaska, E. W. Nelson, 6.7 inches (17 cm.) long, 5.1 inches (13 cm.) wide.) The pottery lamp of St. Lawrence Island has a ridge in the bottom on which the moss wick is laid. The lamp rest and drip catcher also admits of tipping the lamp. (Pl. 41a, fig. 5, Cat. No. 316720, collected by Sheldon Jackson, 5.7 inches (14.5 cm.) long, 4.7 inches (12 cm.) wide, 3.8 inches (9.5 cm.) high.) In southern Alaska the lamps are of hard stone, sometimes sadiron shape and sometimes circular. These appear to be modifications of the Asiatic dish lamp. Plate 41a, Figure 6, is the sadiron shape. These lamps are often very large and remarkable examples of stone working. (Cat. No. 316719, Unalaska, Alaska, Sheldon Jackson, 5.4 inches (14 cm.) long, 4 inches (10 cm.) wide.) Plate 41a, Figure 8, is the oval form. (Cat. No. 316716, Aleuts, southern Alaska, Sheldon Jackson, 5.5 inches (14 cm.) by 4.3 inches (11 cm.) diameter.) Plate 41a, Figure 7, is a concave beach stone which has been used as a lamp. It is from an ancient Aleutian house ruin. Dr. W. H. Dall found similar stones showing use as a lamp. This is an extemporaneous lamp suggesting great primitiveness, as shown in examples described later. (Cat. No. 14892, Uklatka Spit, Alaska, Capt. J. A. Sladen, 8 inches (20.5 cm.) long.)

Many extemporaneous or makeshift lamps have been observed. Sometimes these lamps seem worthy of standing at the beginning of the developmental series, as observed in the beach stone lamps of the Aleuts. Often these lamps are associated with occupations, as Plate 41a, Figure 1, which is a brick with a hole dug in the surface for the reservoir and used some years ago by bakers. (Cat. No. 152532, Oxford, England, Henry Balfour, 8.8 inches (22.5 cm.) by 4.1 inches (10.5 cm.) by 3 inches (7.5 cm.).) Another, used by

---

[5] The Lamp of the Eskimo. Report of U. S. National Museum, 1896, pp. 1025–1056.

printers, consists of a block of wood with a mass of fat inclosing a rag wick set upon it. (Pl. 41a, fig. 2, Cat. No. 325642, New York City, Paul Brockett.) A pottery bowl containing fat and a cloth wick comes from the Zuni Indians of New Mexico. It is an example of adoption from the white man, since none of the aborigines south of the Eskimo had a lamp. (Pl. 41a, fig. 14, Cat. No. 20345, collected by the Bureau of American Ethnology, 5 inches (13 cm.) diameter.) Figure 13 is a lamp consisting of a saucer filled with fat, in which is embedded a sycamore ball as a very effective wick. Such lamps were used on the old frontier of the Middle West. The specimen is a model of those used in Iowa. (Cat. No. 325643, collected by Walter Hough, 6 inches (15 cm.) diameter.) Plate 41a, Figure 12, is a lamp cut out of chalk and used by the flint knappers of England. Chalk lamps apparently date far back in England. (Cat. No. 211910, Brandon, England, Edward Lovett, 3.5 inches (9 cm.) by 2.4 inches (6 cm.) by 3 inches (5 cm.).) In this connection mention may be made of improvised lamps of a hollowed billet of wood or a turnip used in the United States in emergencies.

ANCIENT LAMPS

As a rule ancient lamps refer to those of the historic period, the classical lamps of pottery and bronze which are among the most interesting relics of Greek and Roman times. Their use covers a period of about a thousand years, during which neither the Romans, to whom this type of lamp is accredited, nor the nations among which it spread, gave any heed to its improvement in the matter of effectiveness. Throughout this period the lamp underwent many changes in art and thus can be assigned to period and locality with their various shadings of culture. For this reason there may be selected from the multiplicity of culture forms series showing a quasi-development of the minor appendages of the classical lamp. In the first series both modern and ancient are arranged to show the theoretical progress in the development of the covered reservoir lamps of the Romans. Plate 41b, Figure 13, is a triangular open lamp of soapstone from Skardu, Baltistan. (Cat. No. 164964, Dr. W. L. Abbott.) Following are three baked clay lamps (figs. 10–12), from Mirzapur, India. (Cat. Nos. 164920, 164929, Henry Balfour.) An ancient lamp which shows what must be considered as the first modification of the primitive saucer lamp to form a groove to hold the wick steady is seen in Plate 41b, Figure 9. (Cat. No. 146073, Cyprus, Henry Balfour.) Figure 8 is a pottery lamp from Kashmir in which the reservoir is partly closed over. (Cat. No. 161972, Kashmir, India, Dr. W. L. Abbott.) A lamp from Leros, Greece (fig. 7), shows further progress (Cat. No. 73168, M. A. Carindouas), and

Figure 6 is the typical Roman lamp closed over and having a slight beak (Cat. No. 175584, Asia Minor, A. A. Azeez).

The development of the beak also gives an interesting series leading almost to the spout forms which were in use up to the age of invention. In Plate 42a, Figure 7, is a specimen said to have been found at Thebes, Egypt, and having a rudimentary beak. (Cat. No. 150436, Minor Kellogg.) The next specimen, Figure 6, from Tyre, shows further development (Cat. No. 130910, M. F. Savage). The spout is more marked in Figure 5 (Cat. No. 175558, Asia Minor, A. A. Azeez), and in Figure 4 (Cat. No. 167625, Italy, G. Brown Goode. Figure 3 is an Italian form. (Cat. No. 167629, same donor.) Figure 2 is from Halicarnassus, Greece (Cat. No. 73162, M. A. Carindouas), while Figure 1 is Roman and shows the extreme of spout development (Cat. No. 167632, G. Brown Goode.)

The handle series in Plate 42a has Figures 8 and 9, without handles, from Egypt and Italy, the former from Dr. George W. Sampson and the latter from M. A. Carindouas. A pinched-up handle, perforated (fig. 10), is from Italy, collected by G. Brown Goode (Cat. No. 167642). The fourth specimen (fig. 11) has a stub handle pierced laterally and is from Italy by the same collector. The fifth specimen (fig. 12), from Coos, Greece, has a better developed handle. Figure 13 has a small ring handle in which the finger can hardly be inserted (Cat. No. 167618, Italy, G. Brown Goode). A lamp from Pergamos, Greece (fig. 14), displays an effective handle (Cat. No. 73161, M. A. Carindouas). No. 15 is also furnished with the extreme type of ring handle (Cat. No. 167650, Italy, G. Brown Goode). The series below, Plate 42a exhibits another variety of handle generally crescentic and sometimes floriated. The first lamp (fig. 16) is from Carpathos, Greece, Mr. Carindouas; the second (fig. 17) in bronze, from Italy, G. Brown Goode; the third (fig. 18) in pottery, also from Italy, by the same collector; and the fourth (fig. 19), also of bronze, from Italy, by M. F. Savage (Cat. Nos. 73165, 167656, 167628, 175263).

Sometimes Roman lamps were given a foot, never much elevated. The series here (pl. 42b, first row) displays a crude lamp from Egypt, Minor Kellogg; a well-made lamp with low foot from Baiae, Italy, Captain Chauncey; a smaller specimen from Italy, M. F. Savage; a neat globular lamp from Greece, William Green; and a lamp with bell-shape foot raising it 2.3 inches, Italy, G. Brown Goode (Cat. Nos. 130436, 1355, 17268, 128364, 167646). The ancients made lamps with more than one burner. These are favorite subjects of falsifiers, whose forgeries are common in the more elaborate types of lamps. Beginning to the right of Plate 42b, third row, a one-burner Roman lamp decorated in relief is shown. The next specimen is a fine example of a two-burner lamp in the best style of art. Two-burner lamps are the more frequent of the multiple-burner lamps. The third figure is a three-burner lamp of somewhat doubtful authenticity, yet illustrating this variety. The fourth is a seven-burner lamp of red terra cotta. It is suggested that Roman lamps of multiple burners were used for ceremonial purposes. (Cat. Nos. 167635, 129399, 167653, 167647.) The Henry J. Heinz collection in Pittsburgh contains a nine-burner lamp with a bas-relief of the triumph scene from the Arch of Titus, in which the seven-branch candlestick, or, rather, lamp stand, is borne as spoil. (Pl. 41*b*, fig. 1.) This and the seven-burner described are Roman of the later period.

In Plate 41*b* are shown various antique lamps, some doubtfully old and some recent. In the upper row, Figure 2 is a tortoise-shape lamp from Italy. The second is a Silenus head in bronze and doubtful. The third is a Roman lamp with palm-leaf design. The fourth is a well-modeled head of a satyr in terra cotta, and perhaps recent. In the lower row of Plate 42*a*, Figure 20, is a rude lamp from Chios, Greece; Figure 21 has beautiful relief modeling in the concave; Figure 22 is from Baiae, Italy, with floriated decoration; Figure 23, also from Baiae, is also decorated, and has the potter's mark beneath; Figure 24 is a modern glazed terra cotta from Naples, called a "toe lamp," following an obscure scriptural allusion; and Figure 25 is a modern green and yellow glazed majolica lamp in dolphin shape. (Cat. Nos. (upper row, pl. 42*b*), 167621, 29407, 167630, 167637; (lower row, pl. 43*a*) 73168, 175267, 1356, 1355, 129409, 167654.)

Lamp stands of bronze are among the more successful works in that material produced by the ancients. They appear to descend from the Etruscan sliver candle stands (p. 10) and the footing shows decided Egyptian tendencies, seen in the specimen shown on Plate 43, Figure 5. This stand, perhaps an original, is a fine example of the Roman bronze worker's art. (Cat. No. 169073, Italy; Magruder collection; 34.2 inches (84.5 cm.) high.) A lamp stand of iron secured in Italy by Dr. G. Brown Goode is suggestive of the ancient lamp stands. No data is available to determine the age of this specimen. The stand has every appearance of great age. It has three rudely bent feet and the head has three arms from which hang a rather incongruous set of lamp-tending utensils attached to chains of brass and iron wire evidently of several periods. From one of the chains hangs a boat-shape two-burner lamp of terra cotta with a loop for suspension in the middle. This form of lamp may be late Roman. Three specimens of this lamp are in the Museum collection. They can not be related to any Roman types known here. They may be adaptations produced in the Middle Ages. (Pl. 43, fig. 6, Cat. No. 168134, Italy; G. Brown Goode; 32.75 inches (83.2 cm.) high.)

The lamp beam shown in Plate 43, Figure 7, is of curious interest. The beam is of cast iron, a triform loop in the center and at the ends, crozier heads from which hang chains to which the lamps are attached. At the attachment of the chains are small iron crosses. The design on the bar of the beam is a scallop shell with volutes on either side. The lamps are iron beaten into boat shape, and show traces of wick tongues, as seen in Italian lamps of an early period. The tweezers are of brass. The snuffers are of iron and of old form, but may not be contemporaneous with the rest, as the tweezers would be sufficient for tending the wick. The lamp beam is evidently ecclesiastical and perhaps early seventeenth century. (Cat. No. 168127; G. Brown Goode; 22.2 inches (56.5 cm.) high.) On Plate 43, Figures 1–3, are shown two two-spout hanging lamps and a single burner, all of terra cotta and similar to the specimen attached to an iron lamp stand described on page 49. (Cat. Nos. 167648, 167636, 168154; Italy; G. Brown Goode.) Figure 4 is a curious three-spout terracotta lamp, light brown in color, washed with darker brown. This lamp appears to be authentic and shows marked traces of use. The opening to the reservoir is annular, surrounding a tube arising from the bottom and projecting above the top of the lamp. Through this tube is passed at present a chain with flat brass links having a disk stop at the lower end by which the lamp could be hung. The similarity of this specimen to the lucerna reservoir and burners is complete (see p. 61). The date of the specimen would seem to throw light on the ancestry of the lucerna. (Cat. No. 167651, Italy; G. Brown Goode, reservoir 3.5 inches (9 cm.) diameter.)

The series of lamps, three ancient and one modern, plate 42b, middle row, indicate in a striking manner the persistence in time of a particular form of lamp. Figure 6 is a crude pottery lamp having an open trough for the wick prolonged from the body of the lamp and a neck through which oil is poured. It was collected a few years ago at Yarkand, Eastern Turkestan (Cat. No. 175140), by W. L. Abbott (5.9 inches (15 cm.) long). This recent lamp may be compared with the adjoining specimens. Figure 7 is a glazed lamp, also from Turkestan, dating about the twelfth century A. D. (Cat. No. 259384, Turkestan; Museum of Peter the Great, Leningrad, S. R.) Figure 8 is a lamp having a beautiful glaze of turquoise blue having a more refined form but of the same type as the other specimens. The lamp is of the tenth century. (Cat. No. 9586, Turkey in Asia; Tiffany and Co.; 4.4 inches (11 cm.) long.) Figure 9 is a lamp glazed in colors, having a trough for the wick, but differing in the treatment of the reservoir opening. (Cat. No. 259388, Eastern Turkestan, 12th–13th century; Museum of Peter the Great, Leningrad, S. R.) A lamp of this type is one of the Babylonian star emblems and is found cut on a stone *kuduru* dating about 1800 B. C. (See p. 44.)

FLOAT LAMPS

The lamp consisting of a saucer-like reservoir, in which the wick is floated on oil resting on water, follows nearest the primitive saucer lamps described in the next section. This ancient lighting method appears to be indigenous to the Near East and North Africa, and to have spread from these centers into Europe, and thence in the form of altar lamps and domestic night lights to all quarters of the civilized world. It is probable, or at least worthy of consideration, that the contacts of the Crusades were responsible for the European distribution. It is evident also that the Moorish conquest of Spain brought the float lamp to Europe. This curious installation of oil on water in a lamp originated in Egypt, and, so far as known from archeologic data, is the oldest lamp. Since any convenient dish would serve for the night light, there is practically little survival of an apparatus as with the lamp. The floats, however, are easily obtained. Hanging float lamps which require more or less complicated means of suspension are frequently observed. The Moros of Mindanao, P. I., make a brass cup for the night light, and this is one of the few vessels devoted to this special purpose. (Pl. 44, fig. 3, Cat. No. 329866, E. W. Keyser; 3.3 inches (8.5 cm.) in diameter, 3 inches (7.5 cm.) high.) A hanging float lamp from Tetuan, Morocco, consists of a green glaze saucer with foot, slung in chains fastened to a disk, which in turn is suspended from a flat plate of perforated brass in the form of a bird; also resembling a hand and may be a charm against the evil eye. (Pl. 45, fig. 7, Cat. No. (Williams 96); bowl, 5.1 inches (13 cm.) in diameter, 14.1 inches (36 cm.) high.) Dr. Talcott Williams also collected a float-lamp chandelier for the mosque having 13 green glaze pottery cups hung in chains from the points and angles of a frame made by superimposing two equilateral triangles of strap brass. Each lamp is hung immediately from a disk supported by flat cast-brass two-head birds. One lamp is in the middle and a little higher than the others. (Pl. 45, fig. 8, Cat. No. 192, Talcott Williams; Morocco; 20.5 inches (52 cm.) in diameter.) The Turkish float-lamp glass for hanging installations is calyx shape with knob at the bottom. The wick is clamped in the junction of three twisted brass-wire tentacles which hook over the edge of the glass. (Pl. 46, fig. 1, Turkey; Turkish Commission, World's Columbian Exposition, Chicago, 1893; 3.7 inches (9.5 cm.) in diameter, 5 inches (12.5 cm.) long.) These glasses are seen in the Turkish chandelier shown on Plate 26. A variation of the float lamp is found in the Near East. They are hanging lamps, often of finely worked brass, in which art this part of the world excels. The metal specimens are domed in the upper part, and fitting under the dome is a cluster of generally three collars, in which are placed the glass tubes which are flanged at the upper

border. These tubes are punched up in the bottom, and at the apex
of the cone so formed is affixed a slender glass tube, around which
the wick is wound. Water and oil are poured in to the proper
height. Plate 44a, Figure 2, shows the lamp open; Figure 1 shows
the lamp closed and the function of the chains for suspension. (Cat.
No. 325644, Syria; Walter Hough; 7.7 inches (19.5 cm.) in diameter.)
Another fine specimen from Damascus is of fretted wood inlaid with
pearl shell and bone. From the upper collar hang six lamp tubes
and from the bottom seven tubes. One of the sections opens as a
door, through which the tubes are inserted. (Pl. 44b, fig. 2, Cat. No.
175471; Syria; A. R. Souhami; 13.4 inches (34 cm.) in diameter, 22.9
inches (58 cm.) high.) A beautiful specimen in pierced brass overlaid with silver medallions is in the shape of a flattened vase and is
suspended by three chains, the hook for hanging projecting from the
center of a Turkish silver coin. The float installation is a glass bowl
fitting in the opening of the vase, much of the light thus passing
through the transparent glass and out through the perforations.
(Pl. 46, fig. 2, Cat. No. 175590; Persia; Miss A. A. Azeez; 6 inches
(15 cm.) in diameter, 3.7 inches (9.5 cm.) high.) From Burgos,
Spain, the writer in 1892 procured an altar lamp of brass which is
simple and well designed and may stand as the type of ecclesiastical
float lamps. The church use of the float lamp is quite ancient. The
Ner tamid, or perpetual light, Dr. I. M. Casanowicz informs me,
was a lamp of this kind used in the Temple at Jerusalem. (Pl. 44b,
fig. 1, Cat. No. 167080; Burgos, Spain; Walter Hough; 29.1 inches
(74 cm.) long.) The secular use of the float lamp was widespread
and still is very common in some countries. The immediate basis
for this use was the need for a dim, non-irritating light in a sick
room or as a guide light at night. "Night lights," as they are commonly called, consist of a disk of light wood, cork, or paper, in the
center of which a short bit of taper is fixed. This is allowed to
float alone on the oil or buoyed on a triangular or cross-shape piece
of metal, the points of which are tipped with cork. Nuremburg,
Germany, was a center where enormous quantities of night lights
were manufactured and were distributed over the world from that
city. At present Paris is the city where night lights with modern
improvements are made and sold. Several specimens of night lights
are shown on Plate 47. In Spain in 1892 several varieties of night
lights were on sale. One of Parisian manufacture is called *veilleuses
plongeantes*. The float is of cork, with circular hole cut out in the
middle overlaid with tin having a cross-shape depression in which
"holy crosses" are placed. (Fig. 1.) Another kind, called *veilleuses
unalterables*, has a hollow-glass float in which a short length of taper
is thrust. (Fig. 5.) These specimens (Cat. Nos. 167056 and 167057)
were bought in Madrid. In Spain these lights are called "mari-

posas." A box from Burgos, Spain, bears the inscription: " Mariposas para tres meses," Mariposas for three months, and has a cork and tin float. (Fig. 4.) (Cat. No. 167058.) Night lights made locally were sold at Burgos. The taper is set in a cork float covered with a disk of paper and are self-floating. (Fig. 3.) A box of Nuremberg night lights having a float of tin cut with three arms tipped with cork is in the collection. (Fig. 6.) The lights are disks of wood with the taper set up in the middle, and are packed in an oval veneer wood box containing tin tweezers for picking up and placing the lights. A Nuremberg box with label bearing the name of the device in four languages and a cut of Christ rising from the dead was bought by Dr. Leonhard Stejneger in Russia in 1898. (Cat. No. 324738.) A box without identification, probably from Nuremberg, came also from Russia. The float is a square cross with cork at the tips. The lights are disks of paper with tapers. A box of Nuremberg night lights was received from Philadelphia, where they were said to have been used in 1820. (Cat. No. 130310; George G. Fryer, fig. 2.)

SIMPLE LAMPS

The simplest lamps, not makeshifts, and definitely used over great culture areas of the world are mere saucers with no footing for the wick, which is brought up to the rim at any place, where it hangs insecurely. This was the universal lamp of China and Japan. It is of very ancient origin, perhaps the most ancient lighting vessel designed by man, at a period of culture when his needs required a house light. Perhaps the original model was a shell of smooth outline. There were endless hints that the wick should have a groove at least in which to rest, and this step was taken by most of the lamp-using world, as described in the next section.

Plate 48, Figure 4, is a saucer lamp mounted on a bamboo stand and used formerly in street lighting. Generally the saucer is of pottery, but iron, brass, pewter, and porcelain serve. (Cat. No. 175867, China, W. W. Rockhill; 8.3 inches (21 cm.) high.) Figure 3 is an example of fine porcelain with blue decoration. The stem arises from a saucer and has a cup support for the shallow saucer lamp. The latter has a small stub handle. (Cat. No. 175863, China, same collector; 7.1 inches (18 cm.) high.) Figure 5 is of brass. The saucer has a handle and rests on a cup at the top of a column arising from a bowl. (Cat. No. 175864, China, same collector; 15.7 inches (40 cm.) high.) An ingenious folding pocket candlestick lamp is shown (pl. 49a, figs. 2, 3), joined and ready for use. (Cat. No. 175866, China, same collector; 8 inches (20.5 cm.) high.) An elaborate cast brass hanging lamp from Japan in the collection had for its effective part a simple saucer, and in other Japanese lights the saucer was

used. (Pl. 48, fig. 1, Cat. No. 274922, Mrs. Julian James; 35.1 inches
(89 cm.) long.) The Tibetan is a deeper saucer mounted on a bell-
shape base. (Pl. 49a, fig. 1.) These lamps vary greatly in size, some
of them holding 50 pounds of butter. They are often elaborately
decorated. (Cat. No. 167286, Eastern Tibet, W. W. Rockhill; 3.5
inches (9 cm.) high.) A pair of magnificent bronze temple lamps
from Tibet illustrate the gorgeous setting of a primitive lamp, which
is a shallow bowl at the top of the column. The form of these lamps
would seem to indicate that the artist followed a Persian candlestick
in his design. (Pl. 49b, figs. 1, 2, Cat. No. 216041, Tibet, Howland
collection; 45 inches (114.5 cm.) high.) The Korean lamp is a pottery bowl containing sesame oil and a rush pith wick. In shape it is
like the Tibetan butter lamp. It is often mounted on a wooden
stand having an arm to hold the lamp and another to hold the drip
catcher. A ratchet at the back admits of raising and lowering the
lamp. The specimen is a model from plans by the late Pom K. Soh.
(Pl. 48, fig. 2, Cat. No. 203214, Korea; 36 inches (91.5 cm.) high.)
Here and there in Asia the saucer lamp has been observed and in the
Polynesian Islands of the Hawaiian group stone lamps of this type
and of ancient appearance have been found. They, however, appear
to be accultural, and are most prevalent in Hawaii, being nonexistent
or sporadic in other islands of Polynesia. Of the four specimens in
the Museum collection one is a beach stone having a natural circular
concavity at one end. (Pl. 50, fig. 2, Cat. No. 257876, Hawaii, N. B.
Emerson; 6.5 inches (16.5 cm.) long, 4.2 inches (10.5 cm.) wide.)
Figure 3 is worked from vesicular volcanic rock. (Cat. No. 5891,
Hawaii, S. R. Dowdle; 3.4 inches (8.5 cm.) diameter.) Figure 4 is
well worked from dense red porphyry and shows no traces of oil or
effects of fire. (Cat. No. 5892, Hawaii, S. R. Dowdle; 3.4 inches
(8.5 cm.) diameter.) Figure 1 is of basaltic rock, somewhat eroded
and roughened around the edge of the excavation. (Cat. No. 255723,
Hawaii, E. H. Estep; 5.6 inches (14 cm.) diameter.) The Eskimo
pottery saucer lamp (pl. 41a, fig. 3) is of the class described above.
It is the Southern Eskimo form and is not found north of Norton
Sound. This lamp is of Asiatic origin and appears to have spread
from eastern Asia across the Arctic to America.

WICK CHANNEL LAMPS

It is evident that the installation of the wick in the saucer lamp
where it could only be drawn up to the edge at any point was the
essence of simplicity. Except in lamps remaining stationary the
wick would be displaced and the light put out. Yet millions in the
Far East used such a lamp. The need for a groove or channel to
stabilize the wick appears to have been earliest felt in the Near East

where a saucer lamp in all probability preceded the Roman lamp. This is in accord with the theory of the prehistoric migration of eastern Asiatics from Mesopotamia, supported by numerous similarities brought forward by Terrien Delacouperie and other students. In various older horizons in Cyprus, Asia Minor, and Carthage, in North Africa, are found lamps in which a wick channel has been formed by pinching up the side of a small clay saucer. (Pl. 42.) This is the type of pottery lamp current in North Africa at present. Plate 51, Figure 5 shows a green glazed Moroccan pottery lamp with pinched-up reservoir mounted on a column rising from a saucer base and having a curved handle reaching from the reservoir to the base. This lamp was collected in Morocco by Dr. Talcott Williams, (12.2 inches (31 cm.) high). On the same plate, Figure 6 is an ancient earthenware pinched up saucer lamp from Syria. (Cat. No. 95874; Tiffany & Co.; 3 inches (8 cm.) diameter.) A lamp of faience with two wick grooves shows North African influence. (Pl. 51, fig. 7, Cat. No. 150435, Naples, Italy; Mrs. E. S. Brinton; 9.8 inches (25 cm.) high.) A glazed pottery lamp in form of a two-faced woman bearing the two spout closed-in reservoir on the head is from Holland. (Pl. 51, fig. 4, Cat. No. 175711; M. F. Savage; 12.2 inches (31 cm.) high.) A splendid specimen of Moorish green glaze pottery lamp has the characteristic reservoir with column and handle rising from the center of a basin having small lamps, candle sockets, and modeled ornaments around the border, the whole mounted on a sturdy stem with base. (Pl. 51, fig. 3, Cat. No. 168308, Morocco; W. H. Chandlee; 29 inches (73.5 cm.) high.) An iron lamp, four pointed and with spike for sticking in a base, also from Morocco, shows the open wick groove or fold as in the pottery lamps. (Pl. 52, fig. 4, Cat. No. (57, Williams); Talcott Williams; 17.4 inches (44 cm.) long.) A cast brass standing lamp with three wick channels comes from the Philippines. The circle of the bowl is continued as a slender bridge across the wick channel. (Pl. 54, fig. 7 Cat. No. 232816, Moro, Cotas, Mindanao; Maj. E. A. Mearns; 11.8 inches (30 cm.) high.) This lamp is evidently an inheritance of the Mohammedan culture of the Moro. A well designed but crudely worked mosque lamp of brass shows the simple installation of the wick. The reservoir at the apex of the column has cut in it six incisions, the metal being bent out to serve as a channel for the wick. (Pl. 51, fig. 1, Cat. No. 176519, Near East; Van Gasbeek and Arkell; 35.4 inches (90 cm.) high.) A hanging lamp of brass has the reservoir beaten up to form seven angles, in which the wick is laid. This is an advance on the simpler wick channel lamps which will be seen from the specimens figured having only one wick. (Pl. 51, fig. 2, Cat. No. 205549, Tangier, Morocco; donor unknown; 35.4 inches (89 cm.)

long.) The lamps of India and Ceylon are all of the type under consideration. No simple saucer lamps such as are used in the Far East are found. Minor household lamps are seen among tribes and peoples along the border of Chinese influence, but invariably have wick grooves. Plate 54 shows simple Ceylonese lamps of circular or oval outline brought up to a beak for the wick. Figures 9 and 11 are of a stony composition and Figure 10 is of soft earthenware. (Cat. Nos. 168300, 168301, 168304, Ceylon Commission, World's Columbian Exposition, Chicago, Ill.; fig. 9, 5 inches (13 cm.) diameter; fig. 11, 3.7 inches (9.5 cm.) diameter; fig. 10, 5.5 inches (14 cm.) wide, 11.3 inches (28.5 cm.) long.) Ceylonese metal lamps sometimes in the commoner forms have a square reservoir with wick channels at the four corners. Such a lamp of tin with column and pan base is shown on Plate 45, Figure 6. The more important lamps, like those of India, have multiple light. One of these, of heavy cast brass, has nine small wick channels. The reservoir is placed midway of a roundel stem centered in a dish. A trefoil handle is placed at the apex of the column. (Pl. 52, fig. 3, Cat. No. 234132, Ceylon; St. Louis Exposition; Ceylon Commission; 13.4 inches (34 cm.) high.) Another fine specimen is similar and has seven wick channels in the open reservoir. This lamp is reminiscent of the Italian lucerna, as the reservoir can be raised or lowered on the central support. (Pl. 52, fig. 5, Cat. No. 168205, Ceylon; Ceylon Commission, St. Louis Exposition; 24.8 inches (63 cm.) high.) As mentioned, the lamps of India generally have multiple lights. Plate 52, Figure 1, is of cast brass, the reservoir with four lights mounted on a column and base suggesting European influence. (Cat. No. 92753, Calcutta, India; H. R. H. The Rajah of Tagore; 12 inches (30.5 cm.) high.) On the same plate (fig. 2), is an excellent specimen of quite old, pure Indian work in brass. The simple lamps are stepped on the ends of conventional branches, five in number, supported on a resting bird on a high peak. (Pl. 52, fig. 2, Cat. No. 216067, India; Bennoo-Hodges; 13.8 inches (35 cm.) high.) Another old specimen shows a fabulous animal holding the stem of a one-wick lamp. (Pl. 53, fig. 1, Cat. No. 216068, India; Bennoo-Hodges; 5.5 inches (14 cm.) long, 5.2 inches (13 cm.) high.)

A hand lamp of brass having 12 wick orifices leading into a circular reservoir filled from above is a departure from the usual Indian method. (Pl. 53, fig. 2, Cat. No. 216060, India; Bennoo-Hodges; 3.2 inches (8 cm.) diameter, 8.3 inches (21 cm.) long.) Figure 3 is a lotos pod, the wick being drawn up at four angles. The curved handle and base of the lamp are joined by a straight bar. (Pl. 53, India; Bennoo-Hodges; 4.8 inches (12 cm.) long, 4 inches (10 cm.) high.) Perhaps belonging here is a wooden lamp of the group of Malays inhabiting Simalur Island, East Indies. This crude affair consists of an oblong wooden reservoir attached by mortising to a hook branch. Excluding the idea of independent invention is probably an infiltration from India following the spoon-shape lamp of the West rather than the saucer-shape lamp of the East. (Pl. 54, fig. 6, Cat. No. 237351, Sigoeli, Simalur, Island; Dr. W. L. Abbott; 19 inches (48 cm.) long.) For comparison with the Indian multiple lamps the Jewish *hanuka* is interesting. The *hanuka* is an oriental lamp transported to every clime at the behest of religion. It consists of a row of eight small spoon-shape lamps placed at the base of an ornamental panel like a sconce, reflecting the style of art of the period and country in which it was produced. The *hanuka* may be hung up or set on a surface. The lamps usually have placed under them a drip catcher. Two specimens from the collection illustrate the form of the *hanuka*. Plate 53, Figure 4, is from Morocco and is unusual in being in triptych form, the two side wings hinged and closed in at the sides of the lamp row. A larger lamp is set in the upper middle of the frame. The specimen is of cast brass and a good example of modern Moorish art. The other specimen (pl. 53, fig. 5) is an old Italian *hanuka* of brass, the back two columns with arch and dating in the seventeenth century. (Morocco; Talcott Williams; 8 inches (20.5 cm.) wide, 9.5 inches (24 cm.) high; Cat. No. 168312, Florence, Italy; S. B. Dean; 8.3 inches (21 cm.) wide.) Another old Italian multiple lamp, not ceremonial so far as known, is Figure 10, Plate 53. The back is a floriated shield having a row of three spoon-shape lamps at the base and one near the top. (Cat. No. 153903, Italy; G. Brown Goode; 5.9 inches (15 cm.) wide, 5.9 inches (15 cm.) high.) On Plate 53 are shown several examples of the lamps under consideration. Figure 6 is a crude pottery lamp used on the frontier in Virginia many years ago and of English ancestry. (Cat. No. 130498, Morgantown, W. Va.; Walter Hough; 5.2 inches (13 cm.) diameter, 5.2 inches (13 cm.) high.) Figures 8 and 9 are Javanese brass lamps, one detached and the other mounted on a column and base with feet, a drip catcher placed on the column below the lamp. (Cat. Nos. 311385, 311386, Java; Victor J. Evans; 4.2 inches (10.5 cm.) diameter, 5.5 inches (14 cm.) long.) Figure 7 is a small Algerian pottery lamp which shows the Mohammedan style of reservoir open at the top for filling. (Cat. No. 157435, Algiers; Edward Lovett; 5.2 inches (13 cm.) high.) Examples of what must have been regarded as improvements on the simple lamp shown on Plate 45 consist of bringing the wicks up at more points around the reservoir. Figures 1 and 3 show the parts of a three-wick lamp of brass, the drip catcher having a bowed support with ornamented head. On the support is hung the reservoir. (Cat. No. 169100, Flemish;

S. B. Dean; 9.3 inches (21 cm.) high.) Figure 2 is from Tetuan, Morocco, of brass having four wicks and a hook for hanging. Attention is called to the similarity of this lamp to the Flemish example. (Cat. No. 76484, Morocco; U. S. Department of State; 8.3 inches (21 cm.) high.) An old Italian two-light lamp of copper is a good example of an early device. In the Italian lamps of this type the wick is supported on a small metal channel soldered at the lower end to the bottom. This gives a more secure setting for the wick. (Pl. 45, fig. 4, Cat. No. 153891, Rome, Italy; G. Brown Goode; 3.5 inches (9 cm.) wide, 5.6 inches (14 cm.) long.) Figure 5 is a similar lamp of copper with four wick points. (Cat. No. 153894, same locality and collector; 4.9 inches (12.5 cm.) square.) Figure 6 is the Ceylonese lamp described on page 56. An antique French iron three-wick lamp is of the simple character of its class. It has a long hooked support with swivel for hanging. (Pl. 54, fig. 5, Cat. No. 289436, France; Anton Heitmuller; 15.4 inches (39 cm.) long.) The simple metal lamps of Europe show many variations due to adaptations for local, industrial, and even personal uses. These minor inventions have the essential parts of the lamp, namely, the reservoir and wick installation, in its age-old condition. For purposes of classification we have lamps with and lamps without drip catchers. Some of these in the collection are figured on Plate 55. Figure 10 is of copper and iron, of antique French work, and the ratchet for tilting the lamp is found nowhere else. There was some discussion among French antiquarians as to whether a reservoir was set in the hollow portion of the lamp, but it was decided in the negative. Old French and Italian iron cruisies substantiate this. (Cat. No. 130590, France; John Durand: 3.5 inches (9 cm.) diameter.) Figure 12 is an old Italian cruisie of hammered iron with bowed handle at the back and spike hook of twisted iron for hanging. (Cat. No. 153896, Siena, Italy; G. Brown Goode; 14.2 inches (36 cm.) long when hung.) Another from Siena (fig. 15) has the handle extended and a hook at the end for some special purpose, as a weaver's light. The walls of the reservoir are ornamented with chisel work. (Cat. No. 153895, same locality and collector; 14.2 inches (36 cm.) long.) Figure 16 is a French beaten-iron hand lamp of the fourteenth century with a narrower wick channel than usual in crusies. This lamp has a handle beaten out thin and convenient for moving the vessel. (Cat. No. 216072, France; S. B. Dean; 7.5 inches (19 cm.) long, 2 inches (5 cm.) high.) A wrought-iron crusie from the old manor at Dedham, Mass., has a cruciform handle with hole at the top for fastening the hook. The lamp is much like the French specimen described above. (Fig. 14, Cat. No. 151481, Dedham, Mass., 4.4 inches (11 cm.) long, 3.8 inches (10 cm.) high.) A cast-brass lamp which was in common use in northern France is Figure 11. The body of this is pear shape, connected to a bell-shape apex by four narrow bands, probably representing the chains of a hanging lamp. The spout is straight. The drip catcher is a small simple crusie hung on a hook below. The reservoir is filled by a projection and opening in the side. The hook is of cast brass. (Cat. No. 205377, northern France; S. B. Dean; 12.2 inches (31 cm.) long.)

In Figure 13 is shown a brass standing circular lamp with wick channel bent on the border. A tongue soldered to the bottom of the lamp inclines above the wick channel and is for holding the wick steady. This feature is found in Italian crusies and obviates the use of a separate drip catcher. The date of this improvement is not known. (Cat. No. 207818, Leyden, Holland; H. D. Paxson; 5.9 inches (15 cm.) high.) The crusies next to be taken up have the familiar drip catcher duplicating the reservoir. The specimen shown as Figure 17 is of excellently worked brass. The reservoir is set on a hook projecting from the bowed handle. The shield-shape top of the handle is perforated. Tweezers are attached by a chain; the hook for hanging is missing. (Cat. No. 168317, Belgium; S. B. Dean; 7.5 inches (19 cm.) high, 5.9 inches (15 cm.) long.) Scotch crusies are a characteristic type well and strongly made of iron. It is said that formerly crusie and drip catch reservoirs were hammered out in a stone mold, but probably not many real blacksmiths would care to do it that way. Plate 54, Figure 2, shows one of the ruder Scotch crusies with narrow long reservoir. The reservoir is slipped on a hook on the handle and the latter is bent over in the upper portion at right angles and at the extremity is fastened the hook. (Cat. No. 130411, Scotland; Edward Lovett; 13.8 inches (35 cm.) long.) A very old crusie in the best style is Figure 4. The projection at the back for hanging the reservoir is stepped as in 130411 so that by pulling up the reservoir notch by notch it may be tilted to allow the flow of oil to the wick, a simpler device than in the French lamp described (p. 58). The Spanish crusie (fig. 3) is smaller than the Scotch specimens and is very well made. It also has a notch device for tilting the reservoir as in the Scotch crusie. (Cat. No. 167061, Madrid, Spain; Walter Hough; 11.8 inches (30 cm.) long.) Figure 1 is a pottery lamp suggesting the crusie from Algiers. (Cat. No. 175266; M. F. Savage; 7.1 inches (18 cm.) long.) A typical Spanish crusie property of Mr. Gerrit S. Miller and purchased at Burgos by him shows superior iron work (pl. 54, fig. 8). The development of the crusie shows in an interesting way the course of that of the Roman lamp. The crusie is really the Roman lamp translated into the Iron Age. First the drip catcher was abolished and the wick held on a grooved lip of metal,

long ago adapted to Italian open lamps of metal. Next the crusie
was covered over, the lid hinged for placing the wick and filling.
The handle and hook-and-prick remained. Figure 1 on Plate 55
is a modern Spanish crusie of pressed tin with handle riveted and
soldered on. This has the look of factory manufacture and probably was made in France for Spanish trade; this lamp no doubt
being still used in out of the way places on the Peninsula. (Cat.
No. 167069, Madrid, Spain; Walter Hough; 12.7 inches (32 cm.)
long.) The crusie shown in Figure 2 was made in Washington
about 1820 and especial care was taken in its construction and finish.
The cover of the slot and reservoir moves to the right on a pivot.
The end of the handle is ornamented with a shield as in the Flemish
specimens. (Cat. No. 305620, S. C. Brown; 10 inches (25.5 cm.)
long.) The tin specimen (fig. 3) is a later form made among the
Pennsylvania "Dutch" at a time when the tinner was beginning to
supplant the blacksmith. The specimen is large for a crusie. The
lid is hinged and the hook of bent wire. (Cat. No. 72586, Muncey,
Pa.; N. J. Le Van; 10.6 inches (27 cm.) high.) Almost the last
word in the iron crusie is shown in Figure 4 from the same place
and collector. The handle and the cover of the reservoir are brazed
on, the little door slides on a pivot and the hook-spike is a fine piece
of quaint hammer work. The wick tender is also hand made. The
crusie is file finished. The specimen was probably not made in
America, but may be English or German. (Cat. No. 72588; 8.7
inches (22 cm.) long.) Among the Pennsylvania "Dutch" of past
generations habits of neatness and propriety required stands for
crusies. Formerly the crusie was hung up or stuck up at any convenient vantage point, perhaps usually near or in the chimney. The
stands represent the crusie entering into the intimate life of the
family. Also there were developed fillers for the lamp which could
be put near the fire to keep the grease fluid to pour into the schmutze
lamp, "fat lamp." A tin stand with pan and handle is shown in
Figure 5. This comes from Bucks County, Pa. (Cat. No. 207815;
Henry D. Paxson; 12.6 inches (32 cm.) high.) Stands of turned
wood painted were also used. (Pl. 55, fig. 7, Cat. No. 207816, Bucks
County, Pa.; Henry D. Paxson; 9.1 inches (23 cm.) high.) The lamp
on this stand is from Worms on the Rhine, Germany, presented by
T. Rothrock (Cat. No. 201426). Figure 9 is a crusie sliding on
a rod fastened in a weighted stand. (Cat. No. 207814, Bucks County, Pa.; Henry D. Paxson; 18.8 inches (48 cm.) high.) Figure 6
is a crusie filler of tin from Madrid, Spain. (Cat. No. 167034; Walter Hough; 7.5 inches (19 cm.) high.) Another is shown in Figure
8, also of tin. (Cat. No. 72352, Bainbridge, Pa.; George Bean; 6.1
inches (15.5 cm.) high.)

The farthest development of the lamp whose wick was drawn up at the side is seen in the spout lamp. The development of the spout which may be followed in the classes of lamps previously shown must have taken many centuries, yet was not destined to bring forth the modern central wick lamp. The most attractive of the spout lamps and the ones standing highest in art design are the Italian lucerna. The origin of the lucerna appears to be more immediately in the three-spout pottery lamps (pl. 43) and more distantly in the Roman hanging lamps with two wick orifices on the same plate. The ancient lamp stand may be taken as the support of the lucerna. Lucernas are usually of brass, excellently finished. The survival of this old type of lamp into the modern period in Italy is due to their customary use as lights for the dead. Otherwise they are treasured for their art and curio interest.

The usual lucerna has three spouts, as shown in Plate 56, Figure 3, a rather plain specimen, of brass and having the support on which the reservoir and cover slides rising from a roundel section above the base. (Cat. No. 205548, Italy; donor unknown; 22.4 inches (57 cm.) high.) The four-spout lucerna is also common, but none apparently occur with more than four. Figure 1 is a well-made specimen of the 4 spout lucerna having a longer roundel stem than usual. (Cat. No. 167025, Madrid, Spain; Walter Hough; 15.7 inches (40 cm.) high). A complete four-spout lucerna is shown in Figure 4. From above the reservoir cover depend by chains the objects which should accompany every lucerna, namely, the extinguisher, the pricker for adjusting the wick, and pincers or snuffers. The specimen is of brass, well executed and designed. Cat. No. 168129, Italy; G. Brown Goode; 24.4 inches (62 cm.) high). Another four-spout lucerna is expecially interesting on account of its design. On the gracefully bowed handle are perched three Roman eagles, mice clamber over the reservoir as they were accustomed to do in life searching for spilled olive oil, and in the corners of the base swim three geese. The specimen appears to be old, and this is substantiated by the quaint pricker, pincers, and extinguisher. (Pl. 56, fig. 5, Cat. No. 130656, Italy; Goldsborough & Co.; 18.9 inches (48 cm.) high). Included among the lucernas is a fine specimen of baroque style having two spouts and lobed reservoir, half of the upper section turning back for filling. A figure in classic pose surmounts the lucerna. (Fig. 2, Cat. No. 168133, Italy; G. Brown Goode; 16.4 inches (41.5 cm.) high). A pewter-spout lamp of graceful form has a hinged lid over the reservoir, a curved squared spout with a drip catcher encircling the end. The stem is slender vase shape with slender curved handle. (Pl. 57, fig. 3, Cat. No. 311710, England; Elizabeth S. Stevens; 9.8 inches (25 cm.) high).

Spout lamps of practical purpose were once common in Europe and America, but gave way to less smoky lighting apparatus. One of these from New England was called kyal lamp by the Cape Cod folks. It is of sheet iron, has a cylindrical reservoir with conical lid and upcurving copper spout. The reservoir sets in a bucket-shape base with projecting drip catcher and an iron bail fastened to the side. The specimen dates about 1820. Kyal was identified by Dr. E. B. Tylor [6] as an old Scandinavian name. The kyal is of European derivation, probably Flemish. (Pl. 56, fig. 6, Cat. No. 169103, Middletown, Conn.; A. R. Crittenden; 9.5 inches (24 cm.) high.) A two-spout lamp in the style of the kyal is seen in Plate 56, Figure 8, made of sheet iron. Such spout lamps were used on the whalers of an older period. It was also called "mill lamp." (Cat. No. 75378, New London, Conn.; C. A. Williams & Co.; 8.6 inches (22 cm.) wide, 7.9 inches (20 cm.) high.) A hanging-spout lamp of brass following in form the crusie and having the iron hanging spike of the crusie is Flemish and is shown in Figure 9. The lid with button lift is missing. (Cat. No. 130438, Antwerp, Belgium; Edward Lovett; 7.5 inches (19 cm.) long, 6 inches (15 cm.) high.) A similar lamp with stand is found in the Low Countries. It is of brass of fine yellow. At the back of the reservoir is a loop by which the lamp may be hung, also a wick tender hanging by a chain. The base is weighted with sand. (Pl. 56, fig. 10, Cat. No. 168316, Belgium; S. B. Dean; 10.3 inches (26 cm.) high.) A bucket two-spout lamp of heavy brass is shown in Figure 7. The bucket has a pivoted strap bail to which it attached the hanging hook. Drip catchers project from the sides. The reservoir fits into the bucket and the spouts come in line with the drip catchers. The specimen is well and strongly made. The lamp is classified Flemish seventeenth century. (Cat. No. 22187, Belgium, C. G. Sloan & Co.; 13 inches (33 cm.) wide, 9.8 inches (25 cm.) high.) A lamp with square reservoir of chased brass and up-curving spout having a drip catcher at the wick end is believed to be French (compare fig. 4). (Pl. 56, fig. 13, Cat. No. 175592, France; M. F. Savage; 7.4 inches. (18.5 cm.) long, 4.4 inches (11 cm.) high.) From the Philippines comes a pottery spout lamp used by fishermen in their gourd lanterns. The form of the lamp gives an indication of Mohammedan influence. (Pl. 56, fig. 12, Cat. No. 238386, Pasig, Rizal; C. L. Hall; 7.4 inches (19 cm.) long.) A modern form of the spout lamp is observed in the open-flame miner's lamp (fig. 11), in which the wick tube is nearly vertical and so designed that when the lamp is hooked on the cap it will incline to about the right slant to give oil pressure on the wick. (Cat. No. 325646, United States; Walter Hough; 2.6 inches (6.2 cm.) high.) A rare and at-

---

[6] Journ. Roy. Anthr. Inst., vol. 13, 1883–4, p. 353.

tractive two-spout lamp with reservoir, made to fit into a candlestick, comes from the Stevens collection. The reservoir and cover form a globe from which project the two sharply upcurving spouts. This lamp of silver plate delicately modeled and ornamented, was procured in England, but is of German workmanship. (Pl. 57, fig. 1, Cat. No. 311505, Elizabeth S. Stevens; 11.5 inches (29 cm.) high.) A three-spout lamp of massive construction in cast brass is a product of Ceylonese metal work. The roundel reservoir is screwed to the base. In filling, the reservoir is unscrewed, inverted, oil poured in, and the base screwed on. The lamp is then turned upright and the oil is supplied to the wick by gravity pressure. Evidently this shows the adoption of a western device, notably in the astral lamp. (Pl. 57, fig. 5, Cat. No. 234123, Ceylon; Ceylon Commission, St. Louis Exposition, 1907; 11.8 inches (30 cm.) high.) A rather rudely constructed brass three-spout lamp comes from China. The spouts are enlarged toward the opening and indicate a thick wick, as in the Ceylon specimen. No data is furnished as to the use to which this lamp is put. (Pl. 57, fig. 4, Cat. No. 175873, China; A. E. Hippisley; 9.8 inches (25 cm.) high.) An elaborate three-spout brass lamp with drip catcher and reflectors was procured in Ceylon. Like the lucernae, the lamp with its accompanying parts is adjusted in height on a stem which was originally tipped with the figure of a cock. The lamp shows much wear and appears old. It is undoubtedly of European suggestion and of European construction. Such a lamp might have come from France in the seventeenth century. (Pl. 57, fig. 2, Cat. No. 234124, Ceylon; Ceylon Commission, St. Louis Exposition; 27.9 inches (71 cm.) high.)

WICK-TUBE LAMPS

Mention has been made of a half tube fastened at the lower end in the reservoir of crusielike lamps for holding the wick more steadily in place. The next step would be to inclose the wick in a tube. This is borne out by the fact that the earliest wick tubes were slanted like the wick in the crusie and the reservoir became tightly closed. This was an important step in the development of the modern lamp. Before proceeding, attention is called to Plate 58, Figure 7, an open tin sconce lamp having a wick carrier bent into a tube at the upper portion, leaving a gutter the rest of the way. (Cat. No. 167026, Madrid, Spain; Walter Hough; 4 inches (10 cm.) high.) Also Figure 8, a pewter lamp having a saucer reservoir with the same installation. (Cat. No. 222188, England; C. G. Sloan & Co.; 9.8 inches (25 cm.) high.) An Italian brass lamp of 1589 with closed reservoir and wick holes at the four corners is an example of an approach to conditions which did not reach fruition till several centuries later. (Pl. 59, fig. 10, Cat. No. 153960, Italy; G. Brown

Goode; 7.1 inches (18 cm.) high.)   Figure 9 is a frankly modern
application of the wick tube to the clumsy crusie, the remaining
unchanged features being the bowed handle with its hook spike.
(Cat. No. 167039, Madrid, Spain; Walter Hough; 11.5 inches (29
cm.) high.)   Figure 5 is an old brass lamp with two spouts, a lid,
and a shank for insertion in a plate on a carriage.   The wicks are
carried in tubes.   (Cat. No. 168126, Italy; G. Brown Goode; 3.2
inches (8 cm.) wide, 4 inches (10 cm.) long.)   Figure 6 has four
wick tubes slanted and having a slot as described in the remarks on
crusies.   The slot device for raising the wick was continued for many
years into the nineteenth century.   (Cat. No. 178445, Alexandria,
Va.; Walter Hough; 5 inches (12.75 cm.) diameter, 4.2 inches (10.5
cm.) high.)   Next appears the upright central wick tube, a most
important, almost epochal event in the history of illumination.   The
lamps which were for ages unsymmetrical because the ancients had
drawn the wick to one side of their rude reservoirs gave way to the
balanced, erect lamps with light ascendant, which would be perfected
by modern progress.   One-tube lamps initiate this advance and a
selection of them is on Plate 59.   The oldest of these appear to be the
Pennsylvania "Dutch" grease lamps (figs. 3 and 10), which do not
fulfill the conditions of a closed reservoir, but have an upright central tube for the wick.   (Cat. No. 75353, Bainbridge, Pa.; George
Bean; 7 inches (18 cm.) high, 5.9 inches (15 cm.) diameter.)   Figure
2 is a lamp of heavy brass of plain yet pleasing design.   (Cat. No.
168315, England; S. B. Dean; 8.75 inches (22 cm.) high.)   Figure 11
is a quite old glass one-tube lamp.   The tube is set in a cork and
inserted in the lamp as a cork in a bottle.   This was the first method
with glass reservoir lamps.   Metal lamps admitted of the use of
threads for screwing on the burner.   (Cat. No. 177743, Massachusetts; Dr. Marcus Benjamin; 4.7 inches (12 cm.) high.)   The pewter
lamps (figs. 7, 8) are also old.   They were used as lights to go to
bed by.   The former has a ventilating tube and differs in this respect
from other one-tube lamps.   (Cat. No. 207817, Bucks County, Pa.;
Henry D. Paxson; 3.2 inches (8 cm.) high.)   The other is a graceful
little lamp dating before 1800.   (Cat. No. 151484, Providence, R. I.;
M. F. Savage; 4 inches (10 cm.) high.)   Figure 13 is a Chinese
opium smoker's lamp with one tube and a glass globe.   The base of
the lamp can be screwed over the upper portion.   (Cat. No. 77132,
New York City; Gen. Fitz John Porter; 2.9 inches (7.25 cm.) diameter, 2.8 inches (7 cm.) high.)   Nos. 1, 6, and 9 are lamps current in
Madrid in 1892.   No. 1 is mounted for hanging when required and
the others have a hinged extinguisher cap.   (Cat. Nos. 167422,
167032, 167023; collected by Walter Hough.)   Figure 4 is a tin table
and sconce lamp, excellently made from this material.   (Cat. No.
204681, Guanajuato, Mexico; Walter Hough; 6.7 inches (17 cm.)

high.) No. 14 is a small glass hand lamp with long tube having a sleeve for extinguishing. (Cat. No. 204889, United States; C. A. Q. Norton; 4.8 inches (12 cm.) high.) Figure 5 shows the upright tube applied to the crusie in recent times. (Cat. No. 167053, Madrid, Spain; Walter Hough; 9.8 inches (25 cm.) high.) Lamp No. 12 is a very old French specimen concerning which little is known. It is supposed to have been used by priests on night visitations and to date about the middle of the fifteenth century. The wick tube has a threaded cap which when not in use is secured on a threaded collar, as shown. In the back is a shutter which, raised, discloses a drawer containing flint and steel for striking a light. (Cat. No. 326315, France; Kendrick Scofield; 6.3 inches (16 cm.) long.)

About 1845 the miners of Cerro del Pasco, Peru, wore a crusie in the cap for a work light. The later spout lamp of the gas-free mines of the United States was a short remove from the crusie. Explosive gases in mines and the accidents caused by naked lights brought out Sir Humphry Davy's miner's gauze protected lamp seen in Plate 58, Figure 2. French miners have a characteristic lamp with a napiform cast-iron reservoir hinged to the arms of a yoke and hung by an iron hook. The lamp has one wick tube. (Pl. 58, fig. 3, Cat. No. 168135, France; G. Brown Goode; 23.4 inches (57 cm.) long.) A lamp on the same lines was patented in the United States. This lamp has two wick tubes, a locking cover, and a bent hook spike support. (Pl. 58, fig. 1, Cat. No. 251794, St. Louis, Mo.; U. S. Patent Office; 13 inches (33 cm.) long.)

Two-tube lamps were in vogue in the United States up to the close of the Civil War. The origin of the two-tube burner is better known than the origin of most of the inventions before the Patent Office began. That great natural philosopher, Benjamin Franklin, discovered through experiment that two wick tubes, ranged up side by side and at a certain distance apart, gave a greater amount of light than would be furnished by two single-tube lamps. This was a discovery of great practical value, was taken up at once, and continued in vogue for 100 years, more or less. In practical effect, this position of the tubes gave greater heat to the flame, more draft, and increased oxidation of the carbon particles, bringing them to higher incandescence, therefore more light, which is the first principle of illumination. The next question, "Why not three tubes?" was answered in the negative by the failure of the scheme to work. A "petticoat lamp" with three tubes is shown in Plate 59, Figure 22. The specimen is unused and probably stood on the shelves unsold long before the 45 years since its collection. (Cat. No. 75364, New Bedford, Mass.; J. T. Brown; 5.5 inches (14 cm.) high.) Another lamp of this kind (fig. 20), which has the normal two tubes and shows much use, comes from the same locality and collector (4.7 inches (12 cm.) high). Figure 15 is a heavy cast-brass lamp for the table. (Cat. No. 290443, United States; Mrs. C. E. Bates; 8.3 inches (21 cm.) high.) A similar heavy cast-brass old specimen of hand and table two-tube lamp (fig. 18) is from the same locality and collector. (Cat. No. 290444, 5.9 inches (15 cm.) high.) A hand and table two-tube lamp of pewter is shown in Figure 17. (Cat. No. 30572, United States; Miss H. A. Foster; 5.9 inches (15 cm.) high.) Figure 21 is an old gimbel lamp sconce used on the New London whaling fleet many years ago. The lamp was designed for all conditions for carrying in the hand, hung against the partition, and to care for all sorts of sea motions. (Cat. No. 75467, New London, Conn.; J. T. Brown; 5.5 inches (14 cm.) high.) In 1842 a patent was granted on a two-tube lard-oil lamp (fig. 16). The reservoir of the lamp was filled with a tube plunger bearing at the top the two-tube burner. In the tube two copper strips reached down to the oil, transmitting the heat from the burner to heat the oil. (Cat. No. 207821, Berks County, Pa.; Henry D. Paxson; 5.9 inches (15 cm.) high.) The original patent models are also in the collection. The latest of the two-wick tube lamps is a small hand lamp of gilt brass (fig. 19) filled partly with cotton to absorb the oil and prevent its spilling. Apparently coal oil was burned in this lamp. Collected in Washington, D. C., 1888. (Cat. No. 73385, District of Columbia; Otis T. Mason; 2.4 inches (6 cm.) high.) An interesting reading lamp not uncommon in collections is Plate 60, Figure 1. It is for lard or whale oil and has two wick tubes. Two lenses having hoods are set in sockets at the sides of the reservoir. (Cat. No. 178633, England; Ira F. Harris; 8.7 inches (22 cm.) high.)

Glass lamps were much valued in the older days and many of them have done service under the several burners demanded by different lamp fuels. The glass-lamp series normally have two tubes for burning whale oil earlier and lard oil later. In many cases the base is of pressed glass and the reservoir blown glass, the two being neatly joined. It appears that in the earlier examples the burner was set in cork and thus put in the opening of the reservoir. Later collars of pewter with threading were set on with cement, a method which has never been superseded. Figure 2, Plate 61a, has a blown-glass reservoir and pressed base. (Cat. No. 300541, United States; William Palmer; 7.1 inches (18 cm.) high.) Figure 4 has a cork shod burner, a pressed-glass base, and pear-shape blown reservoir. (Cat. No. 316030, United States; Kendrick Scofield; 11.9 inches (30 cm.) high.) Figure 6 answers to the same description. It has been stated that at times the blown reservoirs were imported from England and the bases added in America, but there is no exact authority for this conclusion. (Cat. No. 204891, United States; C. A. Q. Norton; 8.4 inches (21.5 cm.) high.) Figure 1 is a pressed glass two-tube lamp with pewter collar from the same locality and collector. (Cat. No. 204893; 9.5 inches (24 cm.) high.) Figure 3 is an old pressed-glass lamp still containing the thickened whale oil customarily burned in these lamps before 1829. (Cat. No. 130670, Baltimore, Md.; J. T. Durney; 11 inches (28 cm.) high.) An excellent specimen of pressed-glass lamp with pewter collar is shown in Figure 5. (Cat. No. 204890, United States; C. A. Q. Norton; 6.5 inches (16.5 cm.) high.)

A pewter lamp of good form and with an ornamental handle is of English manufacture. The burner is screwed into a threaded brass collar. (Pl. 60, fig. 2, Cat. No. 311710; Elizabeth S. Stevens; 10 inches (25 cm.) high.)

In the period following the practical disuse of the candle in lanterns the two-tube fish or lard oil burner was adopted, as shown in the mica-window lantern. (Pl. 46, fig. 3), dating about 1800, and collected in Alexandria, Va.

Lamp and candlesticks as adjuncts figured in the state of illumination at the time when the reservoir lamp was superseding the older devices. Lamp reservoirs intended to be set in a stem or joined to a stem and base had a peg at the bottom which would fit into a candlestick. Plate 60 shows a wooden stand for a set of these lamps to be used by hotel guests and when carried to the bed chambers to be set in the candlestick which already furnished the room. The specimen on the left has the burner inverted to show the expansion of the tubes toward the base, which construction was customary in the two-tube lamps. The stand and lamps were used in a hotel at Ellsworth, Me., probably in the early thirties. (Cat. No. 326350, Ellsworth, Me.; D. I. Bushnell, jr.; 13.9 inches (35 cm.) long, 7.1 inches (18 cm.) wide.)

TIME-INDICATING LAMPS

Observations on the gradual wasting away of oil in the reservoir of a lamp suggested to some unknown experimenter a means of marking time, perhaps following up the idea of the sand glass and clepsydra. On this line of thought King Alfred traditionally prepared his time candles (p. 40). Prof. S. P. Langley became interested in primitive chronometrics years ago and initiated the collection of such devices in the National Museum. Among the specimens which Doctor Langley collected for this exhibit was a time lamp of pewter with ovate glass reservoir mounted as in the Argand lamp, delivering oil by gravity to the wick laid horizontally in a spout. The reservoir is encircled vertically with a pewter girdle having on one face the hour and half-hour divisions from 9 to 6 and on the opposite side a handle for convenience in setting the reservoir in place. The lamp was seriously designed as an instrument of precision and may have been adequate at the period (pl. 61*b*, fig. 1). (Cat. No. 208097, Nuremburg, Germany; 14 inches (35.6 cm.) high.) The lamp is dated about 1750. Of curious interest are time lamps which were sold in America as late as 30 years ago. One of these, called "the Weaver time lamp," is of pressed glass, has a round woven wick, and a miniature chimney mounted in brass claws. The hours are from 8 to 6. (Pl. 61*c*, fig. 2, Cat. No. 316031; United States; Kendrick Scofield; 8.8 inches (25 cm.) high.) Another, called "Pride of America," was patented April, 1891 and 1896. It is of pressed glass, with globular opaque glass chimney, and the hours are also from 8 to 6. (Pl. 61*c*, fig. 3, Cat. No. 176091, Philadelphia, Pa.; Stewart Culin; 6.7 inches (17 cm.) high.)

CAMPHINE LAMPS

The search for a good lamp oil which had been earnestly prosecuted in the years following Argand's epoch-making discovery when inventors strove to produce a perfect lamp seemed finished when in the thirties camphine appeared. Properly, camphine is a product secured by the distillation of turpentine over quicklime, namely, pineine, a limpid fluid of agreeable odor, free burning without residue. Spirits of turpentine had previously been used but abandoned on account of its disagreeable odor. Camphine as sold for burning in "fluid lamps" and the Vesta lamp, in which it was originally used, was generally a mixture of turpentine and alcohol. Camphine is very volatile and explosive and about as safe to use in lamps as gasoline. On this account, despite many inventions to make its use practicable, camphine was abandoned about 1850. During the camphine period, which began about 1830, many of the two-tube whale-oil and lard-oil lamps were converted in "fluid" lamps, having two tubes, but longer, and inclined away from each other, as seen on Plate 63. The lamp mentioned has a marble base, brass column, and pressed-glass reservoir with threaded collar cemented on. It was necessary in the camphine lamps to have a cap for each tube to prevent evaporation from the wick, and which also served as an extinguisher. (Cat. No. 178189, Virginia; Walter Hough; 14 inches (36 cm.) high.) Plate 62 shows a variety of camphine lamps. Figure 1 is a fine cut-glass lamp with pressed base and gracefully fashioned. It is complete with the two-wick tube caps. (Cat. No. 13665, Baltimore, Md.; James Russell & Son; 14.2 inches (36 cm.) high.) Figure 4 is the reservoir of an old whale-oil lamp converted to camphine. The base having been broken off, the reservoir was firmly set in a block of wood to extend its usefulness. (Cat. No. 325647, Massachusetts; Walter Hough; 10.4 inches (25.5 cm.) high.) Figure 6 is a pewter two-tube camphine lamp formerly used for whale or lard oil. (Cat. No.

207820, Philadelphia, Pa.; Henry D. Paxson; 11.2 inches (28.5 cm.) high.) A smaller specimen of pewter, also fitted with two tubes, is Figure 7. (Cat. No. 175591, United States; M. F. Savage; 7.1 inches (18 cm.) high.) Figure 5 is an ornate lamp of brass and marble fitted with five tubes and globe. The column bears a bas-relief of Jefferson (?) surrounded with wreath and surmounted by a spread eagle. The column is much older than the reservoir and appears to have been fitted with an Argand type, probably the astral. (Cat. No. 168306, District of Columbia; Walter Hough; 19.7 inches (50 cm.) high.) A bottle lamp with one tube is shown in Figure 3. (Cat. No. 92866, Haiti; Foreign Exposition, Boston, Mass.; 5.2 inches (13 cm.) high.) A tin lamp from the same source is Figure 9. (Cat. No. 92867; 6.8 inches (15 cm.) high.) A small bedroom lamp of glass with one tube and cap hung by a chain is shown in Figure 10. (Cat. No. 207811, Philadelphia, Pa.; Henry D. Paxson; 4.2 inches (10.5 cm.) high.) A typical camphine table lamp with graceful glass reservoir, brass column, and marble base is a converted whale-oil lamp of the later part of the period when that fluid was burned. (PPl. 63, fig. 1, Cat. No. 178189; 13.5 inches (34 cm.) high.) Improvemets on the camphine burner in the interest both of light and safety were brought out in America and Europe. One of these with globular gas chamber and perforated disk burner is shown in Plate 62, Figure 2. (Cat. No. 130430, Broadalbin, N. Y.; F. S. Hawley; 14.2 inches (36 cm.) high.) This lamp has been converted to camphine from whale oil. Another old lamp of pewter is supplied with an improved burner (fig. 8). Cat. No. 130671, Baltimore, Md.; I. T. Durney; 13 inches (33 cm.) high.) An improved camphine lamp based on the gravity principle with stopcock on the line and a fan-shape perforated burner (pl. 63, fig. 2), was brought out in 1860. It is probable that by this plan of separating the fuel to some distance from the flame, as in the faker's gasoline torches of 1875, the use of camphine would have been rendered safe. Coal oil, however, superseded all other lamp fuels within a few years. (Cat. No. 263465, United States; Mrs. Yates Davis Duke; 21.5 inches (54.5 cm.) high.) A chandelier for camphine with improved burners is described on page 30. A wall lamp for camphine (pl. 63, fig. 3) has a horizontal cylindrical tank attached to a sconce. From the bottom of the tank a tube supplies the fluid to an upright secondary reservoir having the burner tube at the top. A tube curved at the end and open leads from the top of the secondary reservoir over the top of the tank. The burner is primed by stopping the end of the curved tube and pumping air into the tank through a vent in the top. When lighted the heat of the burner causes a constant flow of camphine vapor mixed with air. (Cat. No. 325648, Baltimore,

Md.; Anton Heitmuller; 10.9 inches (28 cm.) long.) These lamps
were used in churches and public halls between 1850 and 1860. The
most costly and artistic camphine burners in the collection is a pair
of "torches" which came by some unknown donor to the Library of
Congress and transferred to the United States National Museum.
The reservoir is of repoussee silver swung between two arms and the
handles are of polished ebony. The divergent tubes of the burner
indicate the use of camphine, dating these lamps after 1830. They
were made by Galt & Bro., of Washington. It is suggested that they
were used in one of the great mansions to light guests to their car-
riages. (Pl. 62, figs. 11, 12, Cat. No. 301543, 301544; Library of
Congress; 28 inches (71.2 cm.) long.)

LAMPS OF THE INVENTIVE PERIOD

In the decade between 1860 and 1870, marked by the production
in quantity of the ideal lamp fuel from petroleum, the two-wick tube
lamps burning heavy oil practically disappeared. The glass chimney nearly a century after its application or discovery, and the ventilated burners long seen on certain types of heavy-oil lamps, came
into wide use. Wicks which had given infinite trouble to lamp users
for ages were flattened and raised and lowered by a spurred wheel
on a horizontal axis. The round wick inherited from old times was
insensibly retained by the inventors, who improved the lamp after
the discovery of Argand. The wick was given a tubular form,
recognizing the principle of aeration of both sides of the flame,
which was ventilated through the tube containing the wick. The
flat wick was used in models sent in to the United States Patent
Office as early as 1830. Many of the smaller hand lamps in the
period 1870–1880 were not fitted with chimney, both on account of the
survival of the chimneyless lamp and the uses for which they were
made. Figure 7, plate 64, is a brass lamp gilt, the burner incased
in perforated metal as in the safety lamp. This lamp was patented
in 1863. (Cat. No. 73824, Philadelphia, Pa.; Centennial Exposition,
1876; 4.5 inches (11.5 cm.) high.) Another of the same period has
a round wick and an extinguisher cap (pl. 64, fig. 9). The reservoir
is cotton-filled to absorb the oil. (Cat. No. 204895, United States;
C. A. Q. Norton; 4.3 inches (11 cm.) high.) Lamps collected by the
United States Fish Commission for the fisheries exhibition in the
United States National Museum show interesting adaptations for the
needs of the industry. Figure 10 is a well-made copper binnacle
lamp with socket for a stanchion, weighted and swinging like a binnacle compass. It has a brass ventilated burner for a flat wick, and
was patented in 1864. (Cat. No. 75383, New Bedford, Mass.; J. T.
Brown; 6.1 inches (15.5 cm.) diameter, 5.5 inches (14 cm.) high.)

A brass gilt gimbel lamp for table or bracket was patented also in 1864. The lamp swings in a ring pivoted on the arms of a bell bracket mounted on a base. (Pl. 64, fig. 13. Cat. No. 75,368, Gloucester, Mass.; U. S. Fish Commission; 13 inches (23 cm.) high.) Figure 14, plate 64, is a lamp of japanned tin with burner, patented in 1864. It is swung in a U-shape support riveted in the bottom of a pan like a candle dish, having a ring on the edge by which the lamp may be hung as a wall light. Used in the forecastle of whalers and made by F. M. Loring. (Cat. No. 75384, Gloucester, Mass.; J. T. Brown; 7.9 inches (20 cm.) high.) A lard lamp in which the flat wick and round wick are set in the same reservoir was patented by D. Kinnear, February 4, 1851, shown in Figure 11, plate 64, by a specimen which was used in Pennsylvania many years ago. The round wick tube has a brass rod running down at the side conducting heat to melt the fat. (Cat. No. 75351, Bainbridge, Pa.; George Bean; 7.3 inches (18.5 cm.) high.) The lamp (fig. 12, pl. 64) is a fine specimen of the period 1860–1870. It is of silver, made by Hinks & Sons, Birmingham, England. The wick is flat, the burner ventilated, and the chimney tubular, swelled out in the lower portion. (Cat. No. 316029, England; Kendrick Scofield; 13.8 inches (35 cm.) high.) Some of the early flat-wick lamp models are shown on plate 64. Figure 5 has the sinumbra, " without shadow," type of reservoir, three inclined wick tubes holding coarse woven wicks raised by picking through slots in the metal, and posts with a set screw for securing the globe which acted as a chimney. This lamp was patented March 23, 1831, as a chandelier lamp by William Lawrence. (Cat. No. 251760, United States; U. S. Patent Office; 7.5 inches (19 cm.) diameter.) Figure 6, of the same type, has four wick tubes mounted in inclined position on a ring reservoir having brackets for suspension. This quaint device was patented March 13, 1833, by Couch and Fray. (Cat. No. 251453, United States; U. S. Patent Office; 6.7 inches (17 cm.) diameter.) Figure 8 is a glass lamp with flat wick raised and lowered by the familiar toothed-wheel device.

The flat wick has evidently a more limited history than the tubular wick. It superseded, as has been noticed, the round wicks of the heavy oil lamps which had persisted to the middle of the nineteenth century in defiance of the fact that Argand's great invention had come into the world long before. The reason for this is that Argand's invention and the long line of improvements thereon by known and unknown inventors catered to luxury and not to the needs of the people. These needs were indeed small and easily satisfied. Lamps made for the most part by hand and a modicum of machinery were costly and beyond the means of the many. Therefore, forms of lamps which should have become obsolete held on till machinery should make luxuries necessities.

The investigations at the beginning of the modern oil lamp had to do with wicks, the delivery of oil to the wicks, aeration of the flame, and draft in the burner. The problem of suitable oil was also very difficult. Inventors earnestly worked to make the lamp efficient. By the first quarter of the nineteenth. century the lamps produced had failed in competition with the Argand with its improvements. The Argand supplies oil to the wick by gravity, and when regulated by a valve is delivered at the rate of combustion. The collection of the relics of George Washington in the National Museum includes three lamps of this kind. One of these has tubular chimneys of blue glass, the globes missing. It is of silver plate and is without marks. The other lamps are a pair of silver plate wall, or possibly desk, lamps, without glassware and marks.[7] If these lamps were used in Mount Vernon during the decade before the death of Washington, they would be perhaps the earliest Argands to which a date could be assigned. It can only be ventured that the style and workmanship of these lamps, especially the two-light specimen, appears early. The astral lamp of our forefathers was an Argand of sturdy English manufacture in which labor and material was not spared to make a practicable and enduring product, though less can be said on the point of art. The astral had an extended use among the first families, and from their indestructible character, as stated, and their preservation as ornamental objects for the mantelpiece many have survived to this day. The fine specimen shown on Plate 65a, Figure 2, bears a metal label sweated on the wick tube, " J and I Cox, New York." This inscription was put on in England for the New York vendor. The lamp is massive brass in French rococo style. Even without the lusters, globes, chimneys, and fittings it is an imposing object. (Cat. No. 150434, Baltimore, Md.; T. W. Sweeney; 24 inches (61 cm.) high, 13.8 inches (35 cm.) wide.) Astral lamps were in sets of three, a central two-burner and side one-burner, following the candelabra mantel sets, indicating the special and formal lighting usages of a past period. Plate 66a, Figure 1, is of a side lamp of a set of heavy brass gilt. The set is in good condition and lacks lusters and globes. The globe and chimney support engages the collar containing the wick, which is raised and lowered by turning the support. The lusters were hung from a corona, by which it could be lifted off when the reservoir needed filling. The handle of the shut-off valve is seen below the reservoir. The lamp is inscribed " Manufactured for T. Palmer, Baltimore." (Cat. No.

---

[7] T. T. Belote. Descriptive Catalogue of the Washington Relics in the U. S. National Museum. Proc. U. S. Nat. Mus., vol. 49, 1915, pp. 1–24.

325649, Baltimore, Md.; Walter Hough; 12.2 inches (31.2 cm.) high.)
About 1840 sinumbra, "without-shadow," lamps came into use.
Attempts at arranging the parts of the lamp to prevent shadows are
observed in the specimens of 1831 and 1833 on Plate 64. The sinumbra of real worth was an Argand with ring reservoir furnishing
gravity oil through two supporting tubular arms extending from the
reservoir to the wick tube. The specimen figured on Plate 65a,
Figure 3, is supported on a column of milky glass with base and
pedestal of brass. The globe rested on a flange around the margin
of the reservoir. The lamp was stated to have been in the possession
of a French family since 1847. (Cat. No. 176721, Quebec, Canada;
P. C. Boyle; 21.3 inches (54 cm.) high.) An old astral lamp famil-
iarly called "knitting lamp," being of convenient height when set
on the floor to light up the knitting circle, comes from Orange
County, Va. In its present form the Argand burner and reservoir
have been superseded by a reservoir of about 1850. The column
below the reservoir is French. Traditionally this lamp was used
in the 1800's by Thomas Jefferson. (Pl. 65a, fig. 1, Cat. No. 150442,
Orange County, Va.; Miss Maggie Griffin; 27.2 inches (69 cm.)
high.) Another fine lamp which has been modified in the same way
is shown in Plate 68, Figure 1. The reservoir is of brass with gilt
striping.) (Cat. No. 258916, England; Miss Katherine Noyes.)
One of a pair of pulpit lamps from the Presbyterian Church of
Morgantown, W. Va., is shown on Plate 66b, Figure 3. The reservoir is mounted on a floriated brass bracket hung on a ball-and-
socket joint at the top of the fluted column. In an oval medallion
on the reservoir is the following: "Cornelius & Co. Philad., July
24, 1849 patent: April 15, 1845." The burner was probably for camphine and altered for burning coal oil in the late sixties. The coal-
oil burner is large, ventilated through wire mesh and has no marks.
(Cat. No. 175463, Morgantown, W. Va.; Walter Hough; 24.5 inches
(62 cm.) high.) The collection contains several lamps belonging to the period of intense invention to supply the demand for
better light. It is not possible or desirable, however, to indicate
more than in a very limited way the great and intricate subject having little practical bearing on the history of illumination. This is
borne out by the fact that the mechanical lamp devices which
harassed our ancestors were supernumerary. Chiefly a limpid fluid,
easily combustible without residue, readily drawn up by the wick,
and properly oxidized in the flame, was the thing needed. With the
heavy oils, vegetal and animal, at hand for ages up to 1830, when
camphine was produced, invention was spurred to do the almost
impossible.

One of these lamp curiosities is of French manufacture, inscribed on base, "Lampe Silvant 15589 avec garantie." This lamp has a tubular wick raised and lowered by a ratchet device, the outer brass collar choked. The lamp appears to be one of several similar inventions in which by an arrangement of chambers the displacement of brine and oil was made to force oil to the wick by hydraulic principles long known. They were sometimes called oleostatic lamps. (Pl. 66b, fig. 2, Cat. No. 272261, France; Lemuel Merrill; 15.8 inches (40 cm.) high.)   Another lamp of this type evidently forced the oil up into the wick by direct pressure on the reservoir. This appears to be effected by turning the ornamental key to the left, which works a rack thus lowered to give the proper pressure. The lamp is incased in pressed-brass relief illustrating naval battles.   (Pl. 65b, fig. 1, Cat. No. 130669, Baltimore, Md.; J. T. Durney; 14.9 inches (38 cm.) high.) The specimen is of French manufacture. The Diacon lamp (pl. 66b, fig. 1) is marked "A. Diacon, New York. Patent lamp." There is a clockwork in the base actuating a pump forcing oil through a tube from the reservoir to the wick as in the Carcel lamp. Dates scratched inside the bottom cover by repair man are 1841 and 1849. The lamp is incased in a shell of artistic pressed brass and is of French manufacture. The chimney is tubular with a shoulder at the height of the flame intended to direct the draft and increase the brilliancy of the light. The chimney is 10.7 inches (27 cm.) long.   (Cat. No. 130668, Baltimore, Md.; James Russell & Son; 13.4 inches (34 cm.) high.) The Carcel lamp was reasonably efficient and had considerable use before 1850. It has the Argand burner and tubular wick adjusted, however, by a spur wheel on a horizontal stem as in modern lamps. The base contained a clockwork pump with two valves forcing oil into the wick. Plate 65b, Figure 2, shows the mechanism. (Cat. No. 272259, Boston, Mass.; Lemuel Merrill.) The clock bears the number 23660. Figure 3 is the complete lamp, same locality and collector (15 inches (38 cm.) high). The Hitchcock lamp, patented in 1868 and burning kerosene with a flat wick and without chimney, was quite effective and is still in current use. In this lamp a fan run by clockwork forces air into the flame at the proper point and in the right amount to produce a brilliant light. This lamp may be considered the last of the mechanical lamps, and owes its success to the ideal fluid, kerosene. The development of the kerosene lamp since 1870 is characterized by the perfection to its limit of the flat-wick type and the ascending of the tubular-wick type, which may be said to extend from the Argand to the Rochester lamp. The tubular lamp of 1876 exhibited at the Philadelphia Centennial Exposition as the most advanced product is shown on Plate 67. A pair of lamps combined with candlesticks, the reservoir fitted to the candle socket and removable, is shown in Plate 66a. The inscription on the burner is " F. T. Gale, 128 Oxford Street. Made in Germany." The flat wick is formed by the burner into a tubular wick. The chimney is tubular with a constriction in the lower portion. (Figs. 2, 3, Cat. No. 311510, England; Elizabeth S. Stevens; 18.5 inches (47 cm.) high.) The chimney is by Macbeth.

During his incumbency as Secretary of the Smithsonian Institution, Joseph Henry carried on for the Lighthouse Board experiments to ascertain the relative values of oils suitable for economical use in lighthouses. Sperm oil, due to the diminution in the number of whales from the unrestrained activity of the whalers, had increased in price to such an extent that it was found necessary to cast about for other illuminants. Lard oil and rapeseed oil were the available alternatives for sperm oil, which had for so many years been the mainstay of illumination. Both of these oils were found suitable for the purpose mentioned. Spencer F. Baird, second Secretary of the Smithsonian, continued experiments in the interest of the Lighthouse Board, giving especial attention to improved lamps for the service. The lamp on Plate 68 (fig. 2) is one which Professor Henry used for his scientific work on oils and which was preserved by Professor Baird. This lamp is simple, the oil being raised in the wick by capillarity alone. The wick is tubular, mounted as in the time-honored Argand, but adjusted by a toothed rack engaged by a cogwheel. The wick collar is choked at the wick edge. Ventilation through the wick tube is supplied through holes pierced in the walls of the lamp support. The lamp is made of copper. (Pl. 68, fig. 2, Cat. No. 325650, Washington, D. C., Spencer F. Baird; 18.7 inches (47 cm.) high.) Another lighthouse lamp used by Professor Baird and traditionally devised by him is designed to force oil into the wick at a regular rate by means of a clockwork with strong spring actuating a gear engaged with a rack and pinion. This is practically the Carcel principle and illustrative of the devices necessary before the introduction of petroleum. The burner incorporates all the principles found useful up to the time of this lamp. The latter is entirely of brass and is a good piece of professional work. (Pl. 68, fig. 3, Cat. No. 75373, Washington, D. C., Spencer F. Baird; 16.7 inches (42 cm.) high.)

GAS LAMPS

The subject of gas lighting is very interesting. Few realize that the beginning of gas lighting was 135 years ago and that this form of illumination is the oldest scientific method, introducing gas en-

gineering in an early period of the age of progress. Thus while oil
lamps were subject to endless and mostly unsuccessful experimenta-
tion, gas, though localized on account of engineering problems of
distribut.on, has been from the first a most satisfactory illuminant.
Collections of illumination devices usually contain few examples of
gas burning apparatus. On Plate 1, Figure 22, in the development
of illumination series is shown a Welsbach mantle lamp in which
science has done so much to foster the use of gas as an illuminant.
A gas lamp with improved burner having a lever by which the flow
in the burner is controlled is shown on Plate 65b, Figure 4. In this
specimen the gas issues from a ring of fine orifices on the ring top
of the burner. The flame is ventilated on both sides as in the
Argand. (Cat. No. 325651, Washington, D. C.; Walter Hough;
15.4 inches (39 cm.) high.) This gas lamp dates about 1840.

HEATING DEVICES

The history of fire in heating may be gathered under the following
heads:

Natural.—In response to a need for heat or pleasure in heat man
sought caves and shelters where the temperature remains fairly
constant, built shelters or primitive houses, clothed himself against
weather, and congregated at hot springs.

Artificial.—It seems obvious that from the family fire there should
be lighted in the course of time smaller fires devoted to special uses.
As the result of observations the qualities of stones to retain heat
might have a practical application. It is true that there is a line of
uses based on this princ.ple and persisting through a very long
period to the present. These hot-water vessels, hot stones, bricks,
brazen or iron balls served a valuable purpose at times, but were
not radically important in fathering essential inventions. On the
other hand the first portion of fire set apart and inclosed in a vessel
began the stove and all that implies of usefulness and tremendous
growth.

The descriptions of specimens in the United States National Museum incorporated in this section relate to the application of heat
to bodily wants and mainly to cooking. Under warming the body
and house we have individual appliances, as heated stones and metal,
hot-water vessels, foot stove, pocket stove, and fire pot; family
appliances, as the house, camp, and tent fire, the lamp, brazier, stove,
and accompanying fireplace, chimney, fire tools and irons; and col-
lective appliances, as hot air, water, steam, gas, and electric stoves
and furnaces.

The intention here is to classify the objects described, not as per-
taining to the races and tribes using them, but by their place in the

scale of inventions. In this respect there will be presented an obvious history of development in heating and cooking devices.

Accompanying the heating appliances discussed are adjuncts which have developed with the fire, such as shovels, pokers, tongs, fire fans, bellows, andirons, grates, and cognate objects. Most of these show a considerable development, but some, as the poker, of necessity remain essentially primitive.

There are presented as follow several classifications of the branches of this subject, which will indicate the lines followed in the study of the material. Remarks briefly classifying the early stages in the use of fire for warming the body and house have already been presented.

GENESIS OF COOKING DEVICES

Roasting and broiling:
  Camp fire.
  Broche and skewer (animal in skin).
  Spit.
  Gridiron.
  Grill.
Frying:
  Flat stone.
  Pan.
  Deep fat vessel.
Baking:
  Flat stone.
  Pottery, stone or iron griddle.
  Vessel with cover.
  Oven—
    Hot stones on object.
    Clay cover.
    Pit oven.
    Reflector.
    Baker's oven.
    Dutch oven.
    Oven in range.
    Electric oven.
    Solar oven.
Boiling, stewing, and chafing:
  Cooking vessel.
  Stones in basket.
  Pot over fire.
  Pot on range.
Steaming, sunning, electric, and chemical:
  In can or steaming.
  Over boiling water.
  Exposure to hot sun.
  Above methods.
  By lime and water.

METHODS OF COOKING

Direct heat:
   Roasting—
      Open fire.
      Broche and skewer.
      Spit.
      Gridiron.
      Plank.
      Reflector (direct and reflected heat).
Indirect heat:
   Frying—
      Frying pan.
      Deep fat.
   Baking—
      Hot stones.
      Stone slabs.
      Burying in coals.
      Coating with clay.
      Oven and pit.
      Sand bath.
   Boiling and stewing—
      Basket and hot stones.
      Pot.
      Stewpan.
      Chafing dish.
   Steaming—
      Steamer.
Dessication in sun:
   By heat—
      Sunning—
         In hot sun.
   By air—
      Electric.
      Chemical.

Portions of fire inclosed in simple vessels for personal use, hot-water containers, and heated masses of stone or iron were formerly fairly common in the technology of fire. Many of such adaptations come early in the use of fire and have the appearance of timely devices. Some are frankly the result of more or less urgent need, as the slow match or torch carried to provide a little heat for the hands, or the smothered coal carried by Tibetan herdsmen for igniting at times dry bunches of grass to get a little warmth against the biting cold. It is allowable, however, to see in these rude makeshifts evidences of the methods of handling of fire at the period before there were means of confining fire to vessels, of which the brazier is a type.

BRAZIER

The brazier is of great antiquity, and though treated here as a draughtless vessel for holding fire for personal use, in reality stands near the beginning of the stove and in this sense it will be mentioned later. The examples figured are crude and common vessels of the type which ran the gamut of art embellishment during the period of handicrafts. Gold, silver, bronze, brass, and fine woods entered into the brazier of luxury, which was an important piece of house furnishing. Braziers of solid silver, very massive, were in use in Chile. The brazier of common use in Mexico consisted of an earthenware bowl with three short legs. The specimen (Pl. 69a, fig. 1) is from Durango, Mexico, collected by Edward Palmer (Cat. No. 176486). Such vessels kept a little fire at hand, supplied warmth when required, and over them minor cooking could be done. The portability of the brazier also was much in its favor, facilitating the carrying out of the ashes and cleaning. As to the introduction of the brazier into America from Spain there is no evidence, though European modifications of the native brazier may have occurred. Indigenous censers and braziers antedate the conquest. A bowl brazier has been found in a prehistoric cliff dwelling in New Mexico.[8] The only attempt to ornament the Durango specimens is a wash of red ocher on the border. The specimen is 11.4 inches (29 cm.) diameter, 4.7 inches (12 cm.) high. The Philippine brazier (Pl. 69a, fig. 2) is of earthenware washed with red and ornamented with pleasing designs formed by continuous zigzags and punches, the depressions filled with lime. The vessel is of graceful shape. It has four small holes through the walls in the lower part of the body, which suggest draught holes. The concave of the lid has three bosses which indicate that the lid could be turned over and a vessel set on the bosses to keep food warm. The specimen is from Luzon and probably from the town of Poliacan. (Cat. No. 238321, Philippine Commission, 10.6 inches (27 cm.) diameter, 8.6 inches (22 cm.) high.) The Spanish brazier, which may be taken as a type of European brazier, has a circular ring stand with three feet. In this ring is placed the pan which has two loop drop handles for lifting. The shovel has a circular blade and a cross handle. This model is of cast brass. (Pl. 69a, fig. 3; Cat. No. 167048, Madrid, Spain; Walter Hough; 3.6 inches (9 cm.) diameter.)

HEATED IRONS AND HOT-WATER VESSELS

There is no evidence that the use of heated stones, iron, or hot-water containers has any considerable antiquity, but, as mentioned, it seems reasonable to imagine that the heat-retaining quality of stones and water would be known experimentally very early. The application of this principle for personal use was probably not carried out until a late period. Hot stones, preferably soapstone, hot

---

[8] Culture of the ancient Pueblos of the upper Gila River region, New Mexico and Arizona. (Museum-Gates Expedition.) Bull. 87, U. S. Nat. Mus., Washington, 1914, p. 3.

bricks, flat irons, water bottles, and the like were employed by our ancestors during the rigorous winters. Some of these uses are seen in what we consider modern inventions, as the irons in the fireless cooker.

The specimen shown in Plate 69a, Figure 4, is of excellent cast iron made in Germany. It is a table hand warmer and is charged with a shoe-shape hot iron when in use. (Cat. No. 325301), from Anton Heitmuller, 4.3 inches (11 cm.) high.) The second example (pl. 69a, fig. 5) is a brass pail with bail, of Flemish origin. The lid is a heavy plate of iron covered with sheet brass. The iron is heated by a charcoal pan and the vessel served to warm the hands or feet, and could also be used to dry-iron laces. (Cat. No. 169091, from S. B. Dean, 9 inches (23 cm.) diameter, 5.5 inches (4 cm.) high.) Heated irons were also used in the Colonial smoothing iron (see pl. 93) and in the water heaters or biggins for the table (see pl. 81).

HOT-WATER APPLIANCES

These occur in a number of forms, some extemporary and some manufactured to fill a want. One of the latter is a bottle-shape vessel of Binghampton pottery ware with flat bottom. One side has two concave depressions for the feet. It holds a quart of hot water. Similar vessels were made by English potters in Staffordshire. (Pl. 69b, fig. 1; Cat. No. 303672, from C. S. Smith; measurements, 7.1 inches (18 cm.) wide and 9 inches (23 cm.) high.) For special use in drying boots is a shoe-form hot-water bottle of gray stoneware from Doulton and Watts, Lambeth, England (pl. 69b, fig. 2), and from the same ceramists a concavo-convex bottle for warming the abdomen (pl. 69b, fig. 3). A foot warmer, also English, is shown in Plate 69b, Figure 4. It has a copper hot-water tank inclosed in a padded hardwood foot stool. Dimensions, 13.8 inches (35 cm.) by 11.8 inches (30 cm.) by 4.7 inches (12 cm.).

SLOW-BURNING FUEL DEVICES

The Japanese pocket stove brings forward an interesting invention which, however, has as yet proved of little economic importance. This is of a fuel which, ignited, slowly consumes and gives out heat in a closed receptacle such as the little curved pocket stove in which is placed a cartridge of the fuel. (Pl. 70a, figs. 1, 2; Cat. No. 128139, Tokio, Japanese Department of Education; 4.5 inches (11.5 cm.) long, 2.75 inches (7 cm.) high.) Another example is a tight stove of Japanese cast iron of excellent work decorated with fans and mice. Two cast-iron open-work lifters serve to move the stove about. It appears certain that the slow consuming fuel mentioned, made from powdered charcoal and seaweed, was burnt in this stove. (Pl. 70a, fig. 3; Cat. No. 128135; donor unknown; 8.7 inches (22 cm.) diameter, 6.6 inches (17 cm.) high.) Combustion of fuel without air is the outstanding feature of the stoves of north Europe and Asia. Wood fuel is introduced, ignited, and allowed to burn under a draft for a time, the stove is then closed, and in the heated chamber the combustion goes on, sending out a gentle heat. Wood-burning stoves of iron employing this feature were used in the United States some years ago, but in them the wood was really distilled and the products were disagreeable to the housewife. The Russian stove and the Chinese Kang are examples of slow-burning stoves.

HAND AND FOOT WARMERS

A great variety of hand and foot warmers are found in latitudes and at elevations where their use might be necessary. They consist of a container for holding charcoal and a surrounding case, more or less elaborated in basketry, metal, and wood. Frequently their artistic treatment renders them prized objects. Their survival also may be due in part to the fact that they are small and there might be an exigency when they would be used again. In some parts of the world hand warmers are still current. The Museum has a specimen consisting of an oblong rounded rectangular box of brass with twin handles which fall to either side, an artistically perforated lid and chased sides. (Pl. 71, fig. 2); Cat. No. 315065, China; Mrs. John Van Rensselaer Hoff; 5.8 inches (15 cm.) long, 4.7 inches (12 cm.) wide, 4.5 inches (9 cm.) high.) Another is of copper with finely perforated lid and handle wrapped with cloth and is from western China. It is signed in Manchurian characters. (Pl. 71, fig. 1; Cat. No. 306971; Kendrick Scofield; dimensions 5.5 inches (14 cm.) by 4.3 inches (11 cm.) by 3.2 inches (8 cm.).) Another Chinese form is simply an earthenware bowl inclosed in basket weaving of bamboo. (Pl. 71, figs. 3, 5; Cat. Nos. 14044, 76416, Chinese Commission, Centennial Exposition, Philadelphia, 1876; 6.3 inches (16 cm.) diameter, 7 inches (18 cm.) high, 5.5 inches (14 cm.) diameter, 8.3 inches (21 cm.) high.) An interesting specimen from Srinagar, Kashmir, is also an earthen pot surrounded with an elaborately worked basket of osier and decorated with pendants of rings, plates of mica, and red paper. It has a yoke-shape superstructure and a loop for carrying. The native name is Kangri and this vessel is used for warming the body in cold weather. (Pl. 71, fig. 4; Cat. No. 164967, Dr. W. L. Abbott; 8 inches (20 cm.) diameter, 9 inches (23 cm.) high.) A group of three Italian fire vessels called scaldino are shown in Plate 71 (figs. 6–8). They were collected in Florence by Dr. George Brown Goode. Two are of artistically treated terra cotta glazed in colors, the other of bronze, and from its condition and type may be antique. These were required by ladies going to market in winter or for any other contribution to personal comfort during this season. Some of the scaldini were provided with covers. (Cat. Nos. 165461, 165462, and 165463; middle figure 5.9 inches (15 cm.) diameter, 10.2 inches (26 cm.) high.)

Brass and copper foot warmers of European craftsmanship are frequently worth considering treasures of the past. One of these, of red hammered copper, is decorated with repoussé designs. Over the top is a spider-leg grating of brass rods for resting the feet. The brass handle is artistically bent into shape. (Pl. 71, fig. 12; Cat. No. 169089, Italy, S. B. Dean; 7.1 inches (18 cm.) diameter, 6.7 inches (17 cm.) high.) An oblong brass pail with horizontal ribbed ornament and perforated lid surmounted with a strap-brass foot rest is from France. It has a brass bail with wooden spool. The lid is hinged. Four low brass feet raise the vessel from the ground. (Pl. 71, fig. 11; Cat. No. 205376, S. B. Dean; 4.75 inches (12 cm.) high.) Another specimen is a brass pail with a bail of rolled-up sheet brass. The bowed lid is perforated in heart-shaped pattern. With this specimen is a quaint little spatulate shovel of iron for regulating the coals. The foot warmer is dated 1785, with the initials A. B. (Pl. 71, fig. 13; Cat. No. 169090, France, S. B. Dean; 6.7 inches (17 cm.) high.) A square, perforated brass box on four feet, with repoussé escutcheons on the sides and a bowed perforated top with brass bail is of Dutch workmanship. Like the English and colonial American foot warmers it has a door in the side for inserting the pan of coals. The specimen shows the conscientious work of the craftsmen of the early eighteenth century. (Pl. 71, fig. 9, Cat. No. 289455; Anton Heitmuller; 6.3 inches (16 cm.) square, 6.7 inches (17 cm.) high.) Another Dutch foot warmer of the same period is octagonal with double door and latch on the side. The bail is of brass hooked into two strap-brass loops. (Pl. 71, fig. 10; Cat. No. 289454, Anton Heitmuller; 7.9 inches (20 cm.) diameter, 6.3 inches (16 cm.) high.)

A dovetailed wooden rectangular box lined with sheet iron and having a hinged lid with slats and lined with perforated tin is of English workmanship. Each of the long sides has two perforations lined with brass. The foot warmer has within a sheet-iron pan with bail for the charcoal fuel. It is carried by a bail with a wooden spool and is stained cherry color. (Pl. 70b, fig. 3; Cat. No. 311657, Miss E. S. Stevens; dimensions 10.2 inches (26 cm.) by 7.5 inches (19 cm.) by 4.7 inches (12 cm.).) The specimen just described is close to the type used in America during colonial and subsequent times. These, however, almost always consisted of a sheet-iron perforated box with door placed in a wooden frame or between two tablets of wood forming the top and bottom and held by corner posts of wood or iron rods. From the identity of many specimens it is inferred that the demand for foot stoves prompted a rather extensive manufacture of a certain standard. The specimen figured has a trapezoidal opening in the top while usually cross bars ran across the top. (Pl. 70b, fig. 4; Cat. No. 130623, F. S. Hawley, Broadalbin, N. Y., dimensions 8.7 inches (22 cm.) by 7.9 inches (20 cm.) by 5.9 inches (15 cm.).) The more familiar type has a strong wooden frame with turned corner posts. The sides have a band of baluster piercing, which is more exact than occurs in the usual foot warmers. The piercings and punched designs commonly seen are rows of small holes, hearts, joined hearts, diamonds, and quatrefoils, examples of the quaint symbolism of the times. (Pl. 70b, fig. 2; Cat. No. 325601, donor unknown, New England; dimensions 9 inches (25 cm.) by 7.5 inches (19 cm.) by 5.9 inches (15 cm.).)

Bed warmers were among the conspicuous household impedimenta of the Colonies. They were articles of luxury, and for this reason there are no crude examples such as might have been made by a local artisan. These objects were honestly made by good craftsmen and are both sturdy and graceful. The specimen has a turned maple handle worthy of admiration inserted in an ample brass socket riveted strongly to the side of the pan so that the junction has not worked loose in the past hundred years. The lid is hinged and chased and perforated in several places. (Pl. 70b, fig. 1; Cat. No. 311502, Miss Elizabeth S. Stevens; 11.2 inches (28.5 cm.) diameter, 41.5 inches (1 m. 9 cm.) long.) Hot-water bed warmers were used in south Germany, and sometimes specimens were brought to America by immigrants.

An interesting and artistically complete series of small fire sets to which the name hibachi applies is found in Japan. These are smokers' conveniences, consisting of a tray with pottery fire bowl, or neat cabinets with drawers and pipe holders (pl. 72a, figs. 1–3); and hibachis in variety, which are used for making tea, etc., and for warming (pl. 72b, figs. 2, 3). In most cases the fire receptacle is of pottery, containing a bed of ashes on which the charcoal fire is set. In some instances copper-lined boxes are used. Accompanying the hibachi are rests for the teapot, tongs, shovel, sifter for ashes, fire blower of bamboo, or in the tea ceremony a fan of perfect feathers. (Cat. Nos. 4418, 128140; from the Japanese Department of Education and Romyn Hitchcock; dimensions—fig. 1, 9.8 inches long, 7 inches wide, 3.5 inches high (25 cm., 18 cm., 9 cm.); fig. 2, 10.6 inches square, 7.1 inches high (27 cm. square, 18 cm. high); fig. 3, 6.9 inches diameter, 9.5 inches high (17.5 cm., 24 cm.); fig. 4, 6.7 inches square, 3.1 inches high (17 cm. square, 8 cm. high); fig. 5, 5.3 inches long, 4.9 inches wide, 4.9 inches high (21 cm., 12.5 cm.,

12.5 cm).)   The Chinese fire bowl figured was used by candidates secluded for the official examinations held at Peking. It is of massive brass with relief panels and elephant-head handles. An iron tripod rests in the ashes for supporting the teapot, and a pair of tongs, like larger chopsticks, are shown. (Pl. 72b, fig. 1; Cat. No. 128533, Mrs. W. P. Mangum; 11 inches (28 cm.) diameter, 10.2 inches (26 cm.) high.)   Over the fire is set an iron tripod consisting of a bearing ring with three legs with incurving feet. Two iron rods, hibashi, accompanying the hibachi, and other implements as a blowing tube, ashes leveler shaped like a spatula, etc. We have here in a nutshell the early fire and its belongings.

ANDIRONS

Andirons have been traced from stones or clay cones put in the fire as rests for fuel and later as pot supports. They remained primitive till the iron age, which provided the means at least by which this piece of fire furniture could develop. For a long time the andirons used in the great common house fireplace remained simple rests much as the pair worked from bar iron used by Lewis Wetsel in colonial western Virgina (Pl. 73, fig. 1), property of the writer. Transferred from the great fireplace to fireplaces in rooms in which increasing pride in the furnishings was taken, the andiron demanded ornamentation. A fore piece was added to the humble three-legged iron. On this fore piece was lavished the metal worker's art in the various characteristic periods to the present. Brass was usually the metal selected for the fore piece, but appears to have been preceded by cast iron, of which pleasing and artistic examples exist (pl. 73, fig. 2). In Europe, notably France, where the great fireplace was artistically treated and preserved through conservatism, the andiron took on its highest development. The fore piece became an elaborately worked wrought-iron branched structure from which hung baskets of charcoal for special cooking, and spoons, forks, and other articles of the chef's *batterie de cuisine*. At present in this age of development the andirons serve usually as ornaments frequently to a false fireplace, or, one upon which the luxury of a wood fire may be laid.

SIMPLE STOVES

Simple stoves of the type of the brazier are found in different parts of the world. The line of development of the stove may be begun with them, considering the primitive rests or andirons of three stones or bosses of baked clay as an intermediate step between the brazier-like vessels and the camp fire. A suggestion of this is shown in the cooking vessel set on three supporting overturned pots, from the Haussa of the Niger River, Africa. (Pl. 74a, fig. 4; Cat. No. 249776, Leipzig Museum of Ethnology. (Model.).)   From the Philippines come two small pottery stoves, one a tripod and the other double, having four legs. (Pl. 74a, fig. 1, 2; Cat. No. 238356, Philippine Commission; 5.5 inches (14 cm.) diameter, 4.4 inches (11 cm.) high; and fig. 2, Cat. No. 238356, Philippine Commission, 5.5 inches (14 cm.) long, 3.13 inches (8 cm.) high.) The right central figure is a model of a stove from Laos, French Indo-China. (Pl. 74a, fig. 3, Cat. No. 219640; C. C. Hansen.) Some of the little pottery stoves of the San Blas Indians of Panama are of the brazier draftless type. (See pl. 75, fig. 2–4.) A pottery bowl modified on the rim to form a rest for the pot comes from the Philippines. (Pl. 74b, figs. 3, 4, 5; Cat. No. 238344; Philippine Commission, 7.5 inches (19 cm.) diameter.) Another, from San Fernando, Union, Luzon, has three well-formed rests. (Pl. 74b, fig. 2; Cat. No. 238371; Philippine Commission.) A well-defined expression of the idea of the three fire bosses is seen in a small earthenware stove from the Philippines. (Pl. 74b, fig. 6; Cat. No. 238370, Philippine Commission; 4.7 inches (12 cm.) high, 7.5 inches (19 cm.) diameter.) A large, massive earthenware stove of triangular shape with three bosses is also from the Philippines. (Plate 74b, fig. 1; Cat. No. 235184, Philippine Commission; 15.4 inches wide, 14.6 inches long, and 7.1 inches high (39 cm., 37 cm., 18 cm.).

STOVES WITH RUDIMENTARY DRAFT

The knowledge and utilization of draft grew slowly in the consciousness of man. Its evolution has only been rapid in the latter stages of man's progress. Charcoal also had its effect in retarding the development of draft in the domestic stove. This first manufactured fuel, a *sine qua non* in metallurgy, consumed slowly with a minimum of air and sent out sufficient heat for common purposes. Charcoal played the important part in the early stoves that bituminous coal played in the modern stove. Attention is called to an earthenware stove from Morocco, North Africa. This stove has three spurs or pot rests and three holes perforated through the sides. There is indication here that a little air entering these holes above the fire would aid in combustion. Whether these holes were intended to give draft is not determined. (Pl. 75a, fig. 1, Dr. and Mrs. Talcott Williams; 9.1 inches (23 cm.) diameter, 5.5 inches (14 cm.) high.) An earthenware stove from Durango, Mexico, shows better a rudimentary attempt at draft. Four holes are punched in the vessel above the fire and one of these is larger and suggests a door by which fuel could be put in. This vessel stands on three legs. (Pl. 76a, fig. 2; Cat. No. 176486; Edward Palmer; 13.4 inches (34 cm.) diameter, 9.8 inches (25 cm.)). Some of the small earthenware stoves of the San Blas Indians of Panama, already mentioned, which were for warming and on occasion for burning incense, had small holes in the bottom. As a rule no American censers show evidences of draft. (Pl. 75a, figs. 2–4; Cat. Nos. 327349, 237352, 327343, R. O. Marsh; 6.3 inches diameter, 4.7 inches high; 5.5 inches diameter, 5.9 inches high; 4.4 inches diameter, 5.1 inches high (16 cm., 12 cm., 14 cm., 15 cm., 11 cm., 13 cm.).) An earthenware stove from Colima, Mexico, shows a flat base extending to form a hearth and walls curved in form of a horseshoe on which a cooking vessel may be set. There may be seen here a rudimentary hearth, door, and firebox, which point the way to the stove with draft. (Pl. 75a, fig. 5; Cat. No. 152715, Edward Palmer; 9.9 inches (25 cm.) long.) Small stoves like this were for sale in the public market at Colima in 1896. Another stove from Colima has a hearth, door, and firebox, the latter sealed in, compelling the ingress and egress of air and gases through the door and giving less ventilation than the specimen just described. (Pl. 75a, fig. 6; Cat. No. 152714; Edward Palmer; 7.1 inches diameter, 5.1 inches high (18 cm., 13 cm.).) A similar stove is found in the Philippines, one specimen being rather rudely formed and the other, from Occidental Negros, much better made and provided with a base. (Pl. 74c, figs. 5, 6; Cat. Nos. 238369, 238366, Philippine Commission; 6.7 inches long (17 cm.).) From Sumatra comes a model of a triangular earthenware stove with hook pot rests, the base of the triangle forming the hearth. This stove suggests Hindu origin. (Pl. 74c, fig. 7; Cat. No. 178666; Leiden Museum.) The Siamese form is shown in model. It is well balanced and has an extended hearth. (Pl. 74c, fig. 4; Cat. No. 178338, C. E. Eckels; 6.7 inches long (17 cm.).) The Javanese form consists of a pot with a large opening in the side and a flanged rim on which the cooking vessel rests. (Pl. 77, fig. 4; Cat. No. 178667, Leiden Museum.) A pottery stove with three holes with projecting knob rests comes from the Philippines. The fire placed back under the holes and the perforations in the sides suggest that the maker of this stove was reaching toward the principles of draft. (Pl. 74c, fig. 3; Cat. No. 326157, Luzon, P. I., Victor J. Evans; 9.5 inches diameter, 4.4 inches high (24 cm., 11 cm.).) Another Philippine specimen has sets of three perforations in the side of the bowl. (Pl. 74c, fig. 2; Cat. No. 216687, Philippine Commission; 9.1 inches diameter, 6.3 inches high (23 cm., 16 cm.).)

The Japanese kitchen range is an interesting development of the draftless stove. The specimen in the United States National Museum has three fireplaces with large openings into the fire box. Charcoal is the fuel, as noted for all simple stoves. It will be seen that there is no intentional draft, as the cooking pots fit tightly over the holes, but the large door admits of circulation of air in the fire chamber, the heated current going out at the top of the opening.

(Pl. 75*b*, fig. 4, Japanese Department of Education.) Stoves of this character are found in various parts of the world. They were found at Tonalon, Mexico, in 1900, whence came a well-made model of a three-hole stove elevated on a substructure. (Pl. 77, fig. 3; Cat. No. 132407, Walter Hough; dimensions of model, 5.1 inches by 3.9 inches by 3.6 inches (5.1 inches (13 cm.), 3.9 inches (10 cm.), 3.6 inches (9 cm.).) Another specimen made of clay came from the Philippines. (Pl. 75*b*, fig. 1; Cat. No. 238392, Philippine Commission.) A similar structure with two holes comes from Jogo Kabu, Togoland, Africa. (Pl. 75*b*, fig. 3, Cat. No. 249777, Leipzig Museum of Ethnology.)

Two Etruscan stoves of simple character, dating from the third century B. C., were found in Sovana, Italy, and are now in the private collection of Odowardo Giglioli. They have arcaded openings in the front and circular flaring openings on which pots were set. (Pl. 75*c*, figs. 1, 2; from photographs in the U. S. National Museum; D. I. Bushnell, jr.)

STOVES WITH AIR BOX AND GRATE

The features which mark a great advance in the stove are the grate beneath the fire and the air chamber beneath the grate, together forming a rudimentary flue. With the incomplete data at hand it seems difficult to fix the date of these inventions. It is suspected, however, that they came late in the history of the stove. The simple fire pot, various forms of which have been figured, is often improved by the addition of a grate. These specimens are often contemporaneous with the simple stove which has no doubt been retained by custom. A specimen from Mexico, a model, is of graceful, brazier form with foot and flaring mouth. The grate is the early one of holes pierced through the bottom of the fire box into the air chamber. (Pl. 77, fig. 5; Cat. No. 115798, San Pedro, near Guadalajara, Mexico; Edward Palmer.) A stove model in white clay decorated with red is from Madrid, Spain, and is furnished with grate bars. (Pl. 77, fig. 6; Cat. No. 166997, Walter Hough.) A model from Porto Rico, West Indies, is neatly made from earthenware. It has a single grate bar, leaving two openings. (Pl. 77, fig. 7; Cat. No. 201497, Paul Beckwith.) A model from Guadalajara decorated in colors has holes punched in the bottom of the fire box. (Pl. 77, fig. 8; Cat. No. 175568, Edward Palmer.) A somewhat similar specimen from Caracas, Venezuela, also has a perforated grate. (Pl. 77, fig. 9; Cat. No. 136020, R. M. Bartleman.) A stove from Tetuan, Morocco, worked from a block of tuff, has slits cut through the bottom of the fire box. Originally the stove was hooped with iron bands. (Pl. 77, fig. 2; Dr. Talcott Williams; 10.6 inches (27 cm.) high, 8.3 inches (21 cm.) square.) An earthenware stove from the Philippines has the rim formed into three projecting spurs on which the pot is rested. It has a perforated grate. (Pl. 74c, fig. 1; Cat. No. 216704, Philippine Commission; 8.8 inches (22 cm.) diameter, 8.3 inches (21 cm.) high.) A pottery stove from Sao Christoval, Portugal, made by Amaro Domincos Grillo, was exhibited at the Philadelphia Centennial Exposition in 1876. It is of hard, dark gray sonorous ware, and shows the appreciation of form which the Portuguese potters have transmitted from classical times. This stove has grate bars formed in the clay. (Pl. 78a, fig. 4; Cat. No. 325602; 10.6 inches (27 cm.) high, with cooking pot 16.2 inches (41 cm.) high.) A pottery stove from Santa Lucia, West Indies, shows the highest advance in this material. The fire box has a flat, incurved rim with three bosses on the inner edge. The grate bars are cut in the bottom of the fire box. The hearth is scalloped and the door arched. Above the arch two small holes are punched into the fire box, suggesting over-fire ventilation. Two finger cups on the sides are for lifting. (Pl. 78a, fig. 2; Cat. No. 325603, Jamaica Exposition, 1891; 9.5 inches (24 cm.) diameter, 5.9 inches (15 cm.) high.)

The iron stove used in Tetunan, Morocco, consists of a drum separated in two compartments for the fire box and air chamber by a grate. It has three spear-shape pot rests, a hinged door, three supporting legs, and two ringed handles. A hole into the fire box is seen in the cut. (Pl. 78a, fig. 2; Dr. Talcott Williams; 7.9 inches diameter, 10.6 inches high (20 cm., 27 cm.).) A taller stove of excellent iron and brass work comes from the same locality. The construction is like that of the specimen described. The pot rests are hinged. There are ornamentally pierced openings above the fire. (Pl. 78a fig. 1; Dr. Talcott Williams.)

A stove model collected by the writer in Jalapa, Mexico, seems to be a survival of the temescal or vapor bath form. It has a round and a square hole in the top. In general the rectangular stoves such as were built up of brick of earth in the house, indicating the fixed range in contrast with the fire pot, are the models from which our ranges originated. (Pl. 77, fig. 1; Cat. No. 204663.) The Tibetan fixed stove is sadiron shape, built of mud, has two openings in the top, one a fire box and the other for the pot. At the lower edge, below the pot hole, is an opening forming an ash channel and a flue to the fire box. The fuel is argols, dung of ruminant animals, as the yak. (Pl. 75b, fig. 2; Cat. No. 325604; after W. W. Rockhill.) See also Plate 97, Figure 6, for model restoration.

A stove secured from the Philippines shows an elaboration of the cooking over an open-air fire. It exhibits clay bosses for three pot rests mounted in an elaborately worked bench of bamboo. (Pl. 76b, fig. 1; Cat. No. near 216695; Philippine Commission; 24.6 inches long, 14.2 inches wide, 11.8 inches high (64 cm., 36 cm., 30 cm.).)

It is an almost imperceptible barrier between the simple stoves described and the first examples which are placed in the inventive period. This is due no doubt to the survival of the older forms. Thirty-five years ago in Washington, and no doubt in other parts of America, small cast-iron fire-pot stoves were common; and as the hot chestnut vendors used them, most of the population was familiar with them. Artisans generally required these stoves, which have now practically disappeared. These stoves belong in the period when cast iron was coming into wide use. A specimen of the superior quality of the castings from the Lebanon Valley, Pa., is inscribed " Gotscher." In shape it is like some of the pottery stoves figured. The grate is circular and removable and the handles are wrought iron cast in. (Pl. 78b, fig. 1; Cat. No. 325605; donor unknown; probably a boat stove from the U. S. Fish Commission; 9.3 inches diameter, 7.1 inches high, (23.5 cm., 18 cm.).) A more elaborate stove of this character is of thin and good cast iron. It has a flaring rim with three ribs on which the pot is set. It has a regular grate and also a grating of open work over the fire. The stove is mounted on three feet, has a hearth ornamented on the edge, and an iron bail. This stove was used on whaling ships, the specimen coming from San Francisco, Calif., where it was collected by the United States Fish Commission. (Pl. 78b, fig. 3; Cat. No. 163632; 13 inches diameter, 9.5 inches high (33 cm., 24 cm.).) The Museum lately received from Mrs. Frances Roome Powers a toy fireplace of cast iron with andirons, hanging pot, and spider. Family tradition places this relic to the " time of Washington's father and mother." There is no other history, but the specimen represents the period when fireplaces smaller than the great fireplace were cast entire with hearth, an improvement on the old fire backs figured by Henry C. Mercer,[9] and especially common in Pennsylvania. The fireplace lining may have suggested the first Franklin stove of 1742 and appears to indicate a marked development in iron casting in the eighteenth century. (Pl. 78b, fig. 2; Cat. No. 328725; Virginia, Mrs. Frances Roome Powers; 4.5 inches wide, 4.9 inches high (11.5 cm., 12.5 cm.).)

Before the disappearance of the great fireplace an interesting series of adaptations had been built into its capacious dimensions, in many cases closing it up. These were ovens, hot-water tanks, and finally a grate, the latter often the survivor in a blank wall which hid the fireplace. Sometimes in tearing down old houses

---

[9] Henry C. Mercer, The Bible in Iron, or The Picture Stoves and Stove Plates of the Pennsylvania Germans, with Notes on Colonial Firebacks in the United States, etc. Published for the Bucks County Historical Society, Doylestown, Pa., 1914.

these accumulations are found, with often the old crane in place. At one period there was a great demand for cast ovens and hot-water tanks to be set in the fireplace. It is evident that we have testimony here of the coming together of the various elements that have joined to form the cook stove with all modern conveniences. The warming stove has a more direct lineage from the pot stoves described. The cook stove is an assemblage of things used independently in other stages of progress. It must not be overlooked that fuel has had an important part in the development of the cook stove. The important modifications of the cook stove have occurred since charcoal was superseded by wood and coal; that is, devices were brought forward for consuming these fuels.

The Museum collection contains a curious and interesting relic consisting of a stove of old whaling days. It is a ship's stove with attached warming and cooking oven. It has sheet-iron sides and bottom, and cast-iron top with two holes and lids. In front is a valve with pivoted shutter. On the sides are ring drop handles. There are gadgets on the bottom for receiving the iron plates by which the stove was securely fastened to the floor. The oven is hung on two pins as in the old barn door and is formed to fit against the curved sides of the stove. The stove is provided with joints of stovepipe, pans, etc. It was patented June 22, 1875, by H. L. Dunklee, Boston, Mass. It is said to have been the first sheet-iron stove. Wood was burned in it. (Pl. 78b, fig. 4; Cat. No. 325606, U. S. Fish Commission; 21.3 inches long, 13 inches wide, 11.8 inches high (54 cm., 33 cm., 30 cm.).)

A model gives an idea of the Norwegian stove built of tiles and forming an ornamental piece of house furnishing. In using, wood is placed in the fire box and a flue opened. The wood is lighted, allowed to burn a little while, when the door is shut and the flue closed. The heat generated at first is sufficient to continue the combustion of the wood. The warmth is slowly diffused through the structure of the stove and passed on to the air in contact with the surface of the stove. (Pl. 79, fig. 2; Cat. No. 167114, Mrs. Emma Brinton, model 9.1 inches (23 cm.) high.) Dr. Leonhard Stejneger informs me that the installation of fire in the house was formerly in the ample fireplace as in America and that the tile stove was an introduction from Germany.

There have been many inventions whose idea was the furnishing of compact forms in which small amounts of heat could be applied to temporary uses as the case might require, and others strove to compress in convenient form all that might be demanded of a range completely equipped with cooking vessels. One of these combinations, a stove lamp, was collected in the Philippines during the insurrection. It is probably of Spanish origin. The designer deserves great credit. (Pl. 79, fig. 13; Cat. No. 216668, Philippine Commission; 11.4 inches (29 cm.) high.)

The knowledge that alcohol was a good fuel has probably been known since the beginning of distillation. Alcohol has always borne the name of fire water in Arabic. Its use as fuel for minor purposes, however, does not date very far back. The earlier alcohol burners were lamplike vessels with wick tube and cotton wick. Later improvements to get a larger area of flame were asbestos pads covered with a mesh wire grating. One of these is called "pocket" cook stove, Houchin's Patent. (Pl. 78c, fig. 1, Washington, D. C.; Cat. No. 329466, Walter Hough; 3.12 inches (8 cm.) diameter.) Another form regulated the flame and was called "silver" spirit stove. It consisted of a brass cup, in the bottom of which were set seven brass open tubes, the cup mounted in a three-leg stand with three vertical spurs or rests. A plate used as a cover has three graded openings to regulate draft. (Pl. 78c, fig. 5; Washington, D. C.; Cat. No. 216256, Walter Hough; 4.4 inches (11 cm.) diameter, 1.6 inches (4 cm.) high.) A more recent and quite effective alcohol stove was used in 1915 at the San Francisco Exposition. It is called Universal No. 0 alcohol stove, patented by Frary & Clark, New Britain, Conn., 1908. The burner is primed with alcohol from a pump and when ignited the heat forces the alcohol from the reservoir through pinholes at the base of the burner. The flame is regulated by a sleeve moved by a ratchet. (Pl. 78c, fig. 6; Cat. No. 325607, Connecticut; Panama Pacific Exp., 1915; 6.3 inches (16 cm.) diameter, 5.5 inches (14 cm.) high.)

The means of using artificial gas for heat must be credited to Bunsen, who invented the burner bearing his name about the middle of the eighteenth century. For illumination effects gas does not require any mixture of air, but for heating by means of the blue flame it is necessary to introduce a sufficient quantity of air as an oxidizing agent. All gas stoves therefore have a device for mixing air and gas, consisting of a chamber on the line in which the mixture takes place just before delivery to the burner. A cast-iron gas stove of about 40–50 years ago shows the gas mixer, lacking the movable pierced ring by which the flow of air was regulated. (Pl. 78c, fig. 4; Cat. No. 325608; Smithsonian Laboratories; 4.7 inches (12 cm.) diameter, 3.6 inches (9 cm.) high.)

From time to time and in total a considerable number of devices for utilizing the heat of lamps for warming, cooking, and other purposes have been invented. Such devices are evanescent and rarely survive as examples of wasted inventive talent. One of these is a brass cylinder devised to insure proper ventilation and intended to inclose the chimney of a kerosene lamp. Articles to be heated could be placed on the closed top of the cylinder. (Pl. 78c, fig. 2; Cat. No. 325609, Museum Collections, 1876; 5.9 inches (15 cm.) diameter, 9.1 inches (23 cm.) high.)

Electric heating has recently become of economic value, its use having been retarded by the limited electric power available. Engineers regard electric heating as the most wasteful and costly method of employing electricity and can not predict that it may ever be used for general heating of houses. The conversion of electricity into heat in small units over short periods of time is not unduly expensive and has come into widespread use within a few years. An example is given of an electric-foot stove in use during the winter of 1914–15 at the San Francisco Exposition. This stove has 106–114 volts and 6.8 amperes, and was made by the American Electric Heating Co., Detroit, Mich. (Pl 78c, fig. 3; Cat. No. 325610, Panama-Pacific Exposition; 14.2 inches (36 cm.) wide, 12.6 inches (33 cm.) high.)

STOVES IN COMBINATION: COOKERS, WATER HEATERS, ETC.

There is a large class of vessels from which food or hot water was served, the heating element being a hot iron, a spirit lamp, or charcoal. These vessels are always ornamental and are intended for serving in the dining room. The presence of a heating device associates these vessels with stoves and they may be called stoves in combination. In some cases, as will be noticed, they are actual small stoves with charcoal, fire box, and draft, a type of which is the samovar, "self-cooker," of Russia, probably of oriental origin.

A good specimen of the incorporated stove is from Swatow, China, made of pewter lined with brass. The air box is in the base and has an ornamentally curved opening. The stove with grate stands in the middle of the bowl and the draft opening is through the lid. Food to be cooked or warmed is placed in the bowl and receives heat through the sides of the fire vessel. The lid and vessel have drop handles of brass. (Pl. 80, fig. 3; Cat. No. 75326; Centennial Exposition, Philadelphia, 1876; 8.3 inches (21 cm.) diameter, 4.4 inches (11 cm.) high.) This vessel is almost duplicated in soapstone by the Korean *sin syol lo*, skillfully made and finished in polished black. An opening in the foot leads to the draft chamber, and above this is the tubular fire box with grate. The lid fits down over the bowl and edge of the fire box. The specimen is of the samovar type. (Pl. 80, fig. 5; Cat. No. 77054; Seoul, Korea; J. B. Bernadou; 8⅞ inches diameter, 7½ inches high (22.5 cm. diameter, 19 cm. high).)

Another self-contained stove, made of pewter and brass, represents China's contribution to the inventions connected with the cooking stove. In this stove hot water is utilized in cooking, attended with notable economy of fuel. The stove is drum shape and has an arched opening for draft and feeding. The fire box has a grate and ventilates through the top of the stove by a flue. The surrounding part of the stove forms a reservoir for water, in which hang two tubular pots with lid and a larger vessel also with lid in which food is placed for cooking. The parts in contact with fire are of brass. The Chinese name of this is *samsu*. (Pl. 80, fig. 7; Cat. No. 75340, Amoy, China; Philadelphia Centennial Exhibition, 1876; 13 inches (33 cm.) diameter, 11¾ inches (30 cm.) high.)

An additional specimen is a teapot stove of pewter and brass, also Chinese. The base of pierced brass, ornamented with geomantic and other characters, contains the grate. The teapot has a conical brass hot-air flue ventilating through the lid. It is decorated with incised characters in Chinese. (Pl. 80, fig. 2; Cat. No. 75338; Swatow, China; Centennial Exposition, Philadelphia, 1876; 3.9 inches (10 cm.) diameter, 7.5 inches (19 cm.) high.) Shown with this specimen is a pewter teapot from Chefoo, China. (Pl. 80, fig. 1; Cat. No. 130333, Centennial Exposition, Philadelphia, 1876; 5.5 inches (14 cm.) diameter, 4.4 inches (11 cm.) high.)

In the seventeenth century hot-water vessels for the table tea service were furnished with an iron billet which could be heated at the fire and lowered into a vertical tube in the center of the reservoir. This was the method with the laundry iron of the period. It appears that the use of the stored heat of the hot iron preceded the spirit lamp. The specimen figured is of English craft and is a model of design and execution in hammered copper. The date attributed to the specimen in 1683 but is apparently too early. It is inscribed in ink: " 17th Century English Coffee Urn from an old Welch Coaching Inn of Richard Weeks " and the date 1683 is engraved. The cover is stamped " Best. London Manufac." The handles and spout roundel are of ivory. (Pl. 80, fig. 8; Cat. No. 95829; gift of Richard Weeks; 9.1 inches (23 cm.) diameter, 16.2 inches (41 cm.) high.) An English coffee biggin of tinned iron decorated with pierced work and lion's head drop handles was used in the family of Prof. S. F. Baird, second secretary of the Smithsonian Institution. It consists of three sections fitting together, the top section with a perforated receptacle for holding coffee, the middle section for the percolated coffee, fitted with a brass cock, and the base containing a cup holding an iron disk to be heated. The specimen had come down in the family and is believed to be colonial. (Pl. 81*a*, fig. 2; Cat. No. 75341, gift of Mrs. S. F. Baird; 17.3 inches (44 cm.) high.) Another biggin for hot water is of tinned iron, well shaped, with rigid handles of cast iron, four feet, and a brass cock. The lid is capped with a pheasant in pewter. The base is perforated in baluster pattern and contains a single-tube lamp in which alcohol was burnt for heating water in the reservoir. (Pl. 81a, fig. 1; Cat. No. 130314, Morgantown, W. Va., gift of Mrs. M. L. Casselberry; 8.3 inches (21 cm.) diameter, 15 inches (38 cm.) high.) The Museum has a specimen of hot-water urn of britannia made in England. It is of classic shape with two handles and mounted on four ornamental feet of pewter. The cock is quite old style, of brass with ivory handle. The bottom of the urn is lined with brass to resist the heat from a single-tube spirit lamp. (Pl. 81a, fig. 3; Cat. No. 289433, England, Anton Heitmuller; 18.1 inches (46 cm.) high.)

Preserving the warmth of food by means of hot water was commonly practiced in the eighteenth century and the early nineteenth century. It was effected by means of hollow dishes filled with hot water on which was placed the food to be kept warm during a meal. These dishes were useful in the period when there were no warming ovens and when in some parts of the Colonies food had to be carried some distance through the weather to the table in the mansion. In tavern kitchens there were also great pewter hot-water platters for the purpose mentioned. Specimens of hot-water vessels are scarce and the Museum collection has only one example, a Flemish hot-water dish in fine yellow brass. The dish is oblong-oval, stands on four turned feet, has drop handles, and an ornamentally perforated lid, flanged and recurving in the top of the dish. Upon this perforated area was placed whatever food was suitable to be warmed. It is evident that fluids from roasts or moist food would drain into the water pan. (Pl. 81b, fig. 4; Cat. No. 169099, S. B. Dean; 19.7 inches (50 cm.) long, 11.8 inches (30 cm.) wide, 3.9 inches (10 cm.) high.)

Not many devices have been found in which steam is used as a heating agent. One of these is a pewter vessel with long spout, on the end of which is set an inverted goblet-shape vessel with a small ventilating hole on one side. The vessel is filled with hot water and the steam passing through the spout warms the liquid in the cup. (Pl. 81b, fig. 2; Cat. No. 130332, Chefoo, China; Philadelphia Centennial, 1876; 3.9 inches (10 cm.) diameter, 7.7 inches (19.5 cm.) high.)

A device for getting hot water quickly, especially for shaving, is seen in a conical tin vessel with a hollow flange around the base. Alcohol poured in the flange and lighted burned quickly around the exterior of the vessel filled with water, causing it to boil immediately. The vessel is furnished with a hinged lid and a handle

which disappears inside, the lid being closed over it.   (Pl. 81*b*, fig. 1;
Cat. No. 151485, Massachusetts about 1840, M. F. Savage; 3.9 inches
(10 cm.) diameter, 6.1 inches (15.5 cm.) high.)

VESSELS FOR CONSERVING HEAT

The conservation of heat has been known for a long time by
civilized man.   This object to be carried out requires an experimental
knowledge of the conductivity of materials, seen in the hay baskets
used by the Jews to keep food warm over the ceremonial Sabbath
and mentioned by Juvenal in his satires.   There has apparently
been a progress or at least a continuity from the early heat preservation devices to the fireless cooker.   The Chinese use a padded receptacle for the teapot to keep the tea warm, consisting of an excellently woven basket or an embellished metal box fitted with thick
pads into which the teapot is thrust, leaving only the end of the
spout exposed for pouring.   In the specimen figured the teapot is
pewter, having a perforated tube in which the tea is placed for
steeping.   (Pl. 82, fig. 3; Cat. No. 325611, Canton, China; Philadelphia Centennial Exposition, 1876; 7.5 inches (19 cm.) diameter, 6.7
inches (17 cm.) high.)

As in retaining heat, the cooling of substances depends on the
conductivity of materials.   There is little evidence that the cooling principle was known very far backward in time.   The only
example in the Museum collection is a " Calcutta water cooler "
used in India.   It consists of a glass water jar fitting into a tin
case padded with cloth and having a similar cover sliding down
over the jar.   This device is said to be effective in keeping water
cold.   While this device is commonly known as a feature of Calcutta usage, it does not appear to be native, probably having been
introduced from England.   (Pl. 82, figs. 1, 2; Cat. No. 325612,
Calcutta, India; 6.3 inches (16 cm.) diameter, 7.1 inches (18 cm.)
high.)

FIRE FANS AND BELLOWS

The first aids for blowing up the fire appear to be fans.   These
are found both among uncivilized tribes and civilized peoples.   They
were common at the period of the open fireplace in America and
Europe.   The turkey-wing brush and fan was a familiar object of the
earlier American domestic arrangements.   Palm-leaf fans, whose
normal use was for cooling the face, were also made to serve in an
emergency as a fire fan.   The same may be said of the specimens
shown as fire fans in the rare cases where fans were used for personal
comfort.

The San Blas Indian fan is an excellent piece of weaving, especially marked in the tubular handle.   It is used for blowing the fire
and also in ceremony.   Miss Frances Densmore has collected the

information from Indians brought by the Marsh-Darien Expedition that the guests at a wedding hold a fan of this kind in the hand. (Pl. 83a, fig. 1; Cat. No. 326126; Mrs. G. N. Lieber; 8.3 inches (21 cm.) wide, 15.4 inches (39 cm.) long.) Dr. J. Walter Fewkes brought from Arima, Trinidad, West Indies, a diaper weaving fire fan with handle formed by bundling and crossing the weaving elements at the apex of the blade A smaller specimen has a loop at the apex. (Pl. 83a, figs. 2, 4; Cat. Nos. 231188, 231196; 11 inches (28 cm.) wide, 17 inches (43 cm.) long; 5.1 inches (13 cm.) wide, 8.5 inches (21.5 cm.) long.) A fire fan from Colima, Mexico, has a similar handle formed of two bundles of the rush splints. (Pl. 83a, fig. 3; Cat. No. 152713, Edward Palmer; 7.1 inches (18 cm.) wide, 13.8 inches (35 cm.) long.) A hoe-shape fan from the Arawaks of British Guiana has a cross handle at the apex. (Pl. 83a, fig. 5; Cat. No. 210443, Hassler Coll., Field Museum, Chicago; 10.3 inches (26 cm.) wide, 8.3 inches (21 cm.) long.) A fan made by splitting a palm midrib and interweaving the leaves is also from British Guiana. This clever manipulation of the palm frond occurs frequently in British Guiana and is found in many parts of the East. (Pl. 83a, fig. 6; Cat. No. 325613, donor unknown; 9.8 inches (25 cm.) wide, 8.7 inches (22 cm.) long.) A disk fan with handle of midrib and blade of interwoven leaf is found in Paraguay. (Pl. 83a, fig. 12; Cat. No. 210556, Hassler Coll., Field Museum, Chicago; 11.8 inches (30 cm.) diameter, 15.7 inches (40 cm.) long.) A disk fan of coarse palm braid sewed to a handle and cross brace comes from Merida, Yucatan. (Pl. 83a, fig. 11; Cat. No. 73921; L. H. Ayme; 9.1 inches (23 cm.) diameter, 21.3 inches (54 cm. long.) Also from Yucatan is an excellently woven rush fan suggesting the Paraguay specimen. (Fig. 1.) (Pl. 83a, fig. 10; Cat. No. 325614, donor unknown; 14.3 inches (36 cm.) diameter, 16.9 inches (43 cm.) long.) A square-blade fan mounted diagonally with handle and cross brace comes from Cape Blanco, Morocco. It is woven of split cane and bordered with raffia cord. (Pl. 83a, fig. 7; Cat. No. 14841, Wilkes Exploring Expedition; 9.5 inches (24 cm.) wide, 15.7 inches (40 cm.) long.) An ovate fire fan of esparto from Spain is woven after the fashion of wicker baskets and is in two colors. A loop at one side is for hanging up the fan. (Pl. 83a, fig. 8; Cat. No. 73260, Philadelphia Centennial Exposition, 1876; 12.2 inches (31 cm.) by 13 inches (33 cm.) diameter.) A square-blade fan with branch handle at one corner, made by the Cayapas Indians of Ecuador is woven of palm splints. (Pl. 83a, fig. 9; Cat. No. 68090; William F. Lee; 10.6 inches (27 cm.) wide, 16.2 inches (41 cm.) long.)

Following the fire fan we may presume that the fire-blowing tube came into use. This consists of a bamboo or cane tube with a small hole in the septum at the node, through which the breath was con-centrated on the fire and was an improvement of the most primitive blowing of the fire with puffed cheeks. An example of the tube blower is a bamboo tube such as is customarily used by the Chinese and Japanese. (Pl. 83b, figs. 1, 2; Cat. No. 128147, Japanese Depart-ment of Education; 14.5 inches (37 cm.) long.) In Europe the tubular fire blower had a widespread use. A specimen collected in Madrid, Spain, is a brass tube with collar of iron having a hook for hanging up, and a swallow-tail expansion of iron at the base for stirring and regulating the fire, probably of the brazier. The speci-men is regarded as of ancient type. (Pl. 83b, fig. 4; Cat. No. 169098, Spain, Walter Hough; 26 inches (66 cm.) long.)

Bellows are of great antiquity and of lengendary origin, the classi-cal attribution being to Daedalus. This device is inseparably con-nected with the increasing of fire heat for economic purposes. In general the bellows for domestic use is an outgrowth of the behavior of fuel itself or in different stages of combustion of fuel materials. The familiar bellows of Colonial times hung by the fireplace was regarded as both ornamental and useful. It had a cast-brass nozzle, leather bellows fastened with brass head nails to the two leaves. The hinge necessary to one of the leaves was usually of leather. These specimens were lacquered and decorated with sprays of flow-ers in bright colors, frequently on a dark-green ground. One speci-men in the Museum has bent handles. It is classed as American, but it may have been imported from England. (Pl. 83b, fig. 5; Cat. No. 325615, donor unknown; 18.1 inches (46 cm.) long.) Another has straight handles, a graceful nozzle, and is decorated with rose sprays on a brown background. (Pl. 83b, fig. 7; Cat. No. 289464, Pennsylvania, Anton Heitmuller; 19.3 inches (49 cm.) long.) An interesting bellows of French manufacture secured in Madrid, Spain, in 1892 has a fan actuated through a rack and pinions by means of a crank. Air enters the bellows through an ornamental brass grill and is forced by the fan through the plain tubular nozzle. It is excellently made of fine curly maple wood. (Pl. 83b, fig. 6; Cat. No. 167038, Walter Hough; 14.9 inches (38 cm.) long.) In the Museum collection are a number of bellows used in the arts and industries of various countries. The simplest of these is a Tibetan example consisting of a goatskin bag open at one end and with an iron tuyere at the other. In working it the sides of the bag mouth are pulled apart, closed, and the impounded air pressed through the tuyere against the fire. The specimen was collected by the late W. W. Rockhill. In ancient Egypt and in many parts of Africa the simple bag bellows was used, but improved by placing two bags side by side, connecting with a single tuyere, thus giving a more or less continuous current. The piston bellows originating in some eastern Asiatic center of metal industry is widespread over the East Indies and parts of the continent. It is actuated by plungers in two pistons and is without valves.

The date of the introduction of the valve is not known, but the location was probably Europe. The primitive appearing bellows used by the Navaho silversmith is valved. It is probably an introduction from Spain through Mexico. Plate 84, Arizona, Bureau of American Ethnology collection. A curious method of producing a blast of superheated steam to intensify the fire in melting metals is practised by the Lepcha gold workers in Sikkim, India. The specimen consists of a copper flask with long curved beak having a slight opening at the point. In practice this is heated and submerged in water, the vacuum created drawing much water into the flask. The flask is then set in a fire and the point directed on the fire under the crucible. (Pl. 83b, fig. 3; Cat. No. 326753. Dr. William Clemmons; 3.7 inches (9.5 cm.) diameter, 8.7 inches (22 cm.) high.)

TONGS AND FIRE TOOLS

One of the earliest problems connected with the utilization of fire was fire handling. The poker may be considered the first of the fire tools and may be a branch sharpened and charred in the fire and also serving at times as a temporary, fitful torch. Such pokers are found in universal use around the fires of uncivilized races and specimens are here and there preserved in the cliff dwellings of the southwesten United States. The poker as a simple device remains indefinitely simple at all stages of progress. Two pokers, however, brought together indicate the beginning of tongs, that is, sticks pressed on either side of a brand for lifting it form tongs. Veritable examples can be found in use in the manner of chopsticks to this day in China, Japan, and the northwest coast of America. Apparently the next step is to join these pokers at one end. The Japanese use two iron rods to attend the fire in the hibachi. Sometimes these pokers are joined at the ends with a ring, but beyond this there is no invention in the direction of tongs. (Pl. 86, figs. 4, 5; Cat. Nos. 128275, 128141, Japan, Japanese Department of Education; 11.4 inches (29 cm.) and 14.6 inches (37 cm.) long.) On the northwest coast sometimes the tongs are made by splitting a stick part way. Generally they are of two round sticks, and sometimes joined as mentioned. (Pl. 85, fig. 6.) The Kiowa used a pair of forked sticks to handle the hot stones for the sweat bath. (Pl. 85, figs. 4, 5; Cat. No. 153000, Oklahoma, James Mooney, 14 inches (35.5 cm.) long.) The Washoes of Nevada and some California tribes bent a stick on itself, forming a loop, the implement resembling a tennis racket, and used it for handling hot stones. (Pl. 85, fig. 1; Cat. No. 204473,

Eugene Mead; 24.4 inches (63 cm.) long.) The southwestern tribes generally used a spring tongs formed by bending a strip of wood by fire into shape or by cutting out two tongues in a billet of wood. The smaller implements of this character were useful in handling spiny cactus fruit and the larger for coals of fire. The Apache specimen is strong and well made and has a good spring. It was collected in 1869. (Pl. 85, fig. 2; Cat. No. 9971, Arizona, Edward Palmer; 20.9 inches (53 cm.) long.) The Havasupai specimen is crude and strong. (Pl. 85, fig. 3; Cat. No. 151901, Havasupai Indians, Arizona; Maj. John G. Bourke. U. S. A.; 24.4 inches (62 cm.) long.)

The earlier American and European tongs were hinged at the handle and the two prongs bowed. The grasping ends were flattened into disks. (Pl. 86, fig. 7; Cat. No. 75357; Bainbridge, Pa.; George Bean; 23.2 inches (59 cm.) long.) Improvements added a spring to the pair of prongs and fingers for grasping. (Pl. 86, fig. 6; Cat. No. 284335; Lucy H. Baird; 16.2 inches (41 cm.) long.) A pair of tongs called *kinda*, coming from Denmark, is of bronze and was used for carrying a coal of fire from a neighbor's hearth, following the custom of fire borrowing. This rare specimen was given by Dr. C. A. Q. Norton, of Hartford, Conn., one of the pioneer collectors of illumination devices. (Pl. 86, fig. 3; Cat. No. 151651; 8.7 inches (22 cm.) long.) For handling coals a pincerlike tool of wrought iron was employed in Spain. These were principally for use with the brazier. (Pl. 86, figs. 1, 2; Cat. Nos. 167001, 167068; Madrid, Spain; Walter Hough; 5.1 inches (13 cm.) and 12.6 inches (32 cm.) long.)

GRIDIRONS

Grids of wood preceded grids of iron and were used in parts of the world where iron was as yet unknown. These picturesque grids were erected on four posts over a fire and were made high enough to prevent burning. On these were placed flesh or vegetable foods to be semi-cooked and preserved by drying and smoking. (See pl. 87.) More primitive than the wooden grids were the simple spits consisting of a stick thrust into the substance to be cooked and inclined before the fire. In the salmon area the split fish was fixed on a spit and small sticks thrust across at right angles to hold the fish flat. This suggests the gridiron. From the Bronze Age, so far as may be ascertained, no grids have been found, but in the Iron Age an iron strip bent to and fro appears to be such an object. During the Iron Age it is presumed that the grid came more and more into use, and the simple iron grids of our forefathers might well stand for Iron Age examples.

From Virginia comes a gridiron of honest ironwork which appears capable of surviving indefinitely the wear of time. (Pl. 88, fig. 2; Cat. No. 289436, Anton Heitmuller; 4.7 inches (12 cm.) by 8.3 inches (21 cm.) by 15.7 inches (40 cm.) long.) Later than the specimen mentioned came the use of gridirons of bent wire, which were commonly employed after the first cooking stoves were prevalent. The earlier specimens are single and made of stout wire. The later wire gridirons were double. The camp chest of George Washington, a precious relic in the historical collection of the National Museum, contains a simple gridiron of wrought work. It has four legs, eight bars, and the handle slides into the frame to allow the gridiron to fit into the compartment in the green-baize-lined chest studded with brass nails.[10] The box placed under the grid in the illustration in Mr. Belote's work cited is an oblong tinder box with candle socket on the lid. (Pl. 89, fig. 7; Cat. No. 92621; W. S. Winder collection.) One of the earliest wire gridirons is from Virginia. It is made of a single piece of rod one-fifth inch in diameter, expertly bent, the ends twisted together and forged into a loop. The specimen is over 100 years old. (Pl. 89, fig. 5; Cat. No. 127282, Lynchburg, Va.; Mrs. Ed. Hunter; 18.5 inches (47 cm.) long.) A gridiron which shows inventive thought is of cast iron with wrought-iron side bars and handle. Each grid is concave and is pierced at the end near the handle, allowing some of the drippings to fall into a pan. This gridiron is thought to date earlier than 1840. (Pl. 89, fig. 6; Cat. No. 127283, Lynchburg, Va.; Mrs. Ed. Hunter; 9.5 inches (24 cm.) by 10.6 inches (27 cm.).) A remarkable specimen of Flemish gridiron of the fifteenth century has an oblong frame of seven bars of heart and spiral design, three feet, and a flat handle of dumb-bell shape. It is a splendid specimen of art ironwork applied to articles of common use. (Pl. 89, fig. 1; Cat. No. 205380, Belgium, S. B. Dean; 14.6 inches (37 cm.) wide, 26.4 inches (67 cm.) long.) The revolving gridiron was an improvement in the seventeenth century. It consisted of a circular grid pivoted in the middle of a three-leg spider, from one prong of which extended the handle. This form of gridiron found its way to America and was used here in the colonial period and subsequently. The superior, even artistic ironwork of these gridirons and the honest work of rendering them almost indestructible, have contributed to their preservation. Especially on the handles is the ironworker's skill apparent, as may be seen on the specimen figured. (Pl. 89, fig. 4; Cat. No. 168324, Belgium, seventeenth century, S. B. Dean; 12.6 inches (32 cm.) diameter, 28.3 inches (72 cm.) long.)

MEAT ROASTERS AND TOASTERS

There are described here trivets on which are mounted forks for holding meat to be roasted, in effect a spit. One of these came

---

[10] T. T. Belote. Descriptive Catalogue of the Washington Relics in the United States National Museum. Proc. U. S. Nat. Mus., vol. 49, 1915, pp. 1–24.

down in Mrs. E. J. Stone's family, Washington, D. C., and dates about 1768. It was brought from England by Robert King, sr. It consists of a trivet with cabriolet legs and spade feet surmounted by a ring on which a drip pan could be set. At one side of the ring plate is a pierced tab in which a rod held by a spring is set and is thus capable of being raised and lowered. At the top is a spring slide in which the spit works. The spit has four forks in a row and one placed above, perhaps to hold basting material. (Pl. 89, fig. 3; Cat. No. 130492, England, Mrs. E. J. Stone; height to ring, 9.8 inches (25 cm.).) From Yorkshire, England, comes a tall roaster consisting of an iron grid of five slats having nine forks, and sliding on an upright rod with three ball-toed feet. The upper iron through which the upright rod passes is curved back and has a hole at the end, apparently for hanging the spit on a hook. (Pl. 88, fig. 1; Cat. No. 150885, English, Edward Lovett; 30.8 inches (80 cm.) high.) Another specimen coming from Virginia and believed to date to colonial times is of different type. It is purely of wrought iron. The base is a long, narrow strip mounted on four feet formed by bending a strip of iron in U-shape and riveting to the base near the ends. On the base are mounted two pairs of twisted iron bows set opposite. Two twisted spikes with down-curving ornaments are set under the bows. The handle is hinged to an upright U-shape section and terminates in a loop. (Pl. 89, fig. 2; Cat. No. 233195, Virginia, Walter Hough; 12¼ inches (31 cm.) long, 5½ inches (14 cm.) high.

TRIVETS

This useful utensil from the period of the great fireplace served as a skeleton stove. It was set over coals raked from the fire or hooked on the crane above the fire, the bent-down bars in the front of the trivet giving that impression. The National Museum has a trivet given by Lucy H. Baird. It is of Pennsylvania origin and came down in the family of Prof. Spencer F. Baird, second Secretary of the Smithsonian, whether on the Baird or Biddle side is not known. It is a sturdy trivet with spade feet, a rack for a pan, and a finely perforated brass grid with turned applewood handle polished like amber at the top. (Pl. 90, fig. 1; Cat. No. 284327, Pennsylvania, Lucy H. Baird; 13 inches (33 cm.) high.) A folding trivet of uncertain origin has a beautifully pierced iron rim having four small bosses punched up to accommodate the bottom of the vessel. The handle folds down on itself and has a latch to brace it. The bottom of the pivoted handle forms one of the three feet and the top has a hook for hanging a spoon or fork, and a yoke across for resting the handle of a pipkin or such vessel. This folding device was probably for use in the field and may be in a way the ancestor of the modern field kitchen. (Pl. 90, fig. 4; Cat. No. 168326, probably European; S. B. Dean; 9 inches (23 cm.) high, 10.2 inches (26 cm.) long.) A third trivet is apparently very old and is supplied with a hot iron heating or warming cup placed at the junction of the prongs of the pan rack. The iron is missing. This trivet could be used away from the fire for the purpose of keeping a pan warm, or placed on the fire in the customary way. (Pl. 90, fig. 3; Cat. No. 169095, Flemish; S. B. Dean; 6.7 inches (17 cm.) high, 16.1 inches (41 cm.) long.) A north African trivet from Tetuan, Morocco, shows this utensil in a simple form. It is of iron, triangular in shape, and has three stubs projecting on the inner side of the rim for resting the pot. This trivet is evidently for the open temporary fire of the Arab camps. (Pl. 90, fig. 2; Tetuan, Morocco; Dr. Talcott Williams; 9.8 inches (25 cm.) diameter, 5.5 inches (14 cm.) high.)

POTHOOKS, POT HANGERS

The humble pothook served an ordinary but useful purpose in the great fireplace. Frequently the blacksmith spent time and care in making a pothook that was not only strong, but expressed his idea of art. (Pl. 91, figs. 3, 4, 6; Cat. No. 329468, West Virginia (Virginia), Walter Hough.) It was necessary to adjust the height of kettles above the fire and chains were used in connection with pothooks. (Pl. 91, figs. 2, 5; Cat. No. 329468, West Virginia (Virginia), Walter Hough.) Other inventions were utilized, such as the hole and peg pothook, an ingenious device apparently of the eighteenth century. (Pl. 91, fig. 1; Cat. No. 329468, West Virginia (Virginia), Walter Hough.) European usage developed a rack and stirrup device by which the adjustment could be made easily. Examples of these were brought to the New World in the course of trade and immigration. A specimen from Belgium has a broad saw blade. (Pl. 91, fig. 2; Cat. No. 168323, Belgium; S. B. Dean; 40 inches (105 cm.) long.) A pothook from Finland is slender and roughly beaten out of soft iron. The crane hook is large and simply formed. (Pl. 91, fig. 1; Cat. No. 167870, Finland; J. M. Crawford; 23.2 inches (5.9 cm.) long.)

CURFEW

There have survived from an earlier usage examples of fire covers which were an improvement on the old-time method of keeping fire over night in the ashes. These are low cones of brass punched and perforated with ornamental designs and a curved handle. It is in general like a candle extinguisher. The function of this curfew, as it is called, is to cover a heap of coals raked up from the hearth fire and preserve them under smothered or slightly aerated condition through the night. The curfew as a social institution and the curfew as a material fire cover are thus brought together. (Pl. 92, fig. 5; Cat. No. 289435, Holland; Anton Heitmuller; 9.8 inches (25 cm.) diameter, 4.7 inches (12 cm.) high.)

LAUNDRY IRONS

At one time, as mentioned, the use of a heating iron was quite prevalent, as in the hot-water urns (p. 93) and even in a trivet (p. 102). It is found in the laundry irons of the colonial period when heating an iron and keeping it clean on the open fire was practically impossible. Several of these quaint old irons are in the National Museum. In one of these the heating iron is wedge shape with a hole in the base for drawing it out of the fire. This iron was slid into the hollow body of the laundry iron and closed in by a sliding door. (Pl. 93, fig. 1; Cat. No. 206401, Pennsylvania; Barton A. Bean; 4.7 inches (12 cm.) long, 4.9 inches (12.5 cm.) high, 3.2 inches (8 cm.) wide.) A heavier iron, the shell and bottom joined on, appears also to be a product of the Pennsylvania iron workers, probably from the Bethlehem Valley. It is wrought except the heating iron. The latter, when placed in the iron, rests on an S-shape piece riveted to the bottom. The back of the iron is closed by a pivoted door with knob. (Pl. 93, fig. 2; Cat. No. 298361, Pennsylvania; Dr. P. B. Johnson; 7.9 inches (20 cm.) long, 5.5 inches (14 cm.) high.) A third iron of cast brass is of unknown locality. It is cast in one piece and the handle is riveted on and held in position by a screw. The handle also is of turned brass with a wooden grip projecting forward in the direction the iron would be pushed. The heating iron, which is missing, ran on two ridges cast in the bottom of the hollow of the iron. The door was pivoted and moved in a slot. (Pl. 93, fig. 3; Cat. No. 298362, probably English; Dr. P. B. Johnson; 7.9 inches (20 cm.) long, 7.1 inches (18 cm.) high.)

IRON RESTS

With the use of the flatiron rests became necessary. They come almost invariably cast either of iron or brass and were always artistically treated. The range of folk art displayed in iron rests would correspond to that of the glass bottles so assiduously collected by the present generation. Often the rests were commemorative of some celebrity or had a political or humorous slant. A yellow brass trivet iron rest from England is perforated with crown and plumes design and is of excellent workmanship. (Pl. 92, fig. 1; Cat. No. 168329, S. B. Dean; 8.5 inches (21.5 cm.) long.) Another specimen, of bronze, has an elaborate rococo design. (Pl. 92, fig. 2; Cat. No. 289463, England; Anton Heitmuller; 9.5 inches (24 cm.) long.) A cast-bronze specimen commemorates Jenny Lind posing as goddess of music. (Pl. 92, fig. 3; Cat. No. 289462, United States; Anton Heitmuller; 10.2 inches (26 cm.) long.)

BRANDING IRON

The branding iron reflects a phase of animal industry and a condition of settlement of a country in which grazing territory not under fence is the rule. The type of branding iron shown has been obsolete for many years, having been superseded by the straight iron with which the brand is drawn free hand. (Pl. 92, fig. 4; Cat. No. 127275, Virginia, said to be colonial; Capt. J. J. Dillard; 13.8 inches (35 cm.) long.)

ABORIGINAL COOKING DEVICES

The Virginia Indians at the time of John Smith dried, semicooked, and smoked fish, etc., for the winter provender on a wooden grid. Fish for immediate consumption were roasted on rod spits thrust in the ground around the fire (see Pl. 84), as shown from a model constructed from John White's drawing. Another method which primitive life employed consisted of suspending the paunch of an animal, in previous times that of a buffalo, and boiling meat by means of heated stones placed therein. The sticks of the tripod were lashed together with rawhide near the top, spread, and the paunch hung in the triangle like a Gypsy oven. (Pl. 94, Cat. No. 281261, Teton Sioux, Dakota; Miss Frances Densmore; 62 inches (1 cm., 61.2 cm.) high.) Stone boiling was extensive among the Indians, and the method was practiced also in other parts of the world. Stones definitely so used are rarely collected. (Pl. 95, fig. 3; Cat. No. 178092, Maya Indians, Mexico; Edward Palmer.) Stones worked for use as baking dishes are found in California among recent tribes and in ancient sites. It is possible that stone slabs may have been more widely used and not being worked are unrecognized. The term baking is employed in reference to these stones, and it must be understood that it implies a procedure nearer to frying. (Pl. 95, fig. 1; Cat. No. 77161, Hupa Indians, California; Lieut. P. H. Ray, U. S. A.; 6.5 inches (16.5 cm.) long, 3.5 inches (9 cm.) wide; fig. 2, Cat. No. 30343, Santa Inez Island, Calif.; S. Bowers; 5.1 inches (13 cm.) long, 4.9 inches (12.5 cm.) wide.) These specimens are worked from soapstone.

GRIDDLES

Griddles of pottery and stone are widely distributed where subsistence on cereals prevails. It would appear that " flat bread " is most ancient of the cereal breads. Stone griddles have come down to the present time, especially soapstone, which has the quality of preventing the sticking of the cakes, thus not requiring the application of grease. Dr. Talcott Williams procured from Tetuan, Morocco, a circular stone griddle. The bottom is cut out below, forming three very low feet. (Pl. 95, fig. 5; 11.8 inches (30 cm.)

diameter.)   The Mexican tortilla griddle, *comal*, is of thin earthenware.   It is made by forming the clay on a sand support, allowing it to dry, and baking.   The pottery *comal* is quite fragile.   (Pl. 95, fig. 4;   Cat. No. 176438, Edward Palmer;   16.9 inches (43 cm.) diameter.)   The Pueblo Indian griddle is an oblong slab of stone carefully selected, worked, and prepared for use.   It is mounted at the ends on a low stone wall and the fire built underneath.   The batter is smeared deftly on the griddle with the hand, and the resulting bread is papery.   (Pl. 96, from family group in National Museum.)   Iron griddles of a simple character, consisting of a rectangular plate of thick sheet iron with a loop handle riveted on at one end, have taken the place of pottery gridirons to some extent in Mexico.   (Pl. 95, figs. 7, 8;   Cat. No. 75350, Matamoros, Mexico;   U. S. Department of State;   12 inches (30.6 cm.) by 16 inches (40.7 cm.).)

OVENS

Ovens appear to have begun with pits in the ground heated by means of a wood fire, the food placed in, and the cavity covered with earth.   Such ovens are widespread among uncivilized peoples. Covering an animal with clay and burying the bundle in the ashes is conceived of as a more primitive phase of the oven, but the method is not generally used, is for animal food, and must be regarded as a makeshift.   The oven has its development in the cooking of vegetable food, principally, and has its greatest usefulness in performing this function.   The pit oven is seen in the oven for baking clams and other shellfish.   There are also pit ovens for roasting pig, found among the Pacific islanders.   The barbecue trench oven is allied to the pit oven.   There is a relationship between the oven for cooking and those for baking pottery and smelting metals.   The earth oven, therefore, is presumed to have a very ancient history.   Two classes of earth oven may be distinguished, those requiring a pit dug in the ground and those heaped up on the ground.   In the latter hot rocks performed the cooking, while the pit oven usually cooked by the absorbed heat of the ground subjected to fire action.   Some tribes poured water on the rocks just before closing the oven, thus calling in the aid of steam.

The Hopi Pueblo Indian field oven consists of a bottle-shape hole excavated in the sandy loam of the fields located along the washes. A duct is cut from the bottom of the excavation to the surface for the purpose of draft.   A fire of field débris is built in the hole and maintained for several hours till the earth is very hot.   Roasting ears are then piled in, the draft hole closed, the top hole covered, and a fire built on it.   When opened there issues from the mouth of the oven a tall column of steam.   Corn ears lying near the hot wall of the oven are in reality wasted, and the ears in the mass are thoroughly cooked by steam (pl. 97, fig. 3; model). The same idea is employed in cooking mush, which is put in a jar and set in the hot chamber and cooked by heat radiation from the walls (pl. 97, fig. 4; model; Hopi Indians, Arizona). A curious modification of this type of oven is found among the Zuni Indians. In the heated pit are piled hot slabs of stone alternating with mush. The oven is then covered over and a fire built on top (pl. 97, fig. 2; model in the U. S. National Museum). The heap oven was generally used among the Indians whose habitation was the tipi. In this type the roots, corn ears, and whatever was to be cooked were put in a heap on an area which had been heated by a fire, covered with grass and earth, and a fire built over the heap (pl. 97, fig. 1; model in the U. S. National Museum). From these rude earth ovens there emerges a definite built-up oven in connection with human habitations and among bread-consuming people. A familiar example of these is the dome-shape oven seen in Mexico and in the southwestern United States. It adjoins the house, is built on the ground, and is constructed of mud or stone plastered with mud. The Mexicans invariably use this oven. All the Pueblo Indians have this oven except the Hopi. No archeological traces of this type are found in the Pueblo region, and the inference is that it was introduced from Mexico and to that country from Spain. Such ovens are seen in the Near East, and it is probable that this type is coterminous with the wheat and yeast using peoples. Mounted on legs or foundation, or otherwise installed, this type of "bake oven" was widespread in Europe, parts of Africa, and Asia from ancient times, and was introduced into North America by emigrants from the Old World (pl. 97, fig. 5; model in National Museum).

In the earlier times the oven was a thing apart from the great open fireplace of general utility. Its function was for baking at intervals of an amount of bread sufficient for family needs over a period of time. For smaller bakings of fresh bread the reflecting oven was used. This consisted of a number of forms, but the principle was the reflection of heat rays from a sheet of tin inclined at 90° onto bread or other food in a pan resting horizontally in front of the reflector. Few of the rigid reflectors have survived. The Museum has a folding or camp reflector, Lehnen's patent, patented September 30, 1875, and made by Scoville and Johnson at Marquette, Mich. This is of copper tinned inside. It has two reflecting surfaces, one 90° heating the top and the other 45° the bottom of the pan placed between them on an iron grid which also holds the sides together. This apparatus is set up in front of a camp fire. The older reflectors were stationed in front of a bright fire in

the old-fashioned fire place. (Pl. 95, fig. 6–9; Cat. No. 26843; Scoville and Johnson; 13.4 inches (34 cm.) long, 8.7 inches (22 cm.)
wide, 2 inches (5 cm.) high.)

A very useful fireside utensil and widely known is the Dutch
oven. The Dutch oven indicates the difficulty of cooking over the
open fire in the old fireplace, and it also represents the portable oven
which since the period of cast iron was used over the peripatetic
camp fire as well as on the house fire. Of the variety of handled
three-leg pots which have an ancient ancestry the only one surviving indispensably to this day is the Dutch oven. It is the one
kitchen utensil which renders the miner, prospector, explorer, trav-
eler in wild country, the camper, and others independent in the
matter of cooking. It is awkward to pack and the legs, handle, and
lid loop often damaged the outfit, but in that case it was a necessary
evil. The body of the Dutch oven is like a deep skillet, the latter
having degenerated from some such vessel. It stands on 3 legs and
has a straight handle, for which later, in some cases, a bail was
substituted. The lid is heavy, curved upward toward the border,
and has a wrought-iron loop cast in the middle. In cooking with
the Dutch oven a little bed of coals is raked out of the fire in a
circular heap and the oven is set on and the lid put inplace. More
coals are put on the lid. Between these two fires the cooking goes
on, and after several removals of the lid for inspection, the bread or
such is found nicely baked. The adjustment of the fire top and
bottom is a nice matter. When the wind blows baking is difficult.
(Pl. 98, fig. 3; Cat. No. 130315, United States; Emma Protzman.)
A smaller trivet pot from Alabama is also characteristic. It is
probable that there was a lid like that of the Dutch oven. (Pl. 98,
fig. 2; Cat. No. 216022, Alabama; Louis Drummond; 6.7 inches
(17 cm.) diameter.) An old specimen in cast brass has the handle
projecting from the rim. (Pl. 98, fig. 1; Cat. No. 276122, England;
Frances Benjamin Johnston; 5.3 inches (13.5 cm.) diameter, 4.4
inches (11 cm.) high.) Some of these pots were oval with lid as in
the Dutch oven and were large, for cooking a ham, a joint, or a fowl.

A curious oven is found in Novogachic, southwestern Chihuahua,
Mexico. It is a large jar somewhat flattened on side and bordered
by a ridge. A fire is made in the jar and cakes or meat fried on the
exterior. This resembles the Near East oven or may be classed as
a variant of the baking slab and gridde. (Pl. 98, fig. 4; Cat. No.
115781 Tarahumare Indians; Edward Palmer; 8⅝ inches (22 cm.)
diameter, 12⅛ inches (31 cm.) wide, 14½ inches (37 cm.) long.)

BOILING

The Museum collection contains many pottery vessels, ancient and
modern, for cooking by boiling. The presumption is that boiling

became a standard method of cooking food after pottery began to be made. The use of pottery vessels for cooking has been continuous and in the bronze and iron age metal cooking vessels were not fea‑tured.[11] Regarded as one of the most primitive cooking vessels is a specimen from the Andaman Islands. It is of pottery reasonably thick and strong and rough curried on the exterior. The shape fol‑lows the half coconut. (Pl. 80, fig. 1, Cat. No. 164570; Andaman Islands, from H. H. Giglioli, collected by E. H. Man; 7. 9 inches (20 cm.) diameter, 7.1 inches (18 cm.) high.) The pot is held in a rattan frame for protection when not in use. Pueblo pottery cook‑ing pots are also of coarse heat-resisting paste, allowing them to be put directly on the fire. The specimen shown is from Zuni, N. Mex. (Pl. 80, fig. 3, Cat. No. 41119; J. W. Powell; 7.9 inches diameter, 7.1 inches (20 cm., 18 cm.).) In this connection attention is called to the Korean soapstone pot with lid, and the curious frying pan of the same material on Plate 80 (figs. 4 and 6). In the latter strips of meat are placed on the sloping edge and the juices collected in the central basin. Evidently this vessel is placed over a fire hole.

STEAMING

Steaming food other than takes place in baking in ovens has a narrow distribution. It is connected with rice agriculture except as it occurs in modern cooking of cereals, etc. We find, therefore, aboriginal steamers in the Far East, the specimens in the Museum being from the Malays of the East Indies. (Pl. 98, fig. 6; Cat. No. 247752, Siak River, eastern Sumatra; Dr. W. L. Abbott; 11 inches (28 cm.) diameter, 19.7 inches (50 cm.) high; and pl. 98, fig. 5; Cat. No. 216295, Sibabo Bay, Simalur Island; same collector; 12.2 inches (31 cm.) diameter, 11.8 inches (30 cm.) high.) These specimens are of bark formed into a cylinder and hooped with rattan. A grating of small rods is placed near the bottom of the cylinder. On this is put the rice, and the steamer is set over a pot of boiling water. The top of the steamer is tightly covered during the steam‑ing. The Sumatra specimen is sheathed with palm leaf to retain the heat. A third specimen in the National Museum is from the Dyaks, Landak River, Borneo. The grating is radial of rattan secured to a sleeve which slides in the bark cylinder. It has two loop handles on the side.

WAFFLE IRONS

For baking certain forms of bread in the period when the great open fire was practically the only place in the house where cooking was done there was a device, really a form of oven, called waffle irons. These consisted of two circular disks of equal size in the

---

[11] Guide to the Antiquities of the Bronze Age. British Museum, 1904, p. 29.

·older specimens, mounted to fit up tight one against the other at the end of long tongs. The waffle molds were cast in obverse of what the succulent waffle when properly baked would be when released from the iron. Shorter handle waffle irons with square molds appear to indicate that at a later period, when the great fireplace was more or less boxed in with oven, water tank, etc., the shorter tongs could be used. (Pl. 92, fig. 1; Cat. No. 130312, Morgantown, W. Va. (Virginia); Walter Hough; 37.7 inches (98 cm.) long; fig. 2; Cat. No. 239098, Charmian, Franklin County, Pa.; Mrs. W. H. Comer; 24.8 inches (63 cm.) long.)

TEAKETTLE

The teakettle was an indispensable adjunct to the old fireplace, where it hung by a pot hook from the crane or sometimes was set over the fire on a trivet. The old-time kettle was of beaten copper, made with the idea of endurance uppermost, but always a subject of the metal worker's conception of art. It is said that domestic vessels made by the craftsmen in metal were copied by the potters in their ware, the resulting teapots, sugar bowls, etc., being familiar to collectors of old ceramics. (Pl. 81b, fig. 3; Cat. No. 329472, Colonial, probably English manufacture; Victor J. Evans; 7.9 inches (20 cm.) long, 6.3 inches (16 cm.) wide, 7.5 inches (19 cm.) high.)

FUEL

The materials used for burning to produce heat are of vegetal, animal, and mineral origin. In the first stages of the use of fuel, in which fires are in the open, wood is the common and usual substance for burning. Depending on the environment, we get a great variety of fuels suitable for the open fire. The stage when fuel is burned in a fire having the minimum of confinement between walls or other surrounding devices may be regarded as primitive. In this stage the fuel industry was undifferentiated; every group gathered fuel for themselves. With the progress in housing and knowledge of installing fire in various devices suggesting stoves, proper fuel as to kinds, sizes, etc., became more important. Many fuels suitable for the camp had to be discarded for employment in the habitation. There appear here the rudiments of the manufacture of fuel. This is seen in charcoal, which was a product known to all as derived from the incomplete combustion of wood. The definite, intentional use of charcoal as fuel is the key to the stove. Its importance as a social factor has been unrecognized. It may even be called one of the world's greatest inventions. Upon charcoal rested for a long period the world's advance in fire utilization for heating and other purposes, especially metallurgy. Metallurgy required a fuel freed from volatile constituents and capable of bearing the weight of the ore charge while burning. It is a pure fuel also, imparting no deleterious properties to the metal. The treatment of coal to produce coke may be said to be an extension of the ancient charcoal burner's art.

The collection includes a number of representative examples of native fuels principally from America, described below. Hay fuel, consisting of twists of coarse grass, were used for fuel in the treeless plains of the Dakotas. Hay thus compressed made a hot and excellent fuel. It is remarked that in deforested China similar grass bundles are used for fuel. (Pl. 99, fig. 1; Cat. No. 74216; Kingsbury County, S. Dak., Byron Andrews; 18 inches (45.8 cm.) long.) Another important native fuel coincident with the range of the bison was called "Buffalo chips," the solid excrement of the Bison Americanus. This valuable fuel was used by Indians and others on the Great Western Plains. On the march this fuel was collected around camp. Indian women usually collected the material and formed it into round flat masses which they stored at the village. (Pl. 99, fig. 7; Cat. No. 102226, Bismarck, N. Dak., 1876; Dr. C. E. McChesney; 13.5 (34.3 cm.) inches by 16 (40.7 cm.) inches diameter.) Tablet form masses more appropriately termed chips were also collected. (Pl. 99, fig. 6; Cat. No. 102225; Bismarck, N. Dak., 1876; Dr. C. C. McChesney.) Slabs of material of high fuel value formed from droppings of sheep and goats beaten down on the floor of corrals were used by Hopi Indian pottery makers for firing their ware.

Peat lightly compressed is shown in Plate 99, Figure 4. Other forms of compressed peat formed into tubular briquettes are shown in Figures 3, 6. A block of heavily compressed peat is shown in Figure 2. The specimens are from northern Europe and were exhibited at the Centennial Exposition at Philadelphia in 1876. (Cat. No. 325616, Europe; Centennial Exhibition.)

Charcoal fuel classified as other than the crude product is rarely observed in any other country than Japan. There charcoal made from the twigs, branches, and stems of certain wood growth is selected for some artistic quality and used in the tea ceremony and other expressions of refinements. In Japan also globular briquettes prepared of finely powdered charcoal and other substances are slow burning and useful for keeping fire over night.

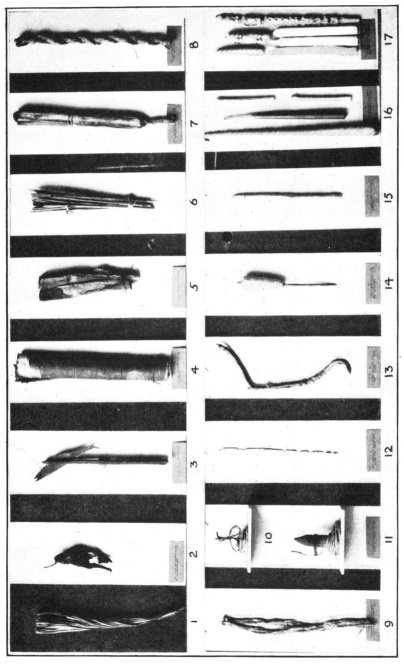

DEVELOPMENT OF THE TORCH AND CANDLE

FOR DESCRIPTION OF PLATE SEE PAGES 2 AND 3

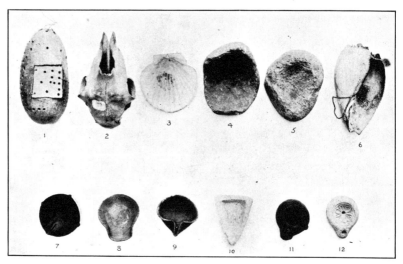

DEVELOPMENT OF THE LAMP

FOR DESCRIPTION OF PLATE SEE PAGES 2 AND 3

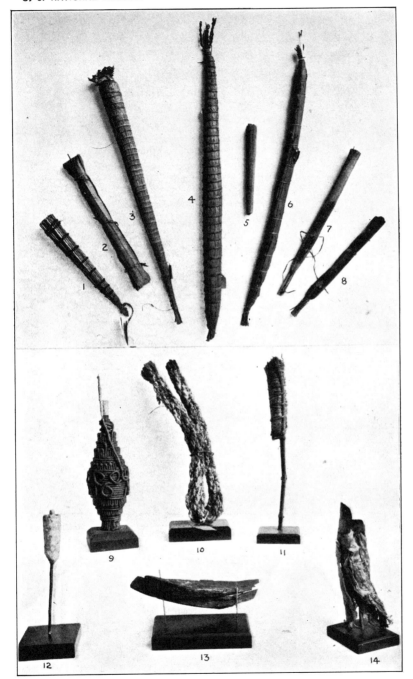

TORCHES AND CANDLES

FOR DESCRIPTION OF PLATE SEE PAGE 4

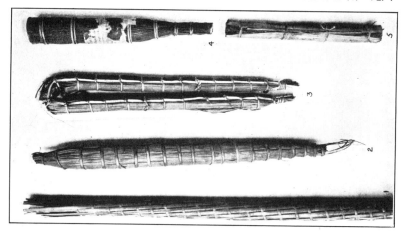

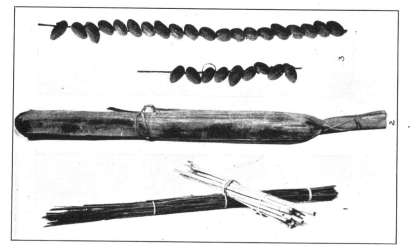

PRIMITIVE ADAPTATION OF ANIMALS FOR ILLUMINATION AND VARIETIES OF TORCHES

FOR DESCRIPTION OF PLATE SEE PAGES 5 TO 9

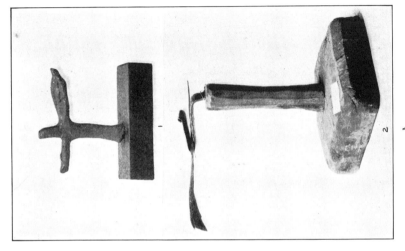

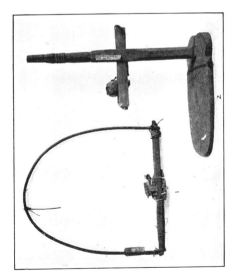

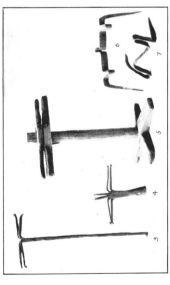

TORCH AND SPLINT HOLDERS

FOR DESCRIPTION OF PLATE SEE PAGES 9 TO 11

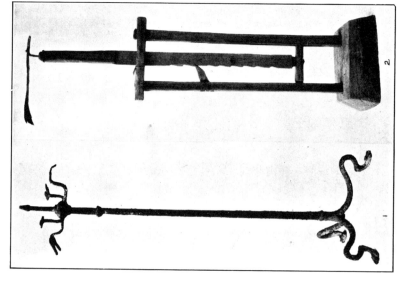

EARLY SPLINT AND CANDLE HOLDERS

FOR DESCRIPTION OF PLATE SEE PAGES 10 TO 12

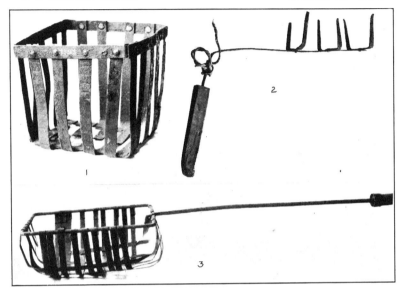

a

b

BASKET TORCHES AND FISHING TORCH

FOR DESCRIPTION OF PLATE SEE PAGES 12 AND 13

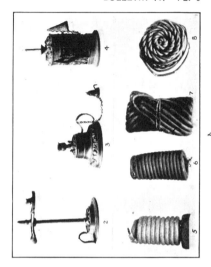

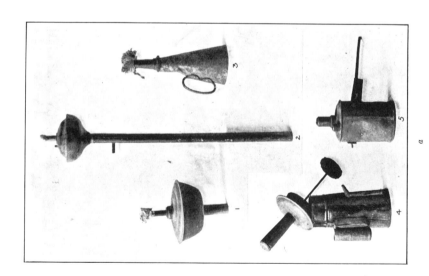

WICK TORCHES, WAX COILED TAPERS, AND TAPER HOLDERS

FOR DESCRIPTION OF PLATE SEE PAGES 12 TO 15

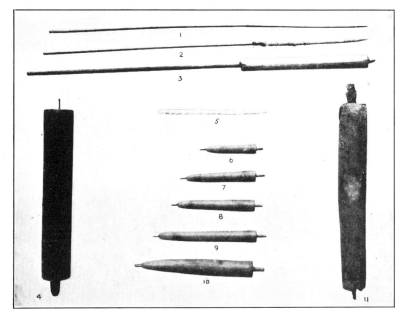

a

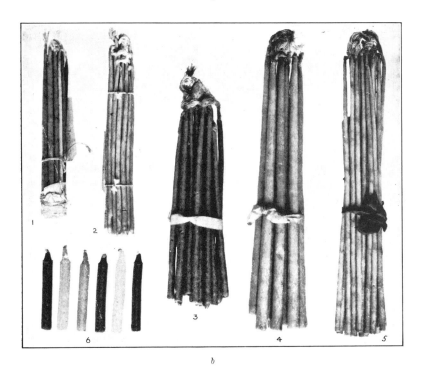

b

CHINESE CANDLE MAKING, AND RELIGIOUS TAPERS

FOR DESCRIPTION OF PLATE SEE PAGES 16 TO 18

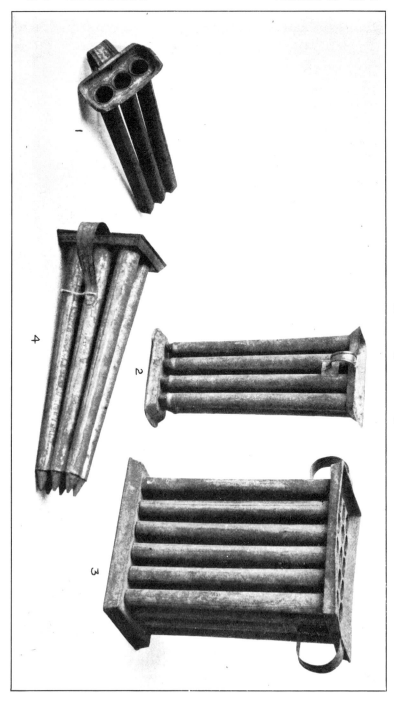

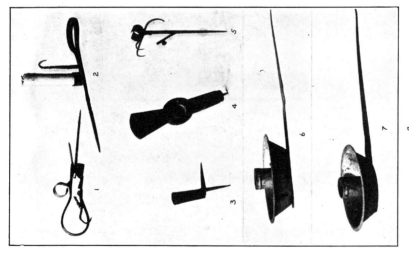

CANDLE HOLDERS AND CANDLESTICKS

FOR DESCRIPTION OF PLATE SEE PAGE 19

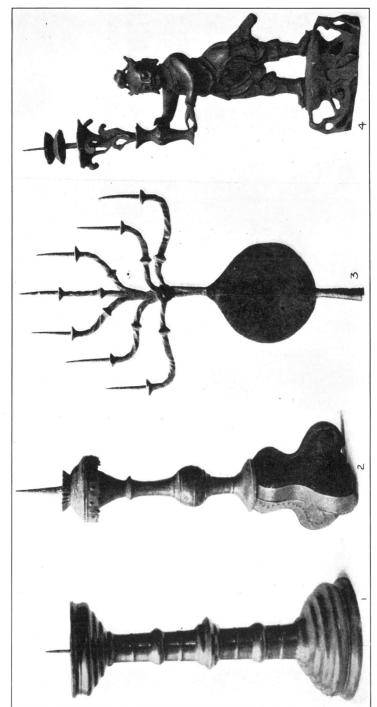

PRICKET CANDLESTICKS

FOR DESCRIPTION OF PLATE SEE PAGE 20

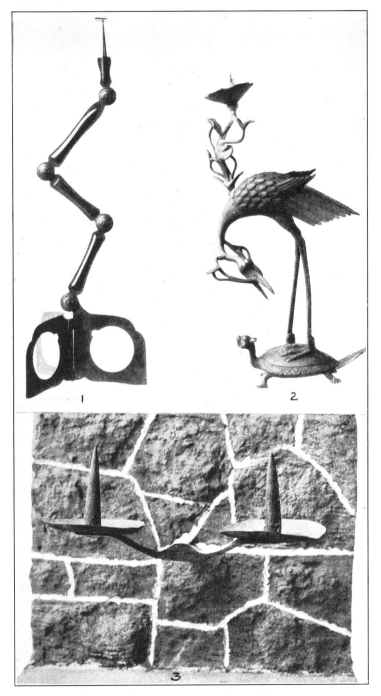

PRICKET CANDLESTICKS AND RUSH HOLDER

FOR DESCRIPTION OF PLATE SEE PAGE 20

CANDLESTICKS OF STONE, WOOD, POTTERY, AND GLASS

FOR DESCRIPTION OF PLATE SEE PAGES 21 AND 22

1   2

GLAZED ROUNDED CANDLESTICK AND TIME CANDLE

FOR DESCRIPTION OF PLATE SEE PAGES 22, AND 40

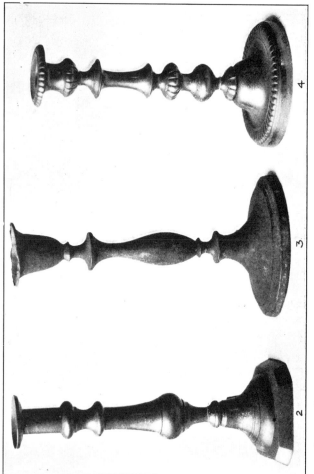

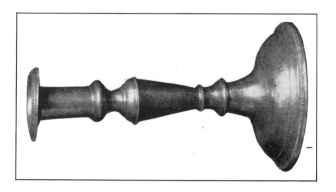

BRASS, COPPER, AND PEWTER CANDLESTICKS

FOR DESCRIPTION OF PLATE SEE PAGES 22 AND 23

SILVER PLATE AND SILVER CANDLESTICKS

FOR DESCRIPTION OF PLATE SEE PAGE 23

PEWTER CANDLESTICKS

FOR DESCRIPTION OF PLATE SEE PAGE 24

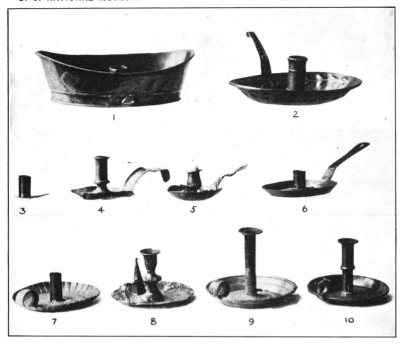

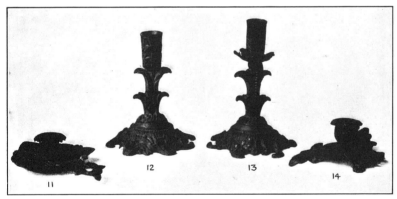

CANDLE DISHES; BRASS AND IRON CANDLESTICKS

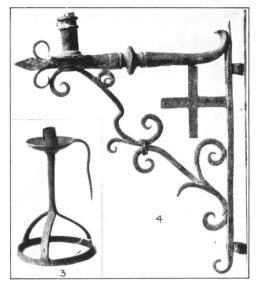

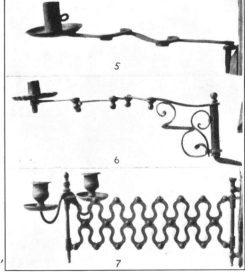

HAMMERED-IRON CANDLESTICKS; CANDLE ARMS AND BRACKETS

FOR DESCRIPTION OF PLATE SEE PAGE 25

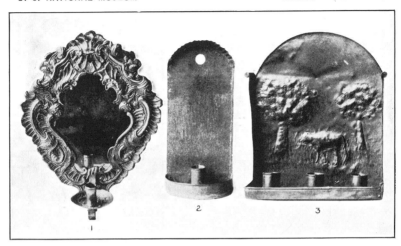

CANDLESTICKS WITH WIND GLASSES, AND SCONCES

FOR DESCRIPTION OF PLATE SEE PAGES 27 AND 29

CANDELABRA

For description of plate see page 28

CHANDELIERS

For description of plate see page 29

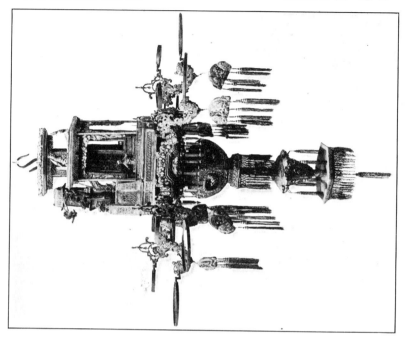

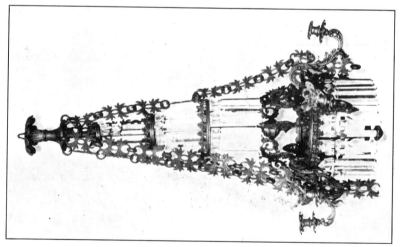

BRONZE CHANDELIER AND CHINESE FEATHERED CHANDELIER

FOR DESCRIPTION OF PLATE SEE PAGE 30

ROCOCO BRASS CHANDELIER AND CAMPHINE CHANDELIER

FOR DESCRIPTION OF PLATE SEE PAGE 30

TURKISH FLOAT LAMP CHANDELIER

FOR DESCRIPTION OF PLATE SEE PAGE 29

a

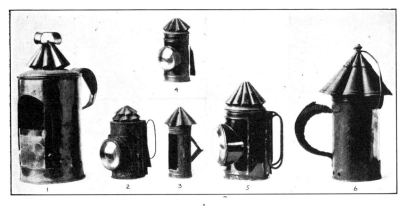

b

VARIETIES OF HORN AND DARK LANTERNS

FOR DESCRIPTION OF PLATE SEE PAGES 30 AND 31

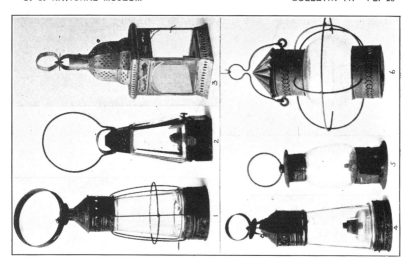

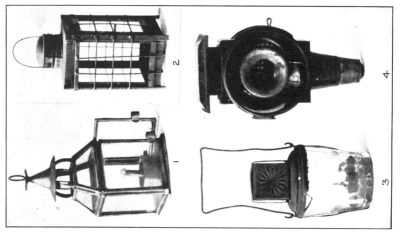

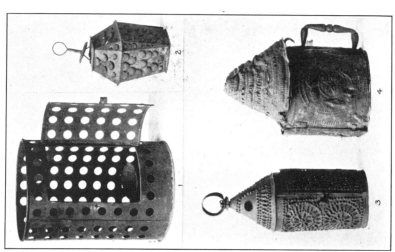

PERFORATED LANTERNS, ARM LANTERNS, SHIP'S LANTERNS, AND SPECIAL LANTERNS

FOR DESCRIPTION OF PLATE SEE PAGES 31, 32 AND 33

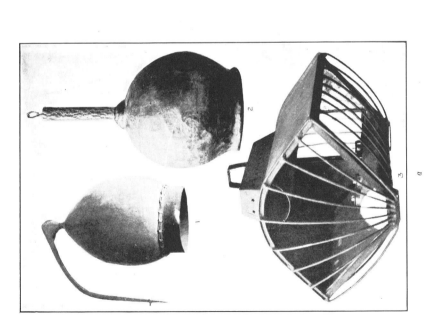

DARK LANTERNS; STANDING HOUSE; AND HAND LANTERNS

FOR DESCRIPTION OF PLATE SEE PAGES 29 AND 38

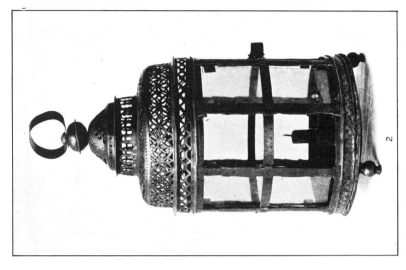

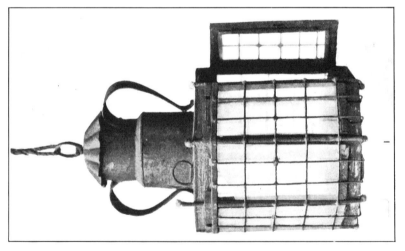

RIGGING LANTERN AND PIERCED COPPER LANTERN

FOR DESCRIPTION OF PLATE SEE PAGES 35 AND 36

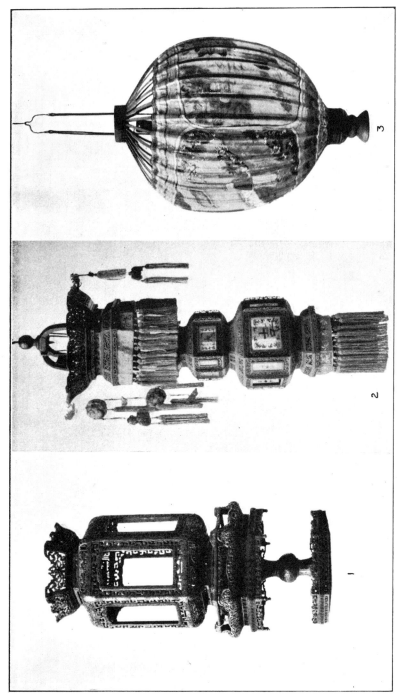

CHINESE LANTERNS

FOR DESCRIPTION OF PLATE SEE PAGE 38

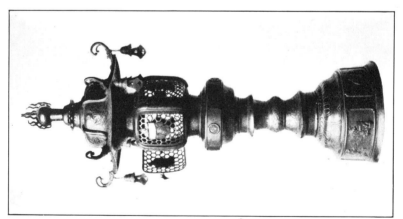

JAPANESE LANTERNS

FOR DESCRIPTION OF PLATE SEE PAGES 37 AND 38

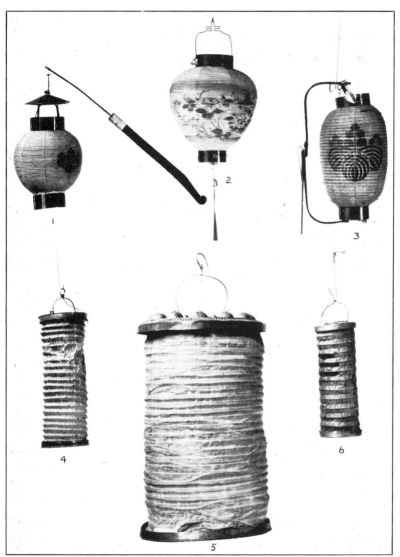

PAPER AND CLOTH COLLAPSING LANTERNS

FOR DESCRIPTION OF PLATE SEE PAGE 38

COLLAPSING LANTERNS WITH MICA WINDOWS

FOR DESCRIPTION OF PLATE SEE PAGE 39

CHURCH CANDLESTICKS

FOR DESCRIPTION OF PLATE SEE PAGE 39

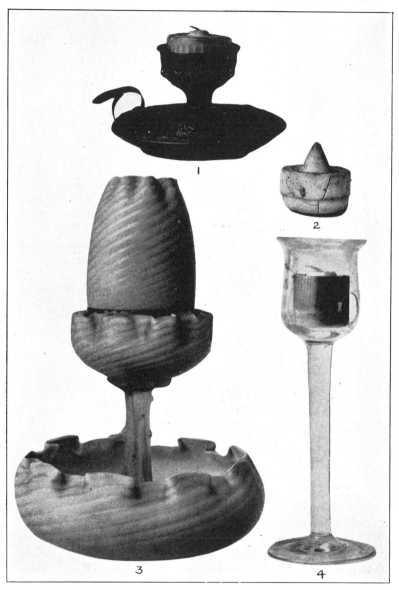

NIGHT LIGHT CANDLES AND HOLDERS

FOR DESCRIPTION OF PLATE SEE PAGE 40

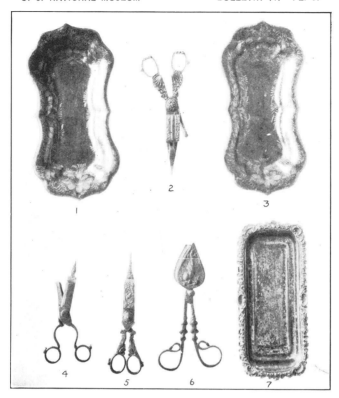

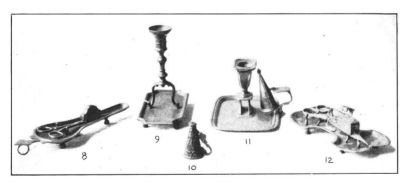

SNUFFER TRAYS, SNUFFERS, AND EXTINGUISHERS

FOR DESCRIPTION OF PLATE SEE PAGE 41

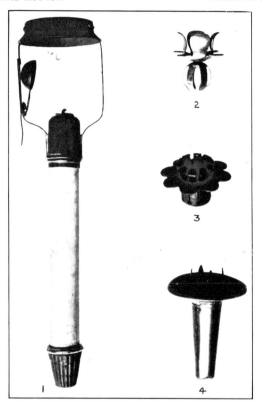

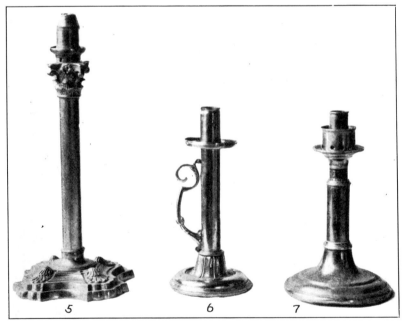

SPRING CANDLESTICKS AND OTHER DEVICES

FOR DESCRIPTION OF PLATE SEE PAGE 43

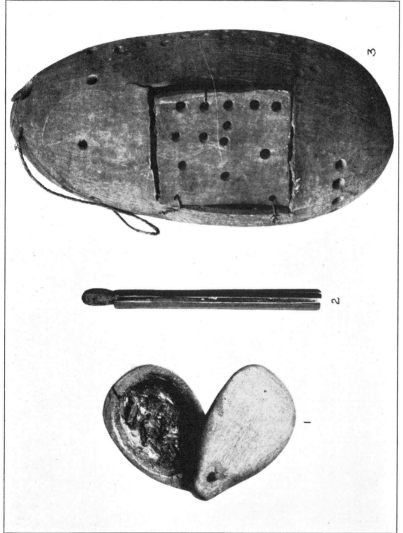

FIREFLY LIGHTING DEVICES

FOR DESCRIPTION OF PLATE SEE PAGES 44 AND 45

SIMPLE LAMPS AND FIREFLY LANTERN

FOR DESCRIPTION OF PLATE SEE PAGES 44, 45, AND 46

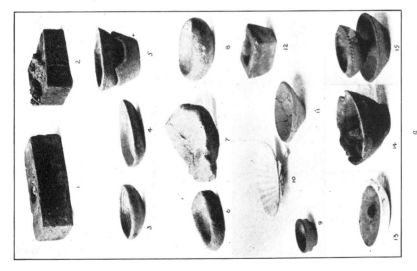

SIMPLE AND MAKESHIFT LAMPS

FOR DESCRIPTION OF PLATE SEE PAGES 45, 46, AND 47

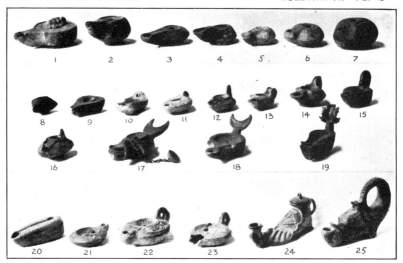

a

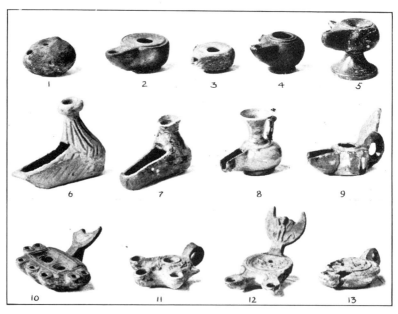

b

QUASI-DEVELOPMENT OF FEATURES OF ANCIENT LAMPS

FOR DESCRIPTION OF PLATE SEE PAGES 48 AND 49

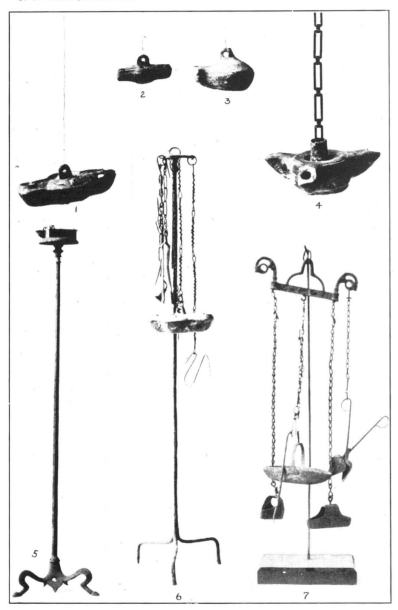

ANCIENT HANGING LAMPS AND STANDS

FOR DESCRIPTION OF PLATE SEE PAGE 49

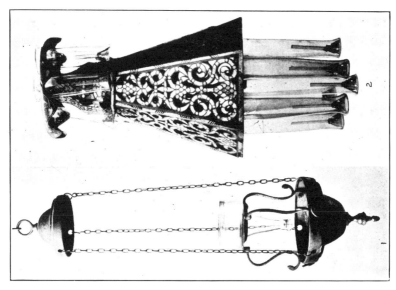

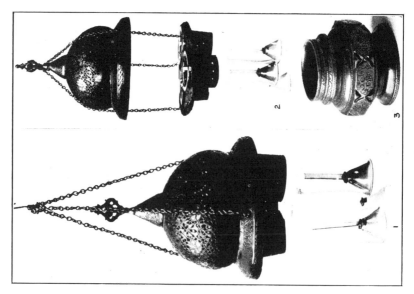

HANGING FLOAT LAMPS AND CUP FLOAT LAMPS

FOR DESCRIPTION OF PLATE SEE PAGES 51 AND 52

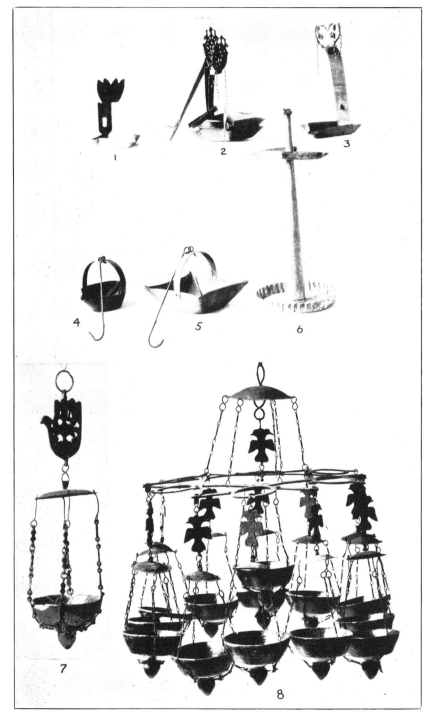

FLOAT LAMPS AND WICK CHANNEL LAMPS

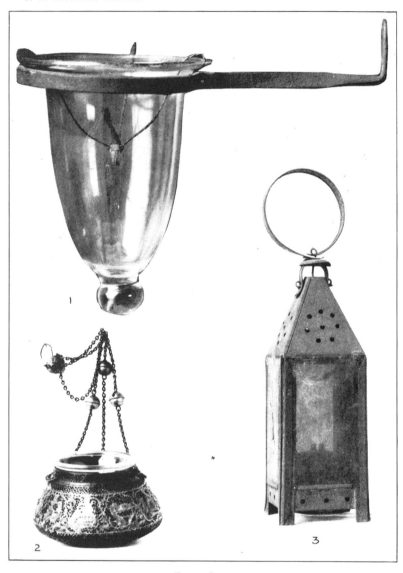

FLOAT LAMPS

FOR DESCRIPTION OF PLATE SEE PAGES 51 AND 52

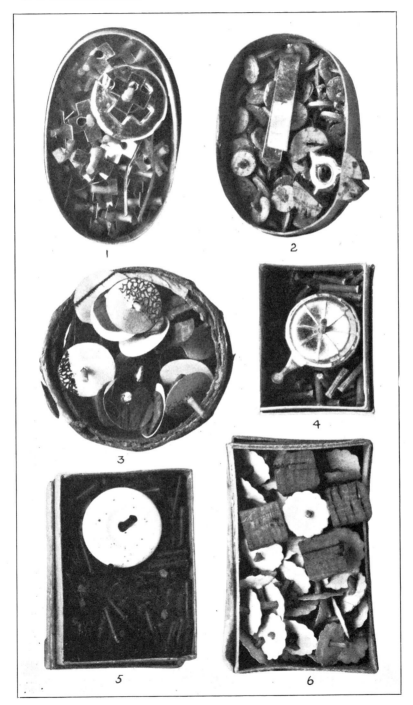

BOXES OF FLOAT WICKS

FOR DESCRIPTION OF PLATE SEE PAGES 52 AND 53

SIMPLE SAUCER LAMPS

FOR DESCRIPTION OF PLATE SEE PAGE 53

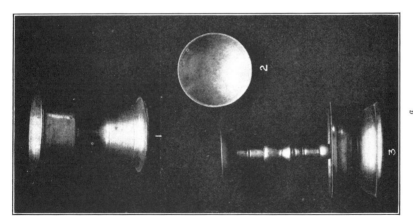

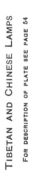

TIBETAN AND CHINESE LAMPS

FOR DESCRIPTION OF PLATE SEE PAGE 54

HAWAIIAN STONE LAMPS

FOR DESCRIPTION OF PLATE SEE PAGE 54

WICK CHANNEL LAMPS FROM NEAR EAST, EUROPE, ETC.

WICK CHANNEL LAMPS FROM INDIAN AND NORTH AFRICA

FOR DESCRIPTION OF PLATE SEE PAGE 56

WICK CHANNEL LAMPS FROM INDIA, JAVA, EUROPE, ETC.

FOR DESCRIPTION OF PLATE SEE PAGE 57

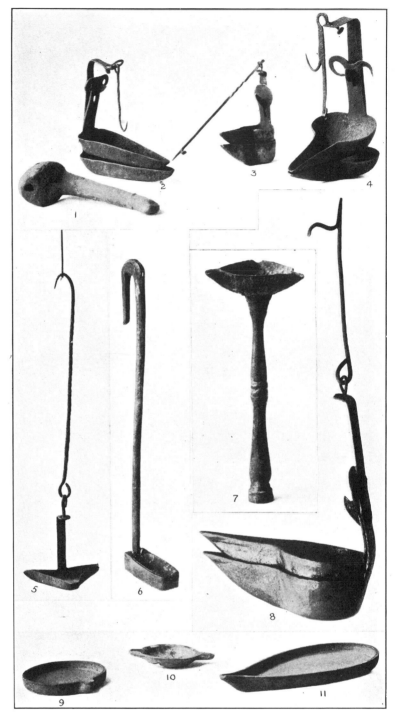

WICK CHANNEL LAMPS AND CRUSIES

FOR DESCRIPTION OF PLATE SEE PAGE 59

CRUSIES OF VARIOUS TYPES

FOR DESCRIPTION OF PLATE SEE PAGE 60

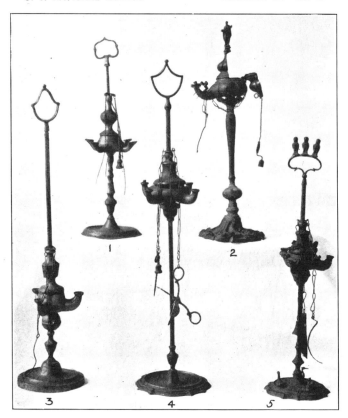

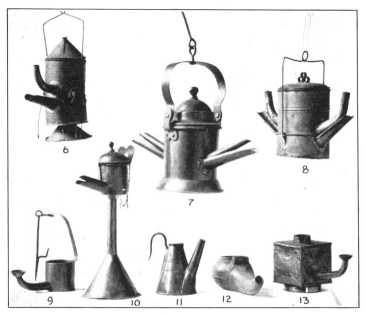

SPOUT LAMPS FROM EUROPE AND PHILIPPINES

FOR DESCRIPTION OF PLATE SEE PAGES 61 AND 62

SPOUT LAMPS FROM EUROPE AND CEYLON

FOR DESCRIPTION OF PLATE SEE PAGE 63

WICK TUBE LAMPS FROM EUROPE

FOR DESCRIPTION OF PLATE SEE PAGE 63

SINGLE AND DOUBLE WICK TUBE LAMPS

FOR DESCRIPTION OF PLATE SEE PAGES 64 AND 65

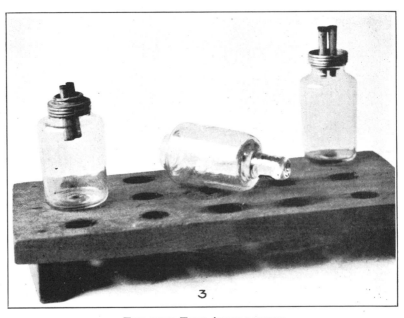

TWO-WICK TUBE INSTALLATIONS

FOR DESCRIPTION OF PLATE SEE PAGE 67

a

b

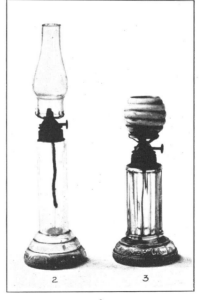

c

GLASS TWO-TUBE LAMPS; OIL AND TIME-INDICATING LAMP

FOR DESCRIPTION OF PLATE SEE PAGES 66 AND 67

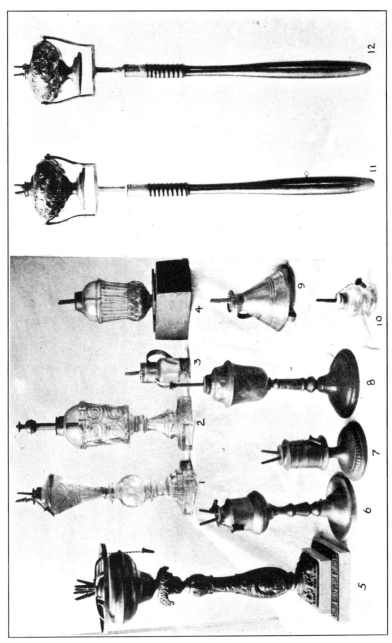

CAMPHINE-BURNING LAMPS

FOR DESCRIPTION OF PLATE SEE PAGE 68

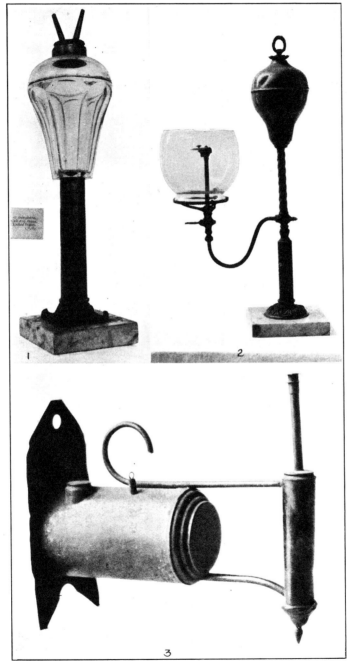

CAMPHINE-BURNING DEVICES

FOR DESCRIPTION OF PLATE SEE PAGE 69

LAMPS WITH FLAT WICKS; CANDLE LAMPS AND TORCH BURNER

a

b

ASTRAL, ARGAND, AND SINUMBRA LAMPS, ETC., AND GAS LAMP

FOR DESCRIPTION OF PLATE SEE PAGE 72

a

b

AN ARGAND MANTEL SET AND LAMP CANDLESTICKS, ETC.

FOR DESCRIPTION OF PLATE SEE PAGE 73

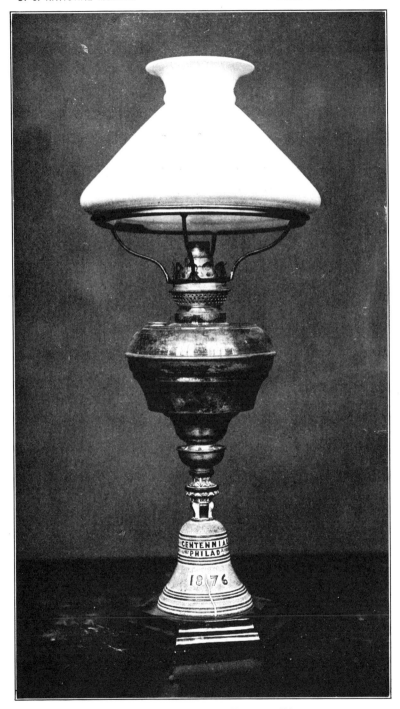

TABLE LAMP, 1876, WITH TUBULAR WICK

FOR DESCRIPTION OF PLATE SEE PAGE 75

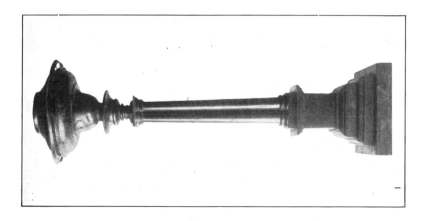

LIGHTHOUSE LAMPS AND MODIFIED ASTRAL

FOR DESCRIPTION OF PLATE SEE PAGE 76

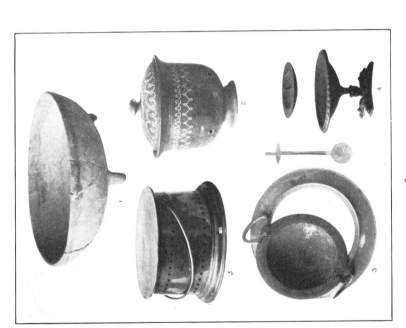

BRAZIERS AND HOT-WATER APPLIANCES

FOR DESCRIPTION OF PLATE SEE PAGES 79 AND 80

WARMING DEVICES

FOR DESCRIPTION OF PLATE SEE PAGES 80, 81, AND 82

HAND AND FOOT WARMERS

FOR DESCRIPTION OF PLATE SEE PAGE 81

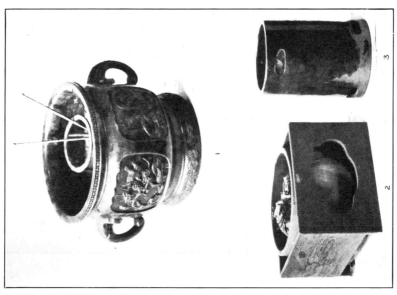

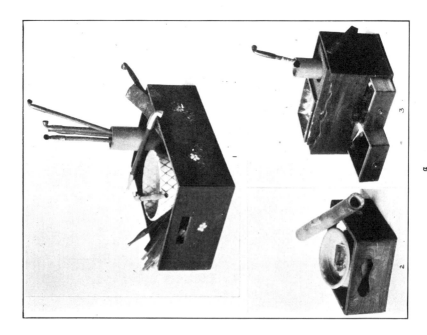

JAPANESE HIBACHIS AND CHINESE FIRE BOWLS

FOR DESCRIPTION OF PLATE SEE PAGE 83

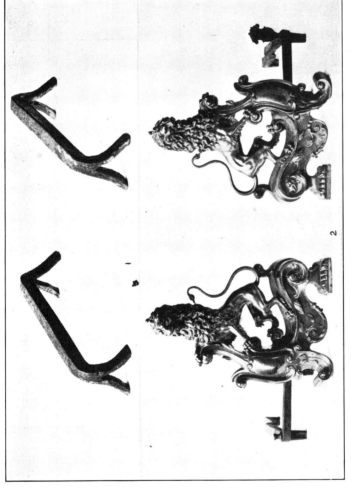

HOMEMADE AND ELABORATE ANDIRONS

FOR DESCRIPTION OF PLATE SEE PAGE 84

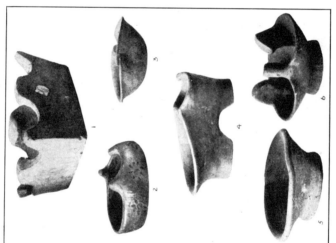

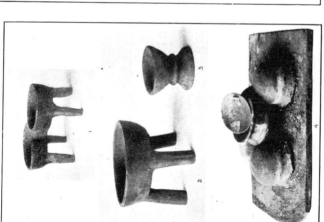

SIMPLE DRAFTLESS STOVES AND STOVES WITH RUDIMENTARY DRAFT

FOR DESCRIPTION OF PLATE SEE PAGE 84

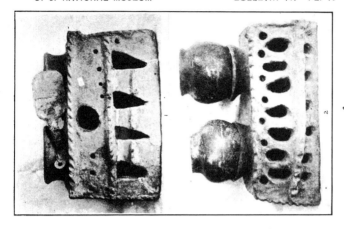

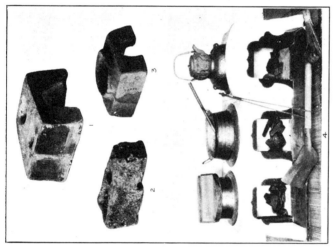

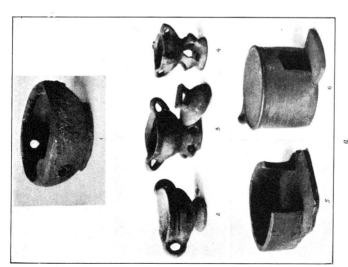

STOVES WITH RUDIMENTARY DRAFT

FOR DESCRIPTION OF PLATE SEE PAGES 85, 86, AND 87

a

b

STOVE WITH DRAFT AND COOKING POTS; SIMPLE RANGE

FOR DESCRIPTION OF PLATE SEE PAGES 85 AND 88

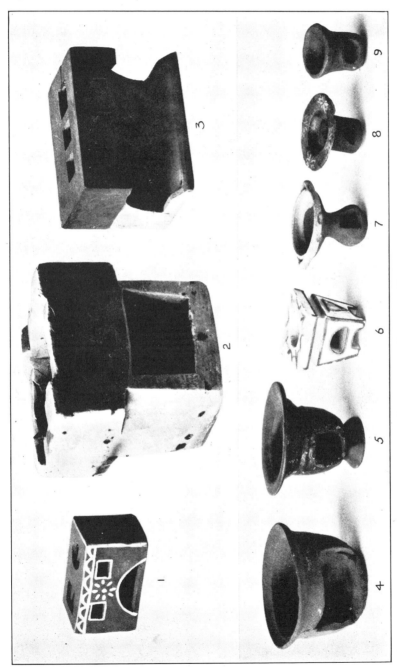

STOVES WITH DESIGNED DRAFT

FOR DESCRIPTION OF PLATE SEE PAGE 87

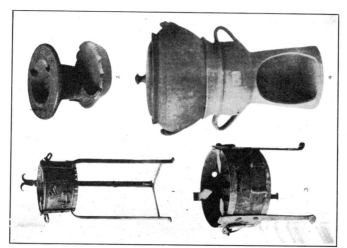

STOVES WITH AIR BOX AND GRATE; STOVES OF THE INVENTIVE PERIOD

FOR DESCRIPTION OF PLATE SEE PAGES 88, 89, AND 90

STOVES OF THE INVENTIVE PERIOD

FOR DESCRIPTION OF PLATE SEE PAGE 90

SELF-CONTAINED HEATER DEVICES

FOR DESCRIPTION OF PLATE SEE PAGES 92 AND 93

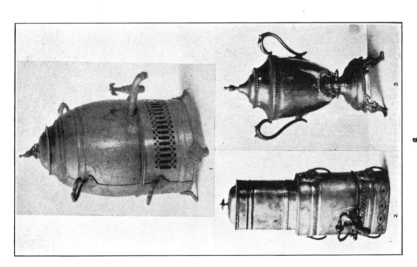

STOVES IN COMBINATION WITH VESSELS; VARIOUS HOT-WATER DEVICES

FOR DESCRIPTION OF PLATE SEE PAGES 93, 94, AND 109

PRESERVING WARMTH AND COOLING DEVICES

FOR DESCRIPTION OF PLATE SEE PAGE 95

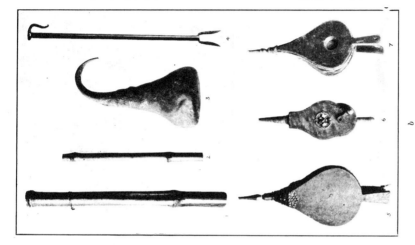

FIRE FANS, BLOWERS, AND BELLOWS

FOR DESCRIPTION OF PLATE SEE PAGES 95 AND 96

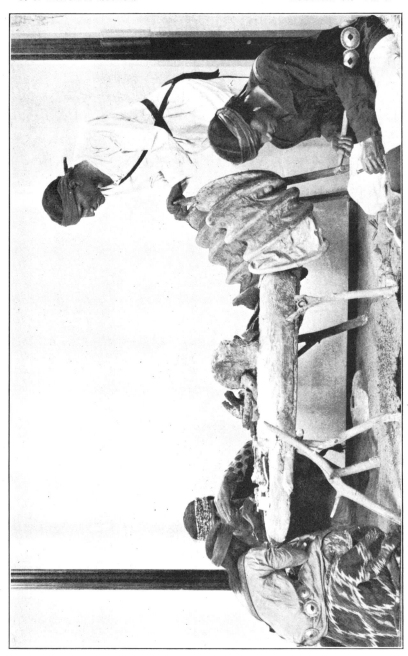

NAVAHO DOUBLE VALVE BELLOWS

FOR DESCRIPTION OF PLATE SEE PAGE 98

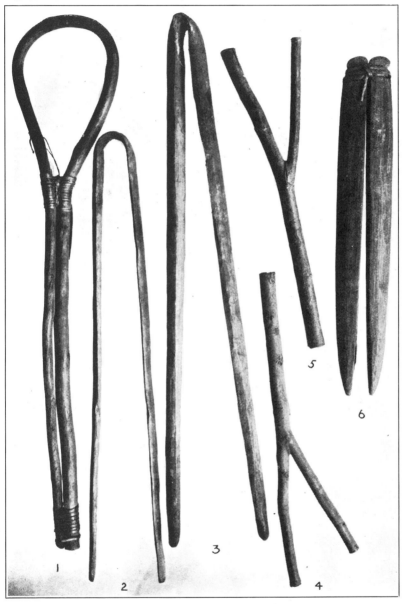

PRIMITIVE TONGS

FOR DESCRIPTION OF PLATE SEE PAGE 98

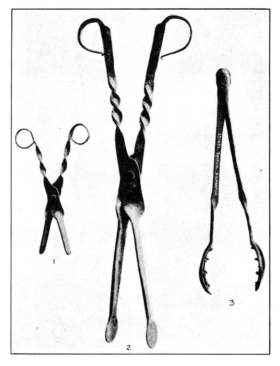

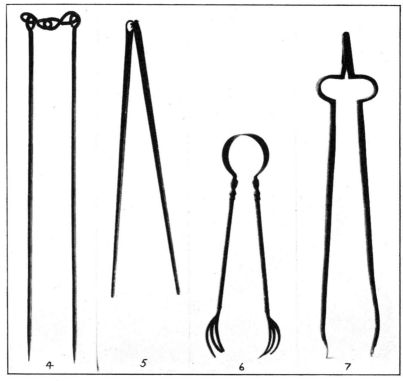

TONGS OF METAL

FOR DESCRIPTION OF PLATE SEE PAGE 99

SPITS AND GRID, VIRGINIA INDIANS

FOR DESCRIPTION OF PLATE SEE PAGE 99

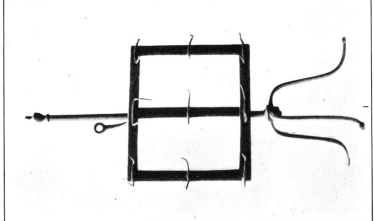

GRIDIRON AND ADJUSTABLE TRIVET ROASTER

FOR DESCRIPTION OF PLATE SEE PAGE 100

GRIDIRONS, TOASTERS, AND ROASTERS

FOR DESCRIPTION OF PLATE SEE PAGE 100

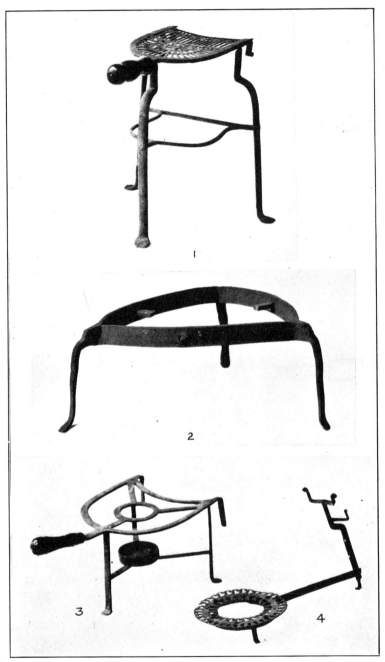

TRIVETS

FOR DESCRIPTION OF PLATE SEE PAGE 101

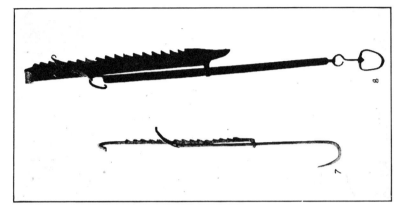

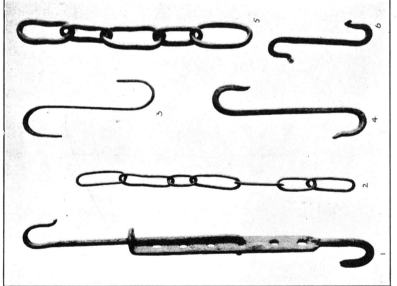

POTHOOKS AND HANGERS

FOR DESCRIPTION OF PLATE SEE PAGE 102

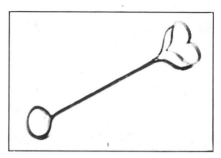

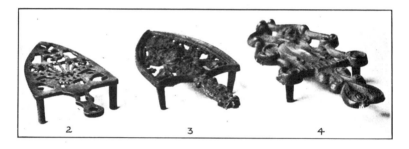

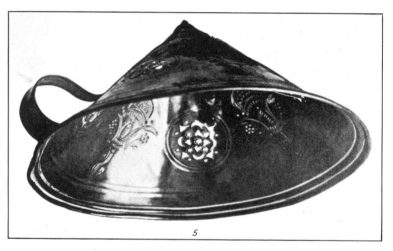

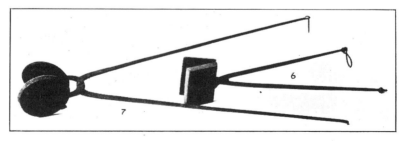

BRANDING IRON, IRON RESTS, CURFEW, AND WAFFLE IRONS

FOR DESCRIPTION OF PLATE SEE PAGES 102, 103, AND 108

SADIRONS

FOR DESCRIPTION OF PLATE SEE PAGE 103

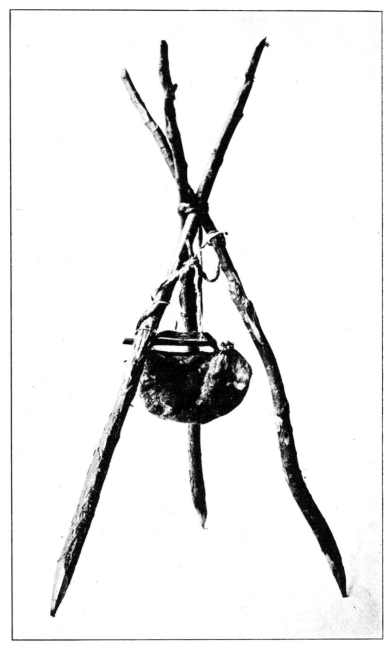

TRIPOD PAUNCH VESSEL FOR COOKING

FOR DESCRIPTION OF PLATE SEE PAGE 104

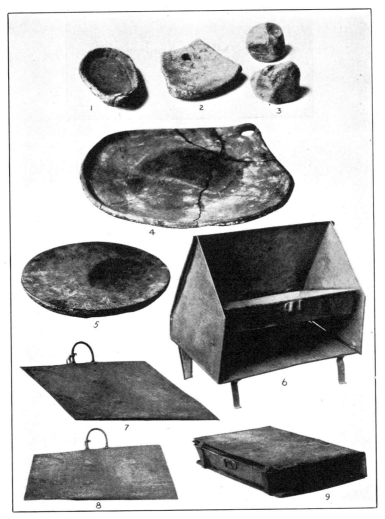

COOKING STONES, GRIDDLES, AND COLLAPSIBLE OVEN

For description of plate see pages 104, 105, and 107

SIMPLE OVENS

FOR DESCRIPTION OF PLATE SEE PAGES 105 AND 106

SPIDERS, DUTCH OVEN, POTTERY OVEN, AND STEAMERS

FOR DESCRIPTION OF PLATE SEE PAGES 107 AND 108

FUEL

For description of plate see pages 109 and 110

INDEX